Best of the Best from the

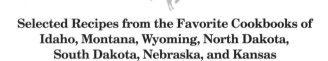

Cookbook

Selected Recipes from the Favorite Cookbooks of
Idaho, Montana, Wyoming, North Dakota,
South Dakota, Nebraska, and Kansas

An ocean of low, rolling hills make up the Palouse region of north Idaho, which ranks among the world's leaders in the production of soft white winter wheat. Idaho ranks fifth in the nation for total wheat production.

Best of the Best from the
PLAINS
Cookbook

**Selected Recipes from the Favorite Cookbooks of
Idaho, Montana, Wyoming, North Dakota,
South Dakota, Nebraska, and Kansas**

EDITED BY
Gwen McKee
AND
Barbara Moseley

Illustrated by Tupper England

QUAIL RIDGE PRESS
Preserving America's Food Heritage

Library of Congress Cataloging-in-Publication Data

Best of the best from the Plains cookbook : selected recipes from the
  favorite cookbooks of Idaho, Montana, Wyoming, North Dakota,
  South Dakota, Nebraska, and Kansas / Gwen McKee and Barbara
  Moseley. — 1st ed.
    p. cm. — (Best of the best regional cookbook series)
  Includes index.
  ISBN-13: 978-1-934193-25-9
  ISBN-10: 1-934193-25-9
    1. Cookery, American. 2. Cookery--Great Plains. I. Moseley,
  Barbara. II. Title
  TX715.M1397 2009
  641.5978--dc22   2008047312

ISBN-13: 978-1-934193-25-9 • ISBN-10: 1-934193-25-9

Book design by Cynthia Clark • Cover photo by Greg Campbell
Printed in South Korea by Tara TPS

First printing, May 2009 • Second, July 2010

On the cover: Chili on a Stick, page 136; Prairie Biscuits, page 30;
and Garlicky Green Beans with Mushrooms, page 111.

QUAIL RIDGE PRESS
P. O. Box 123 • Brandon, MS 39043
info@quailridge.com • www.quailridge.com

CONTENTS

South Dakota's Black Hills provide the backdrop for Mount Rushmore National Memorial. Presidents George Washington, Thomas Jefferson, Teddy Roosevelt, and Abraham Lincoln are the most famous men in rock.

Quest for the Best Regional Cooking

It seems that everywhere Barbara and I travel, we find that people love to talk about food. Invariably they mention specific dishes that have been an important part of their family's heritage and tradition, and do so with exuberance and pride.

"My mother always serves her fabulous cornbread dressing with our Thanksgiving turkey, and it is simply 'the best.'"

"Aunt Susan's famous pecan pie is always the first to go."

"No family occasion would be complete without Uncle Joe's chicken salad sandwiches."

Well, we heard, we researched, and we captured these bragged-about recipes so that people all over the country . . . and the world . . . could enjoy them.

My co-editor Barbara Moseley and I have been searching for the country's best recipes for three decades, and home cooks everywhere have learned to trust and rely on our cookbooks to bring them fabulous meals their friends and family will love! We always choose recipes based first and foremost on taste. In addition, the ingredients have to be readily available, and the recipes simple, with easy-to-follow instructions and never-fail results.

While touring the country and tasting the local fare, we delight in finding the little secrets that make the big difference. We have eaten buffalo in Wyoming, halibut in Alaska, lobster in Maine, gumbo in Louisiana, each prepared in a variety of creative ways. Finding out about conch in Florida and boysenberries in Oregon and poi in Hawaii . . . . No matter where we venture, this part of our job is always fun, often surprising, and definitely inspiring!

In grouping the plains states of Idaho, Montana, Wyoming, North Dakota, South Dakota, Nebraska, and Kansas, we covered a huge amount of territory. It's big country! Wheat fields waving in the wind, potato fields as far as the eye can see, and droves of cattle, buffalo, and sometimes elk are nothing short of patriotically gorgeous against the big blue sky. Early pioneers passed on their knack and zest for outdoor cooking . . . the game and fish they caught, the campfire

stews they concocted, the bounty they enjoyed bringing home
. . . . And oh my, the home cooking is so warm and welcoming. There are also so many fine restaurants and cozy bed and breakfast establishments in major cities offering choice recipes that have become local favorites. In this book, you'll find a sampling of regional taste as big as the land. It's all *just plain good!*

Gwen McKee

Gwen McKee and Barbara Moseley, editors
of BEST OF THE BEST STATE COOKBOOK SERIES

BEVERAGES and APPETIZERS

PHOTO BY SHAWN MCKEE

Old Faithful is not the highest, largest, or most regularly erupting geyser in Yellowstone National Park, Wyoming, but it is the most recognized. Old Faithful erupts 18 to 21 times a day, reaching an average height of 130 feet. About 5,000 to 8,000 gallons of water are discharged during each eruption.

Homemade Orange Julius

This is nice to serve as a refresher on a busy day in glasses that have been turned upside-down in orange juice, then dipped into granulated sugar and let dry for one hour. Top with a slice of orange, twisted.

1 (6-ounce) can frozen orange
  concentrate, thawed
¼ cup sugar
½ cup half-and-half

1 teaspoon vanilla
6 ounces cold water
12 ice cubes

Put first 4 ingredients in blender and blend on LOW speed. Gradually add cold water and 12 ice cubes. Blend at HIGH speed until slushy. Serve immediately to 4 guests.

FOR A LOW-CALORIE DRINK USE:

1 (6-ounce) can frozen orange
  juice concentrate, thawed
1 teaspoon low calorie
  sweetener

⅓ cup nonfat dry milk
2 teaspoons vanilla
6 ounces cold water
12 ice cubes

Cooking with Iola (Nebraska)

Cranberry Cheesecake Shake

1 (3-ounce) package cream
  cheese
½ cup milk
2 cups vanilla ice cream

1 (8-ounce) can jellied
  cranberry sauce
1 cup fresh cranberries

Soften cream cheese. Place all ingredients in blender container and blend until well combined. Serve immediately.

Recipe from MacKenzie Highland Ranch, Dubois, Wyoming
Tastes & Tours of Wyoming (Wyoming)

 Fifty-three of Montana's fifty-six counties are larger in area than the state of Rhode Island.

Graduation Punch

1 (46-ounce) can unsweetened
  pineapple juice
1 (46-ounce) can apricot
  nectar
2 (12-ounce) cans frozen
  concentrated lemonade

2 (12-ounce) cans cold water
2 (32-ounce) bottles 7-Up
Ice cubes
Lemon slices

Mix all together and float lemon slices on top of punch. Makes about 50 (6-ounce) punch cups.

Cooking with the Ladies (Wyoming)

Wassail

1 quart hot tea
1 cup sugar
1 (32-ounce) bottle cranberry
  juice
1 (32-ounce) bottle apple juice

3 cups orange juice
¾ cup lemon juice
2 cinnamon sticks
12 whole cloves

Combine all ingredients in a large kettle. Bring to a boil and boil for 2 minutes. Reduce heat; simmer 20 minutes. Delicious hot or cold. Serves about 25.

Recipe from Prairie Breeze Bed & Breakfast, Laramie, Wyoming
Tastes & Tours of Wyoming (Wyoming)

French Iced Coffee

3 cups very strong brewed
  coffee
2 cups sugar

1 pint cream (or half-and-half)
1 quart milk
3 teaspoons vanilla

Dissolve sugar in hot coffee. Cool. Add cream, milk, and vanilla. Pour into milk cartons or ice cream buckets. Freeze. Remove from freezer several hours before serving. Remove carton. Chop up with knife until slushy. Serve very icy.

Cooking with Iola (Nebraska)

Hot Buttered Rum
(Non-alcoholic)

This is an elegant drink—but so easy.

½ cup (1 stick) butter
½ cup brown sugar
1 cup vanilla ice cream,
  softened

4 teaspoons rum extract

Melt butter. Stir in brown sugar until heated. Pour hot mixture over ice cream. Beat by hand until smooth. Add rum extract.

To serve, put ¼ cup mixture in a cup and add ¾ cup boiling water. Sprinkle with nutmeg. Yields 1¾ cups mix or 7 cups hot buttered rum.

Mom's Camper Cooking (Kansas)

Spicy Hummus

This hummus variation contains sweet bell peppers and a touch of cayenne.

1 (15-ounce) can chickpeas,
  drained and rinsed (about 2
  cups boiled)
6 tablespoons tahini
6 tablespoons fresh lemon
  juice
3 tablespoons plain yogurt
2 tablespoons olive oil
4 cloves garlic, crushed
  (about 2 teaspoons)

1 teaspoon ground cumin
¼ teaspoon cayenne pepper
¼ cup minced jalapeño pepper
¼ cup red bell pepper, seeded
  and diced
Salt and freshly ground black
  pepper to taste

In a food processor or blender, purée chickpeas, tahini, lemon juice, yogurt, and oil until smooth, adding water a little at a time as needed to make a creamy mixture. Transfer the purée to a medium bowl. Add garlic, cumin, cayenne, jalapeño, and bell pepper, and mix well. Season with salt and pepper. Cover and chill 2–4 hours to allow the flavors to blend. Garnish with cayenne pepper just before serving. Makes about 4 cups, approximately 16 servings.

The Pea & Lentil Cookbook (Idaho)

Black Bean Salsa

2 (15-ounce) cans black beans, drained
½ cup diced sweet red pepper
½ cup diced yellow pepper
¼ cup diced purple onion
¼ cup diced cucumber
2 tablespoons diced celery
2 tablespoons tomato juice
2 tablespoons red wine vinegar
1 tablespoon fresh lemon juice
1½ tablespoons chopped fresh thyme
½ teaspoon ground cumin
2 tablespoons chopped cilantro

Combine all ingredients. Refrigerate. Makes 1 quart.

Columbus Community Cookbook (Montana)

White Bean Dip

4 cloves garlic
2 (15-ounce) cans white kidney beans, rinsed, drained
¼ cup fresh lemon juice
½ cup virgin olive oil
1 tablespoon ground cumin
1 teaspoon cayenne, or to taste
Salt and white pepper to taste
¼ cup cilantro leaves
Chopped cilantro (optional)

Place garlic in food processor container. Process until finely minced. Add kidney beans and lemon juice; process until smooth. Add olive oil, cumin, cayenne, salt and pepper; process until well mixed. Add cilantro leaves; process for 30 seconds with on-off pulses. Transfer dip to bowl. Refrigerate, covered, until chilled or overnight. Sprinkle with chopped cilantro. Serve with tortilla chips or as a dip for crudités. Yields 8–12 servings.

Cheyenne Frontier Days "Daddy of 'em All" Cookbook (Wyoming)

Nacho Cheese Dip

2 pounds ground beef, browned and drained
2 pounds Velveeta cheese, melted
1 can cream of mushroom soup
1 (8-ounce) jar picante sauce

Combine ingredients and serve hot with tortilla chips. Crock pot works well.

The Joy of Sharing (Nebraska)

Shoe Peg Corn Dip

1 (15-ounce) can shoe peg
  corn, drained
1 tomato, peeled, seeded and
  diced
½ green bell pepper, diced
½ red pepper, diced
10–15 ripe olives, sliced
½ cup diced red onion
Juice of 1 lime

½ cucumber, chopped
3 green onions, chopped
1 jalapeño, chopped
2 tablespoons sour cream
1½ tablespoons chopped
  cilantro
Seasoned salt and pepper to
  taste

Combine all ingredients and mix well. Refrigerate until well chilled. Serve with crackers or chips. Best prepared a day ahead.

From the High Country of Wyoming (Wyoming)

Gazpacho Dip

½ cup vegetable oil
3 tablespoons vinegar
1 teaspoon salt
1 teaspoon garlic powder
½ teaspoon pepper
4 or 5 green onions, thinly
  sliced
2 or 3 tomatoes, chopped

1 teaspoon coriander
1 (4-ounce) can chopped black
  olives, undrained
1 (4-ounce) can chopped green
  chiles, undrained
1 teaspoon chopped parsley
2 ripe avocados, chopped

Combine vegetable oil and vinegar in bowl; blend well. Add salt, garlic powder, and pepper; mix well. Add green onions, tomatoes, coriander, black olives, green chiles, and parsley; mix well. Chill. Fold in avocados just before serving. Serve with Doritos. Yields 10 servings.

Cheyenne Frontier Days "Daddy of 'em All" Cookbook (Wyoming)

Major Grey's Delightful Dip

Sweet and smoky, a cocktail hour hit!

1 pound cream cheese,
  softened
2 cups shredded Cheddar
  cheese
2 teaspoons curry powder
2 tablespoons plus 2 teaspoons
  dry sherry

1 cup peach or mango chutney
1 pound bacon, cooked crisp
  and crumbled
6 scallions, chopped

Blend cheeses with curry powder and sherry until creamy. Spread in an even layer on the bottom of a 9-inch quiche dish or pie plate. Spread chutney on top of cheese mixture. Top with bacon, then scallions. Serve at room temperature with sturdy crackers. Makes 12 servings.

Jackson Hole à la Carte (Wyoming)

Idaho Caviar

1 (16-ounce) can black-eyed
  peas or crowder peas,
  drained
⅓ cup finely chopped green
  pepper
⅓ cup finely chopped onion

3 cloves garlic, finely minced
⅓ cup Italian salad dressing
Salt, pepper, and Tabasco to
  taste
1 jalapeño pepper, finely
  chopped

Mix all ingredients together and serve with tortilla chips.

A Century of Recipes (Idaho)

Idaho's nickname is "The Gem State." Gems from all around Idaho give credence to its nickname—jasper from Bruneau, opal from Spencer, and jade, topaz, zircon, and tourmaline from around the state. The same geological processes that gave Idaho its mountains also gave it Star Garnets, the state gem. This stone is considered more precious than either Star Rubies or Star Sapphires. The color is usually dark purple or plum.

Fresh Fruit with Sour Cream Grand Marnier Dipping Sauce

Delightful for pre-brunch or pre-luncheon munching!

1 (8-ounce) carton sour cream
2 tablespoons orange juice
2 tablespoons Grand Marnier
  liqueur

1 teaspoon grated orange rind
½ cup confectioners' sugar,
  sifted
Fresh fruit for dipping

Combine sour cream with orange juice, Grand Marnier and orange rind. Stir in confectioners' sugar. Place sauce in a small serving bowl. Chill, covered, 1–2 hours to blend flavors.

To serve, place bowl of sauce in the center of a serving platter. Surround sauce with attractively arranged fresh fruit. Use toothpicks to spear fruit for dipping. Makes 1½ cups sauce.

Note: This may also be presented as a salad at luncheons. Amaretto may be substituted for the Grand Marnier.

Jackson Hole à la Carte (Wyoming)

Apple Dip

A very delicious dip or ball that may be served with apples for a wonderful appetizer. Especially good for those health-conscious souls.

2 (8-ounce) packages cream
  cheese, softened
¾ cup sugar, scant
½ cup pecans, chopped
½ cup raisins, chopped
½ cup coconut
½ cup maraschino cherries,
  diced and drained

½ cup crushed pineapple,
  well drained
¼ teaspoon lemon juice
2 teaspoons vanilla
⅛ teaspoon nutmeg
⅛ teaspoon ground allspice
⅛ teaspoon mace (optional)

Mix all ingredients together until spreadable. Cool slightly in refrigerator, then roll into a ball. Makes about 4 cups.

A Cooking Affaire II (Kansas)

Artichoke Heaven

MMMmmmmm! Delicious!

6 small jars marinated
  artichoke hearts, drained,
  and chopped into bite-size
  pieces
3–4 cups low-fat (or not)
  mayonnaise

8 cloves garlic, chopped
1 cup grated low-fat mozzarella
  cheese
½ cup grated Parmesan
  cheese, divided

Combine artichoke hearts, mayonnaise, garlic, mozzarella, and ¼ cup of Parmesan in a bowl. Place in lidded ceramic casserole, sprinkling with remaining Parmesan cheese. Cover and bake at 350° for 40 minutes. Uncover and continue to bake for 10–15 additional minutes, or until lightly browned. Serve hot with favorite crackers (Triscuits are highly recommended) or sliced baguettes.

Potluck (Montana)

Artichoke-Tomato Tart

1 refrigerated unbaked pie
  crust
1 (8-ounce) package shredded
  mozzarella cheese
8 Roma tomatoes
1 (14-ounce) can artichoke
  hearts, drained, chopped

1 cup loosely packed fresh
  basil leaves
4 cloves garlic
½ cup Hellmann's
  mayonnaise
¼ cup grated Parmesan
  cheese

Bake pie crust according to package directions in a 9-inch quiche dish. Remove from oven. Sprinkle ¾ cup of the mozzarella cheese over the baked pie shell. Cut Roma tomatoes into wedges; drain on paper towels. Arrange tomato wedges atop the cheese in the baked pie shell. Sprinkle artichoke hearts over the tomato wedges. In a blender, combine basil leaves and garlic and process till coarsely chopped, and sprinkle over the tomatoes. Combine remaining mozzarella cheese, mayonnaise, and Parmesan cheese and spoon over basil mixture, spreading evenly to cover the top. Bake in a 375° oven for 35 minutes or till top is golden and bubbly. Serves 8.

Recipes & Remembrances / Buffalo Lake (South Dakota)

Holiday Pinwheels

2 (8-ounce) packages cream
  cheese, softened
1 (1-ounce) package Hidden
  Valley Ranch Salad
  Dressing Mix
3 green onions, minced fine
1 (4-ounce) jar pimento, diced

1 (4-ounce) can green chiles,
  diced
1 (2¼-ounce) can black olives,
  diced
1 (3-ounce) package dried beef,
  cut fine
4 (12-inch) flour tortillas

Mix all ingredients together (except tortillas) and spread on flour tortillas. Roll tightly and wrap in Saran Wrap. Chill for at least 2 hours. Slice and place on serving tray.

Cooking with Iola (Nebraska)

Cowboy Cheese Puffs

1 loaf firm, unsliced white
  bread
¼ pound sharp Cheddar
  cheese

1 pound Velveeta cheese
¼ pound butter
2 egg whites, stiffly beaten

Remove crust from bread and cut into 1-inch cubes. Melt and stir cheeses and butter in top of double boiler over hot water until smooth. Remove from heat. Fold in stiffly beaten egg whites. Dip bread cubes in cheese mixture until well coated. Place on a cookie sheet, cover, and refrigerate overnight.

Bake in 400° oven for 12–15 minutes or until puffy and brown. Yields 4 dozen.

Wyoming Cook Book (Wyoming)

Sausage Squares

1 pound sausage
½ cup onion, chopped
¼ cup grated Parmesan
cheese
½ cup grated Swiss cheese
1 egg, beaten
¼ teaspoon Tabasco
1½ teaspoons salt
2 tablespoons parsley, chopped
2 cups Bisquick
⅔ cup milk
¼ cup mayonnaise
1 egg yolk

Cook sausage and onion over low heat until brown. Drain off fat. Add cheeses, whole egg, Tabasco, salt, and parsley. Make Bisquick dough by mixing with milk and mayonnaise. Spread half of dough over bottom of greased 8-inch square pan. Cover with sausage mixture and top with remaining dough mixture. Brush with beaten egg yolk. Bake 25–30 minutes at 400°. Cut in squares. May be served for a brunch, or coffee, or as appetizers. Makes 16 squares.

Home at the Range I (Kansas)

Onion Sausage Sticks

1½ cups finely chopped onions
(Idaho-Eastern Oregon)
½ pound bulk pork sausage,
fried and drained
⅓ cup sausage drippings or
vegetable oil
1 cup buttermilk baking mix
½ teaspoon salt
4 eggs, beaten
1 cup shredded Cheddar
cheese
2 tablespoons minced parsley

Combine onions with remaining ingredients. Spread into greased 9x13-inch baking pan. Bake at 350° for 20–25 minutes or until golden. Let stand 5 minutes before cutting into sticks. Makes about 4 dozen appetizers.

Onions Make the Meal Cookbook (Idaho)

Classic Onion Bloom

2–4 large onions   **Vegetable oil for frying**
  (Idaho-Eastern Oregon)

To cut onion into bloom: Peel onion. Cut ½ inch off top end. Trim root end slightly, but do not cut outer layer. Top-side-up, cut onion into quarters, cutting deeper into the outer layers than into inner layers, like a pyramid. Do not cut through the root base. Turn onion upside down. Insert knife ½ inch below root base and cut each quarter into 4 more sections by cutting downward. Turn onion right side up; gently pull petal open, leaving core intact. If petals do not open easily, make cuts slightly deeper. Letting cut onion stand in ice water will also help the onion "bloom." Once onion is cooked, cut out the core to create individual petals.

BATTER:

3 tablespoons cornstarch   **1 teaspoon each salt and black**
1½ cups all-purpose flour   **pepper**
2 teaspoons garlic salt   **2 (12-ounce) cans beer**
2 teaspoons paprika

Mix dry ingredients. Add beer; mix well. Place onion in batter, root end first. Roll onion all around, making sure the batter gets between the petals. Lift onion out and set it upside down to drain, squeezing lightly, to remove excess Batter. Allow to drain for 15 seconds.

BREADING:

2 cups all-purpose flour   **3 teaspoons garlic powder**
4 teaspoons paprika   **½ teaspoon black pepper**

Mix Breading ingredients. Place the battered onion on a tray, petals up. Shake Breading mixture over petals. Separate petals so that breading gets down inside layers. Carefully squeeze the petals together to press and seal Breading. Very important— allow onion to sit right-side-up for 2 minutes once breaded. The Batter and Breading must merge. Turn onion over, and gently tap out excess Breading. Heat enough oil in deep pan to cover the onion. It is critical that the oil is at the right temperature, 375°–400°. Using tongs, place the onion upside down in oil for 4–5 minutes, or until golden brown. Lift onion with slotted spoon and let oil drain. Turn right side up (this can be done by putting a

(continued)

(Classic Onion Bloom continued)

bowl on onion and flipping onion and bowl over together). Cut out 2-inch core from center of onion. This allows petals to separate. Place Dipping Sauce in a small dish and place in center of onion. Serve immediately. One 4-inch onion serves 4.

DIPPING SAUCE:

2 cups mayonnaise	**½ cup bottled chili sauce**
2 cups sour cream	**½ teaspoon cayenne pepper**

Combine well; cover and refrigerate until ready to serve.

Onions Make the Meal Cookbook (Idaho)

Tater Wedges

2 sticks butter	**2 teaspoons garlic powder**
4 large Idaho russet potatoes,	**1 teaspoon seasoned salt**
cut lengthwise into wedges	**Parsley flakes**
½ cup grated Parmesan	
cheese	

Melt butter in 12-inch Dutch oven and add potato wedges. Stir to coat well and arrange in a circular pattern. Mix the grated cheese and spices, and sprinkle over the tater wedges. Sprinkle with parsley flakes. Bake about 40 minutes or until the taters are done with 5 or 6 briquets underneath and 16–18 on the lid. Serve as either an appetizer or as a side dish.

Cee Dub's Ethnic & Regional Dutch Oven Cookin' (Idaho)

Potato Logs

5 medium potatoes	**Salt and pepper to taste**
¼ cup butter	**¾ cup grated Cheddar cheese**

Wash potatoes thoroughly; microwave or boil until fork pierces easily. Peel and mash, adding butter, seasoning, and cheese. Set aside to cool.

FILLING:
12 Little Sizzlers Pork Sausages

Preheat oven to 400°. Cook sausages thoroughly. Drain on cookie sheet lined with paper towels. While sausages are cooling, on a floured surface, pat potato mixture out to ¼ inch thick. Divide into 12 equal parts. Place 1 sausage in the center of each piece. Using a spatula or scraper, lift from work surface and mold potato mixture around sausage. Place wrapped sausage in a greased baking dish, being sure to make only 1 layer; do not stack. Bake approximately 20 minutes or until golden brown.

Elegant Cooking Made Simple (Idaho)

Hot Potato Skins

Bake potatoes until tender. Cool, cut in quarters lengthwise, then in half crosswise, to form 8 sections. Scoop out potato pulp, leaving about ¼ inch. Brush skins on both sides with melted butter and a little soy sauce. Bake at 500° until crisp, about 10–12 minutes. Serve with assorted dips or add shredded cheese and crumbled, cooked bacon, then heat until cheese melts.

Red River Valley Potato Growers Auxiliary Cookbook
(North Dakota)

The Red River of the North defines the east boundary of North Dakota. It probably got its name from a Sioux word for bloody in reference to battles there. The place in legend called the Red River Valley is hard to recognize as a valley at all; it is more like a plateau. The rich black soil in this valley is so fertile that few places on earth compare to it.

Stuffed Mushrooms

16 (2-inch) mushrooms
2 tablespoons butter
2 teaspoons finely chopped
   onion
½ (10-ounce) box frozen
   chopped spinach, thawed
   and squeezed

¼ cup grated Swiss cheese
¼ cup Parmesan cheese

Remove and chop mushroom stems into small pieces. Then sauté stems and onion lightly in butter. Add chopped spinach and Swiss cheese; stir lightly and remove from heat. Fill caps with mixture and sprinkle with Parmesan cheese. Place in a warm Dutch oven and bake at medium heat for 10–15 minutes, until cheese is melted. Serves 4–6.

Recipes Stolen from the River of No Return (Idaho)

"Devil" Eggs

6 eggs
2 tablespoons mayonnaise
1 tablespoon prepared
   horseradish
1 tablespoon vinegar
1 teaspoon mustard
1 teaspoon dill relish

½ teaspoon salt
½ teaspoon pepper
1 teaspoon sugar
Salsa (optional)
Sliced canned jalapeño peppers
   (optional)

Put eggs in medium saucepan and cover with cold water. Bring to a boil. Remove from heat and let stand, covered, 10 minutes. Drain. Peel shells from eggs while holding them under cold running water. Cut eggs in half lengthwise. Remove yolks and mix with mayonnaise, horseradish, vinegar, mustard, dill relish, salt, pepper, and sugar. Use mixture to fill egg whites. Garnish with a dab of your favorite salsa and top with a slice of jalapeño on each. Makes 6 servings.

Note: These are hot! The faint-hearted might want to start with one teaspoon horseradish, then add more to taste.

Recipes Worth Sharing (Kansas)

Cocktail Quiches

PASTRY:

1 (3-ounce) package cream
    cheese, softened

⅓ cup butter, softened
1 cup flour

In a medium bowl, cream together cream cheese and butter. Mix in flour and chill overnight. Form dough into 24 small balls and press into mini-muffin tins.

FILLING:

1 cup milk
1 egg, slightly beaten
¼ teaspoon salt
¼ teaspoon pepper

½–1 tablespoon chopped
    chives
1 cup grated sharp Cheddar
    cheese

In a medium bowl, mix together milk, egg, salt, pepper, and chives. Evenly distribute cheese over Pastry in muffin tins. Pour milk and egg mixture gently over grated cheese. Bake at 350° for 30 minutes. Serve warm. Makes 24 servings.

Bound to Please (Idaho)

Apricot Chicken Wings

The wings can be made ahead of time and held over for those late-comer guests.

1 small jar apricot jam
1 (8-ounce) bottle Russian
    dressing

½ package dry onion soup mix
3–4 pounds chicken wings

Mix the jam, Russian dressing, and onion soup mix together and pour over the chicken wings in an oven-proof baking pan. (It is easiest if you microwave the jam first.)

Bake at 350° for 2 hours. If your guests are late, turn temperature down and continue baking. Can leave wings in oven for 2–3 hours for those very late guests.

Best-of-Friends, Festive Occasions Cookbook (Montana)

Beef in a Bread Bowl

½ cup chopped onion
2 tablespoons butter
1 tablespoon cornstarch
1 cup evaporated milk,
  undiluted
½ cup water
1 (3-ounce) package cream
  cheese, diced

1 (5-ounce) package dried beef,
  rinsed and diced
¼ cup chopped green
  pepper
8–10 drops of Tabasco
1 teaspoon prepared mustard
1 large or 2 small uncut loaves
  round crusty bread

Sauté onion in butter over medium heat. Stir in cornstarch and mix thoroughly. Gradually add milk and water. Cook mixture over medium heat, stirring constantly until the mixture just comes to a boil and thickens. Stir in cream cheese, dried beef, green pepper, Tabasco, and mustard. Continue to cook and stir until the cheese is melted. Cut the top off the crusty bread and pull the center of the bread out to form a bread bowl. Tear the bread top and center pieces up to use as dippers. Just before serving, spoon the hot beef mixture into the hollowed bread and serve. Makes 2⅔ cups.

Recipes & Remembrances / Buffalo Lake (South Dakota)

Teriyaki Tidbits

1 (10-ounce) jar apricot jam
½ cup barbecue sauce
1–2 tablespoons teriyaki
  sauce
1 pound wieners, cut into
  1-inch pieces, or 1 pound
  cocktail franks

1 (15¼-ounce) can pineapple
  chunks, drained
1 large green pepper, cut into
  ¾-inch squares

In large saucepan over medium heat, combine preserves, barbecue sauce, and teriyaki sauce. Heat until hot and bubbly, stirring constantly. Stir in wieners, pineapple, and green pepper. Heat thoroughly. Transfer mixture to chafing dish, keeping warm over low heat. Serve with toothpicks. (Stick pretzels can be used instead.)

We Love Country Cookin' (North Dakota)

Smoked Salmon Cheesecake

Different and always a hit! I serve as an appetizer, but could be a luncheon or brunch entrée. Very rich!

WALNUT CRUST:

2 cups bread crumbs
½ cup chopped walnuts
½ cup butter, softened
¼ cup shredded Gruyère cheese
1 teaspoon dill

Preheat oven to 350°. Combine bread crumbs, walnuts, butter, cheese, and dill in a bowl. Mix well and press firmly into bottom and sides of a buttered 9-inch springform pan, and chill.

1 medium onion, minced
3 tablespoons butter
1¾ pounds cream cheese, softened
⅓ cup half-and-half
¼ teaspoon pepper
½ cup shredded Gruyère cheese
4 eggs
½ pound smoked salmon, finely chopped

Sauté onion in butter until tender. Combine cream cheese and half-and-half, and whip until smooth. Add onion, pepper, and Gruyère cheese. Mix well. Add eggs, one at a time, beating slowly until incorporated in mixture. Stir in salmon and mix well.

Pour into Crust and bake for 1–1½ hours. Unmold and serve with small rye or pumpernickel bread or crackers. Serves 16.

Ketchum Cooks (Idaho)

Homemade Fiddle Faddle

2 cups brown sugar
2 sticks margarine
½ cup white corn syrup
1 teaspoon salt
1 teaspoon butter flavoring

1 teaspoon maple flavoring
¼ teaspoon cream of tartar
1 teaspoon baking soda
7 quarts popped corn
2 cups mixed nuts

In saucepan, combine brown sugar, margarine, corn syrup, and salt. Boil for 6 minutes, stirring constantly. Add flavorings, cream of tartar, and soda. Pour over popped corn and nuts, mixing thoroughly. Bake in 200° oven for one hour.

Cooking with Iola (Nebraska)

Munchies

1 (10-ounce) package
    mini-pretzels
5 cups Cheerios cereal
5 cups Corn Chex cereal
2 cups salted peanuts

1 large bag of M&M's
2 (12-ounce) packages white
    chocolate chips
3 tablespoons vegetable oil

In a large bowl combine first 5 ingredients; set aside. In a microwave-safe bowl, heat chips and oil on MEDIUM or HIGH for 2 minutes; stir. Microwave on HIGH for 10 seconds; stir until smooth. Pour over mixture and mix well. Spread onto wax paper-lined cookie sheets. Cool—break apart and store in an air-tight container. Makes 5 quarts.

Recipe from Bonnie's B&B, Kalispell, Montana
Recipes from Big Sky Country (Montana)

Flowing more than 425 miles, Idaho's Salmon River is the longest free-flowing river within one state in the Lower 48. Dropping more than 7,000 feet between its headwaters above Sawtooth Valley and its confluence with the Snake River, its discharge is 11,060 cubic feet per second, giving this fast-moving waterway the nickname "River of No Return." Salmon River's canyon is deeper than most of the earth's canyons, including the Grand Canyon of the Colorado River.

Sesame Thins

1¾ cups all-purpose flour
½ cup cornmeal
2 tablespoons sugar
½ teaspoon baking soda
½ teaspoon salt

½ cup butter or margarine,
  divided
½ cup water
2 tablespoons vinegar
2 tablespoons sesame seeds

In large bowl, mix flour, cornmeal, sugar, soda, and salt; with pastry blender cut ¼ cup butter into flour mixture until it resembles coarse crumbs. Stir in water and vinegar. With hands knead until well blended. Preheat oven to 375°. Divide dough into 30 small balls. On lightly floured board with floured rolling pin, roll balls in 4½-inch paper thin circles (edges may be ragged).

Place circles 1 inch apart on ungreased cookie sheet. Melt remaining butter (¼ cup). With pastry brush, lightly brush each circle with butter. Sprinkle with sesame seeds and press seeds firmly with pancake turner. Bake 8–10 minutes until lightly browned. Remove to wire rack to cool. When thoroughly cooled, store in tightly covered container. Makes 30.

Editor's Extra: These are superb just to pick up and eat! Also great as dippers, especially with salsa and pesto, and excellent to serve under or alongside a meat dish or in the bread basket.

Feeding the Herd (Wyoming)

BREAD and BREAKFAST

PHOTO © JOHN REDDY PHOTOGRAPHY, INC.

Fields and trees glisten in the sun on a frosty morning in the serene Wolf Creek area in southwestern Montana's Gold West Country. Rich in history, the Gold West Country is located between Glacier and Yellowstone national parks. Its history is marked by the great Gold Rush days, and sprinkled within its territory are ghost towns, museums, mines, and ranches.

Prairie Biscuits

2 cups flour (Natural White™)
½ cup lard
1 teaspoon salt
½ teaspoon baking soda
4 teaspoons baking powder
¾ cup buttermilk

In bowl of flour, make a "well." Mix in lard (crumble the lard and flour with your hands) and work in the salt, baking soda, and baking powder. Sprinkle buttermilk into dough. Form a ball, knead on a floured surface or in hands. Form dough into size of biscuits desired and bake in hot Dutch oven over coals, or on greased cookie sheet in a preheated 450° oven until tannish in color.

Wheat Montana Cookbook

Auntie Em's Cheddar Biscuits

The lost recipe that could have bribed Miss Gulch, saved Toto, and spared Dorothy her concussion-induced hallucinations of talking scarecrows, friendly lions, and tin men. These are delicious served with country ham or as a topping to chicken pot pie.

10 cups unbleached
all-purpose flour
4 tablespoons baking powder
½ cup sugar
1 teaspoon salt
2 cups heavy cream
2 cups buttermilk
1 pound (4 sticks) unsalted
butter, melted
2 cups grated sharp Cheddar
cheese
2 tablespoons chopped fresh
chives

Preheat the oven to 375°. Cover a large baking sheet with parchment paper and set aside. Sift together the flour, baking powder, sugar, and salt. In a separate large bowl, mix together the cream, buttermilk, and unsalted butter. With a wooden spoon, blend together the dry ingredients with the buttermilk mixture. The dough should pull together, but still be crumbly. Fold in the cheese and chives. On a floured surface, roll out the dough to 1 inch in thickness. Cut with a 2-inch biscuit cutter, and place biscuits on the prepared baking sheet. Bake for 20 minutes, or until tops are golden brown. Makes 5 dozen.

Pure Prairie (Kansas)

Buttermilk Biscuits

2 cups flour	3 tablespoons soft butter or
¾ teaspoon salt	shortening
3 teaspoons baking powder	1 cup buttermilk
½ teaspoon baking soda	Melted butter

Preheat oven to 450°. Sift flour once before measuring. Then sift together into a large bowl the flour, salt, baking powder, and baking soda. Add butter or shortening and beat about 2 minutes or until mixture is the consistency of coarse meal. Add buttermilk and beat about 1 minute, just enough to mix thoroughly. Be certain to scrape sides of bowl while beating.

Turn out onto a lightly floured board and knead gently by folding over 2 or 3 times, until texture is even. Roll out to ½-inch thickness. Dip cutter in flour and cut biscuits. Place on ungreased baking pan and brush with melted butter. Bake 12–15 minutes until golden brown. Makes 12 or more biscuits, depending on cutter size.

Matt Braun's Western Cooking (Idaho)

Grandma's 60 Minute Rolls

2 packages dry yeast	3 tablespoons sugar
¼ cup warm water	2 heaping tablespoons butter
1¼ cups milk	or margarine, softened
2 eggs	4 cups flour
1 teaspoon salt	¼ cup butter, melted

Dissolve yeast in warm water. Scald milk and let cool to lukewarm. Beat eggs, then add salt, sugar, and butter to eggs. Add yeast and egg mixture to milk. Add flour until a nice soft dough forms. Let rise for 20 minutes, covered. Turn out on floured board, roll and spread with melted butter, and cut for Parker House rolls. Put in buttered pan and let rise until double. Bake in 400° oven for 15–20 minutes.

Mackay Heritage Cookbook (Idaho)

Easy Refrigerator Rolls

2 packages active dry yeast
2 cups warm water
  (110°–115°)
½ cup sugar

2 teaspoons salt
¼ cup soft shortening
1 egg
6½–7 cups flour

Mix yeast with warm water. Stir in sugar, salt, shortening, and egg. Add flour, stirring in enough to form soft dough. Cover and place in refrigerator. About 2 hours before baking, shape dough into rolls, coffee cake, etc. Cover; let rise until double. Bake at 400° for 12–15 minutes. Can be made into rolls as soon as mixed.

Centerville Community Centennial Cookbook (Kansas)

Fool-Proof Popovers

2 eggs
1 cup milk

1 cup flour
Scant teaspoon salt

Break eggs into bowl. Add milk, flour, and salt. Mix well. Grease an 8-cup muffin tin. Divide mixture into 8 parts, and fill tin. Turn oven heat to 425°. Put popovers into COLD OVEN. Bake 37 minutes. Do not peek!

North Dakota: Where Food is Love (North Dakota)

North Idaho Spoon Bread

3 cups milk, scalded
1 cup white cornmeal
1 teaspoon butter or
   margarine

1 teaspoon sugar
1 teaspoon salt
3 egg yolks, beaten
3 egg whites, stiffly beaten

Add scalded milk gradually to cornmeal, and cook 5 minutes, stirring constantly. Add butter or margarine, sugar, and salt. Add beaten egg yolks; beat well, then fold in beaten egg whites. Turn into greased baking dish, and bake at 350° for 45–50 minutes. Serve hot from baking dish with plenty of butter. Makes 4–5 servings.

Recipes Logged from the Woods of North Idaho (Idaho)

Lily's Beer Bread

Beer bread used to be made out of necessity rather than as a novelty the way it is today. The beer acted as a yeast and allowed the bread to rise.

4 cups flour
3 teaspoons baking powder
3 tablespoons sugar
½ teaspoon baking soda

Pinch salt
2 tablespoons butter, softened
12 ounces beer

Sift dry ingredients together. Add butter and cut in well. Add beer, but make sure it is not cold, even a little warm will help. (The cold will drastically slow down the "rise.") If you need more moisture to make a good dough, add a little warm water.

In a greased bowl, set in a warm place to rise for several hours, covered with a towel. Put in a well-greased bread pan and bake at 350° for approximately an hour.

Note: You can brush the top with butter or egg during the last 15 minutes of baking, and it will make a nice crisp crust.

Sowbelly and Sourdough (Idaho)

Bread in an Onion Ring

Very good with fish and coleslaw.

2 large onions
  (Idaho-Eastern Oregon)
¼ cup yellow cornmeal
½ cup all-purpose flour
½ teaspoon salt
¼ teaspoon cayenne pepper

2 teaspoons sugar
1½ teaspoons baking powder
½ cup milk
1 egg
¼ cup bacon drippings or
  vegetable oil

Peel onions and cut crosswise into ½-inch slices. Remove centers of slices to leave ½-inch-thick rings. Prepare batter by mixing rest of ingredients in order given. Place onion rings on griddle that has been coated liberally with oil and heated to 350° (medium heat). Fill each onion ring with batter and cook on one side. Turn and cook on other side. Serve hot.

Onions Make the Meal Cookbook (Idaho)

Cheezy Hot French Bread

1 long loaf French bread
½ cup margarine, softened
1 tablespoon prepared
  mustard
¼ cup minced onion

2 tablespoon poppy seeds
1 (8-ounce) package sliced
  Swiss cheese, cut in thirds
2 slices bacon, cooked and
  crumbled

Slice loaf horizontally into two large pieces. Combine margarine, mustard, onion, and poppy seeds. Spread on bread and top with cheese. Place slices in a foil "boat" and sprinkle bacon on top. Bake 15 minutes in 375° oven; cut in serving pieces. Serves 8–12.

Home at the Range IV (Kansas)

PHOTO BY ANDREW YOOL.

Carhenge, in Alliance, Nebraska, is an exact replica of England's Stonehenge constructed of vintage American automobiles, all covered with gray spray paint. Built by Jim Reinders, it was dedicated at the June 1987 summer solstice. In 2006, a visitors' center was constructed to service the site.

Patio Bread

½ cup grated mozzarella
  cheese
½ cup margarine
½ cup mayonnaise
¼ teaspoon dill weed
¼ cup black olives
¼ cup green olives
¼ cup pimento
½ teaspoon garlic salt
¼ cup onion
French bread

Spread mixture on French bread sliced to desired thickness. Can top with pepperoni. Bake uncovered 20 minutes at 350°.

Sharing Our "Beary" Best II (South Dakota)

Parmesan Puffs

Guests' favorite!

¼ cup milk
¼ cup water
½ stick unsalted butter (¼
  cup)
¼ teaspoon salt
½ cup flour
2 large eggs
1 cup freshly grated Parmesan
  cheese
Pepper to taste

In a heavy saucepan combine milk, water, butter, and salt and bring to a boil over high heat. Reduce the heat to moderate, add flour all at once and beat mixture with a wooden spoon until it leaves the side of the pan and forms a ball. Transfer the mixture to a bowl and whisk in eggs, one at a time, whisking well after each addition. Stir in Parmesan cheese and pepper to taste. Drop the batter in 8 mounds on a buttered baking sheet. Bake the puffs in upper ⅓ of a preheated 400° oven for 20 minutes, until crisp.

Recipe from Paradise Gateway B&B, Emigrant, Montana
Recipes from Big Sky Country (Montana)

Poppy Seed Bread with Orange Glaze

2 eggs	1 cup milk
¾ cup vegetable oil	1 teaspoon butter extract
1½ cups sugar	1 teaspoon almond extract
2 cups all-purpose flour	1 teaspoon vanilla extract
1 teaspoon salt	1 tablespoon poppy seeds
1 teaspoon baking powder	Orange Glaze

Preheat oven to 350°. Combine eggs, oil, and sugar in large bowl; mix well. Combine flour, salt, and baking powder in bowl. Add flour mixture to egg mixture alternately with milk, mixing well after each addition. Add butter extract, almond extract, vanilla, and poppy seeds; mix well. Pour into greased and floured 6x10-inch loaf pan. Bake for one hour. Remove from pan. Let cool on wire rack.

Brush Orange Glaze on top, sides and bottom of bread with pastry brush. Repeat frequently until all glaze is used. Wrap in waxed paper, then in foil to store. Freezes well. Yields 10–12 servings.

ORANGE GLAZE:

½ cup sugar	½ teaspoon almond extract
⅓ cup orange juice	½ teaspoon vanilla extract
½ teaspoon butter extract	

Combine sugar, orange juice, butter extract, almond extract, and vanilla in bowl; mix well.

Cheyenne Frontier Days "Daddy of 'em All" Cookbook (Wyoming)

Wheat isn't native to Kansas, but for many people across the country, when they think wheat, they think Kansas. The state has the nicknames "Wheat State" and "Breadbasket of the World" for good reason: Kansas leads the nation in wheat production.

Flatwillow Colony Zucchini Bread

The colony makes dozens and dozens of loaves of this bread and sells them at the Billings, Montana, Country Market.

6 eggs	1 teaspoon cinnamon
2 cups oil	2 teaspoons mace
4 cups sugar (scant)	2 teaspoons nutmeg (or more)
3 cups white flour	½ teaspoon ground cloves
3 cups whole-wheat flour	(optional)
2 teaspoons baking soda	4 cups peeled, grated zucchini
1 teaspoon salt	6 teaspoons vanilla
1 teaspoon baking powder	1½ cups chopped nuts

Preheat oven to 350°. In your mixer, place the eggs, oil, and sugar and beat well. Add flours, soda, salt, baking powder, spices, zucchini, and vanilla; mix well. Add nuts. Pour batter into 4 greased loaf pans and bake at 350° for 45–50 minutes, or until center springs back.

Heavenly Recipes and Burnt Offerings (Montana)

Rhubarb Bread

Wyoming gardens are often filled with rhubarb in the spring. You can freeze the sliced fresh rhubarb in 1½-cup batches and then make the bread whenever you choose. The bread freezes well, also.

½ cup butter, softened	1 teaspoon baking powder
1 cup sugar	½ teaspoon baking soda
2 eggs	½ teaspoon salt
½ teaspoon orange extract	½ teaspoon nutmeg
1½ teaspoons dairy sour	1½ cups sliced rhubarb
cream	(⅛- to ¼-inch pieces)
2 cups sifted flour	1 cup chopped nuts

Cream butter and sugar. Add eggs, one at a time, mixing well after each addition. Blend in orange extract and sour cream. Sift together the dry ingredients and combine with the butter mixture. Stir in rhubarb and nuts. Pour into 1 greased 9x5x3-inch loaf pan (or 2 small loaf pans). Bake at 325° for 1 hour and 20 minutes for the large pan, about 1 hour for smaller pans.

Wyoming Cook Book (Wyoming)

Sausage Bread

Great on Christmas morning. Can have ready to bake and stick in oven when opening gifts.

1 loaf fresh or frozen bread
  dough
1½ pounds sausage, cooked
  and drained

8 ounces skim mozzarella
  cheese, grated
¼ onion, diced small
1 tablespoon butter

Roll bread dough as to make cinnamon rolls. Layer dough with sausage, cheese, and onions. Roll like a cinnamon roll. Raise in greased pan. When double, bake at 350° until golden brown. Take a fork and run butter over baked loaf. Let cool before cutting.

Recipes from the Heart: 100 Years of Recipes and Folklore (Kansas)

Skillet Cornbread

3 eggs
½ cup sugar
1½ cups flour, sifted
1 cup cornmeal
2½ teaspoons baking powder

½ teaspoon baking soda
1 teaspoon salt
1½ cups buttermilk
⅓ cup butter, melted
1 teaspoon butter

Beat eggs with sugar until blended. Sift together flour, cornmeal, baking powder, baking soda, and salt. Add dry ingredients alternately with buttermilk to the egg/sugar mixture. Stir thoroughly after each addition. Stir in melted butter. Melt the 1 teaspoon butter in a 9-inch cast-iron skillet. Pour batter into warm skillet. Bake at 400° for 30 minutes or until top begins to brown. Serve warm in wedges from the skillet.

Ashton Area Cookbook (Idaho)

Spicy Corn Muffins

½ cup butter or margarine,
  softened
½ cup sugar
5 eggs
1 cup buttermilk
1 (4-ounce) can chopped
  green chiles, drained
1¼ cups cornmeal
1 cup all-purpose flour

½ teaspoon salt
2 teaspoons baking powder
1 cup whole-kernel corn,
  drained
1 cup shredded Cheddar
  cheese
1 cup shredded Monterey Jack
  cheese

In large mixing bowl cream butter and sugar. Add eggs, one at a time, beating well after each addition. Beat in buttermilk and chiles; mix well. Combine dry ingredients; gradually add to creamed mixture. Fold in corn and cheeses. Fill well-greased, cast-iron-shaped muffin pan or regular muffin cups with about ⅓ cup batter. Bake at 375° for 20–25 minutes or until a toothpick comes out clean. Cool for 5 minutes before removing from pans to wire rack. Serve warm with butter.

Ranch Recipe Roundup IV (Wyoming)

The Corn Palace in Mitchell, South Dakota, was built around 1892 to encourage settlement and prove the richness of eastern South Dakota soil. The Moorish Revival palace is decorated inside and out with thousands of bushels of native corn, grain, and grasses. The exterior corn murals are replaced and redesigned each year with a new theme by local artists and is celebrated with a citywide festival, the Corn Palace Festival. Besides being a tourist attraction, the Corn Palace also serves the local community as a venue for concerts, sports events, exhibits, and other community events.

Toffee Delight Muffins

2 cups flour
1 cup sugar
1 cup water
4 eggs
1 small package instant
  vanilla pudding

1 small package instant
  butterscotch pudding
2 teaspoons baking powder
1 teaspoon salt
¾ cup vegetable oil
1 teaspoon vanilla

TOPPING:

1 cup firmly packed brown
  sugar

¾ cup chopped pecans
1 teaspoon cinnamon

Mix together all except Topping. Beat 2 minutes. Using ½ of batter, pour and fill each muffin cup ⅓ full. Mix together topping. Sprinkle ½ of Topping on muffins. Add remaining batter to fill each muffin cup ⅔ full, then put rest of Topping on. Bake 15–20 minutes at 350°.

Heavenly Recipes (North Dakota)

Pumpkin Chip Muffins

4 eggs
2 cups sugar
1 (16-ounce) can pumpkin
1½ cups vegetable oil
3 cups flour
2 teaspoons baking soda

2 teaspoons baking powder
1 teaspoon ground cinnamon
1 teaspoon salt
2 cups (12 ounces) chocolate
  chips

In a large mixing bowl, beat eggs, sugar, pumpkin, and oil until smooth. Combine flour, baking soda, baking powder, cinnamon, and salt. Add to pumpkin mixture and mix well. Fold in chocolate chips. Fill greased or paper-lined muffin cups ¾ full. Bake at 400° for 16–20 minutes or until muffins test done. Cool in pan 10 minutes before removing to a wire rack. Makes about 24 standard-size muffins.

Recipes from the Heart / Epsilon Omega Sorority (Nebraska)

Peach Upside Down Muffins

2 cups flour
1½ cups sugar
1 tablespoon baking powder
½ teaspoon salt
¼ cup shortening, melted
2 eggs, lightly beaten
1 cup milk

6 tablespoons butter or
  margarine
1 cup plus 2 tablespoons
  packed brown sugar
3 cups sliced peeled ripe
  peaches

In a mixing bowl, combine flour, sugar, baking powder, and salt. Add shortening, eggs, and milk; mix until smooth. In bottom of 18 greased muffin cups, place one teaspoon butter and one table-spoon brown sugar. Place in a 375° oven for 5 minutes. Arrange peaches in the muffin cups. Fill each cup half full with batter. Bake at 375° for 25 minutes or until browned. Turn out of pans immediately.

Heavenly Recipes (North Dakota)

Almond Rusks

3 eggs
1 cup sugar
1 cup vegetable oil
3½ cups all-purpose flour

1 cup finely chopped almonds
1½ teaspoons baking powder
1 teaspoon salt

In a mixing bowl, beat eggs. Add sugar and oil; mix well. Combine flour, almonds, baking powder, and salt. Gradually beat into the sugar mixture. Chill the dough until firm. Divide into three pieces. Roll each piece into an 8x2-inch rectangle. Place on a greased baking sheet. Bake at 350° for 15–20 minutes or until firm to the touch. Cool on a wire rack for 15 minutes. Reduce heat to 300°. Carefully cut rectangle into ½-inch slices. Place slices with cut-side-down on baking sheet. Bake 8–10 minutes longer. Yields 4 dozen.

Sharing God's Bounty (Kansas)

Trapper Peak Huckleberry Yogurt Muffins

2 cups baking mix (Bisquick)
2 tablespoons sugar
¼ teaspoon baking soda
¼ cup butter, melted

1 egg
1 (8-ounce) container plain
  yogurt
1 cup huckleberries, drained

In large mixing bowl combine baking mix, sugar, and baking soda, and mix well with wooden spoon. Add butter, egg, and yogurt. Mix until moist. Mix in huckleberries. Fill muffin cake tins ½ full. Bake in preheated 400° oven 15–20 minutes until golden brown. Remove from oven and place on cooling rack. Makes 12 muffins.

Bitterroot Favorites & Montana Memories (Montana)

Mocha Vanilla Huckleberry Muffins

1 tablespoon instant coffee
  granules
¼ cup warm milk
1¾ cups flour
2 teaspoons baking powder
½ teaspoon baking soda
½ cup packed brown sugar
½ cup ground walnuts

2 teaspoons pure vanilla
  extract
1 egg, lightly beaten
1 cup sour cream
½ stick (¼ cup) margarine,
  melted
1¼ cups huckleberries

In a small bowl, dissolve instant coffee in milk. Mix flour, baking powder, baking soda, brown sugar, and walnuts. Add remaining ingredients, except huckleberries, stirring until just moistened. Gently fold in berries. Spoon batter into paper cup-lined muffin pans. Bake at 400° about 20 minutes. Makes a dozen.

Huckleberry Haus Cookbook (Idaho)

Lemon Huckleberry Scones

Huckleberries are not available commercially but are very similar to the widely available blueberry.

2 cups flour
⅓ cup plus 2 tablespoons
** sugar, divided**
2½ teaspoons baking powder
¼ teaspoon kosher salt
⅛ teaspoon ground nutmeg
½ cup (1 stick) cold butter,
** cut into chunks**

1 egg
½ cup milk
2 teaspoons grated lemon zest
¾ cup fresh or frozen
** blueberries**
1 tablespoon melted butter

Preheat oven to 400°. Stir together flour, ⅓ cup sugar, baking powder, salt, and nutmeg. Cut in the butter with pastry blender or by hand until mixture resembles coarse crumbs. Beat the egg with milk and lemon zest. Pour egg mixture over flour mixture and stir once or twice, then add the blueberries and stir just until moist.

Gather dough into a ball and place on greased baking sheet. Pat dough into a 9-inch circle, about ¾ inch thick. With a sharp wet knife, and without cutting all the way through, score the dough into 8 wedges. Do not separate the dough. Brush the tops with melted butter and sprinkle with remaining 2 tablespoons sugar. Bake until golden brown, about 20–30 minutes. Remove from oven and cool 2 minutes. Separate the scones into 8 pieces and serve. Makes 8 scones.

Editor's Extra: It helps to grease your hands, too, for easier patting. Maybe add a little extra zest on top. Delicious!

Recipe from Triple Creek Ranch, Darby, Montana
The Cool Mountain Cookbook (Montana)

Wall Drug Store is a tourist attraction in Wall, South Dakota. Pharmacist Ted Hustead bought Wall Drug in 1931, located in a 231-person town in "the middle of nowhere," and strove to make a living. Business was very slow until Hustead's wife, Dorothy, got the idea to advertise free ice water to parched travelers heading to the newly-opened Mount Rushmore monument sixty miles to the west. From that time on business was brisk. By 1981 Wall Drug was giving away 20,000 cups of water per day during the peak tourist season. It is now a sprawling shopping mall consisting of a drug store, gift shop, restaurants, and various other stores.

Cranberry Walnut Scones

6 tablespoons butter
2 cups flour
¼ teaspoon cinnamon
2 tablespoons sugar
3 teaspoons baking powder

½ cup milk
½ cup maple syrup
½ cup cranberries
½ cup chopped walnuts
1 egg, beaten

Cut butter into flour until coarse in texture. To this mixture, stir in cinnamon, sugar, and baking powder. Add milk and maple syrup. Stir until just blended. Add cranberries and nuts. Blend until distributed. If needed, add more liquid or flour to form a nice biscuit dough. Divide into 2 balls. Pat each half into a circle about ¾–1 inch thick. Cut each circle into 8 wedges, as if cutting a pie. Brush with egg glaze. Bake on ungreased cookie sheet at 425° for 15 minutes or until golden. Makes 16 scones.

Breakfast and More (Wyoming)

Quick Caramel Rolls

½ cup butter
½ cup vanilla ice cream
½ cup brown sugar

½ cup white sugar
2 packs Big Country Biscuits

Melt butter and vanilla ice cream; stir until well blended. Add brown sugar and white sugar. Mix together well and pour over biscuits in Bundt pan. Bake at 350° for 25 minutes. They should be lightly browned. After removing from the oven, let set for a few minutes and tip pan upside down onto serving tray.

We Love Country Cookin' (North Dakota)

James Cash Penney opened his first store, The Golden Rule Store, in Kemmerer, Wyoming, on April 14, 1902. Five years later, Penney bought The Golden Rule Store chain; six years after that, in 1913, he changed its name to JCPenney. Stores now number more than 1,000 and are located throughout the United States.

Opal's Double Butterscotch Crescent Rolls

1 package dry yeast
¼ cup warm water
1 (3-ounce) package
  butterscotch pudding mix
1½ cups milk

½ cup butter, melted
2 eggs
2 teaspoons salt
4½–5½ cups flour

Soften yeast in warm water. Prepare pudding mix using 1½ cups milk; when thickened, add melted butter. Blend unbeaten eggs, salt, and softened yeast into pudding. Gradually add flour to form a stiff dough, beating well after each addition. Cover and let rise in a warm place about 1½ hours.

FILLING:

¼ cup butter, melted
⅔ cup brown sugar
2 tablespoons flour

⅔ cup grated coconut
⅓ cup pecan pieces

Combine melted butter, brown sugar, flour, coconut, and pecan pieces.

Divide dough into thirds and roll each part into a 15-inch circle; cut dough into 12 wedges, using a pastry wheel. Place rounded teaspoon of Filling onto each wedge and roll up, starting with the wide end. Place on cookie sheet in crescent form. Let rise in warm place about 1 hour. Bake at 375° for 12–15 minutes.

GLAZE:

½ cup brown sugar
2 tablespoons water

2 tablespoons butter
1 cup powdered sugar

Combine brown sugar, water, and butter in saucepan. Bring to boil and boil 1 minute. Stir in powdered sugar; thin with milk, if necessary. Glaze rolls while still warm. Makes 3 dozen rolls.

Recipe from Bessemer Bend Bed & Breakfast, Casper, Wyoming
Tastes & Tours of Wyoming (Wyoming)

Cake Mix Sweet Rolls

4–5 cups flour
1 (9-ounce) white cake mix
  (Jiffy)
2 packages rapid-rise yeast
1 teaspoon salt
2 cups warm (120°–130°) water
Butter
Sugar
Cinnamon

In large mixing bowl, combine 2½ cups flour, cake mix, yeast, salt and warm water. Mix until smooth. Add enough of remaining flour to make a soft dough. Turn out on a floured surface and knead until smooth. Roll dough into a 9x18-inch rectangle. Spread with butter and sprinkle with sugar and cinnamon. Roll jellyroll-style, starting with long edge. Slice into 1-inch circles and place on greased cookie sheets. Cover and let rise until doubled, about 15 minutes. Bake at 350° for 15–18 minutes. Frost, if desired. Makes 18 very large rolls.

Tried & True II (North Dakota)

Victory Baked Apple Rolls

APPLE LAYER:
3–4 apples, peeled and thinly
  sliced
¼ cup sugar

Combine apples and sugar; set aside.

DOUGH:
½ cup flour
3 teaspoons baking powder
1 teaspoon salt
3 tablespoons shortening
½ cup milk
1 tablespoon butter

Mix first 5 ingredients and roll out on floured board. Spread with Apple Layer, dot with butter, and roll jellyroll-style; cut into rolls.

SAUCE:
¾ cup sugar
½ cup brown sugar
½ teaspoon nutmeg
⅛ teaspoon salt
1 teaspoon cinnamon
2 cups water

Bring ingredients to boil and pour into 9x13-inch pan. Place cut rolls in hot Sauce. Bake at 400° for 30 minutes.

Quilter's Delight, Busy Day Recipes (Idaho)

Frosted Orange Rolls

CREAMY ORANGE FILLING:

3 tablespoons soft butter
1 tablespoon grated orange
 rind

2 tablespoons orange juice
1½ cups sifted, powdered
 sugar

Combine all ingredients and beat until creamy and smooth. Set aside.

60-MINUTE SWEET DOUGH:

½ cup milk
1 teaspoon salt
1 tablespoon sugar
1 cake yeast or dry yeast

1 egg
2 tablespoons soft shortening
2–2½ cups sifted flour

Heat milk to lukewarm; remove from heat and add salt and sugar. Crumble yeast into mixture; stir until dissolved. Stir in egg and shortening. Add flour. Mix just enough to handle easily and knead until smooth. Roll dough into 12x17-inch rectangle. Spread surface with ½ of Creamy Orange Filling.

Roll up dough as for cinnamon rolls; cut into 12 slices. Grease round 9-inch pan. Let rise until double in size. Bake at 375° or 400° (depending on oven) for 10–15 minutes. Watch closely. Remove from pan. Spread remaining Creamy Orange Filling over top.

Can double or quadruple the recipe. If small tea rolls are preferred, use half the amount of dough, and cut the same amount of slices (12). Double the recipe will fill a jellyroll-size pan.

Be Our Guest (Idaho)

Cinnamon Sunrise Bread

2 teaspoons bread machine
  yeast
1⅓ cups flour (Natural
  White™)
2 cups whole-wheat flour
  (Prairie Gold®)
1½ tablespoons dry milk
3 tablespoons brown sugar
1 teaspoon salt
4 tablespoons butter
2 teaspoons cinnamon
1⅓ cups water
1 cup raisins

Combine all ingredients, except raisins, in bread machine basket. Add raisins after the rest of the ingredients have mixed for a while. Follow instructions for baking in your bread machine. (I set my machine on whole-wheat and select the 5-hour setting.) Makes 1 loaf.

Wheat Montana Cookbook (Montana)

Almond Apple Coffeecake

⅓ plus ¾ cup sugar, divided
½ cup sliced almonds
  (optional)
2 teaspoons cinnamon
½ cup butter or margarine
2 eggs
1 teaspoon vanilla
2 cups flour
1 teaspoon baking powder
1 teaspoon baking soda
½ teaspoon salt
1 cup sour cream
1 medium apple, pared, cored,
  and sliced

Mix together ⅓ cup sugar, almonds, and cinnamon, and set aside. Cream butter and gradually add ¾ cup sugar; beat until fluffy. Add eggs and vanilla. Sift together flour, baking powder, baking soda, and salt. Add to butter mixture. At LOW speed, add butter/flour mixture alternately with sour cream, beating well after each addition. Spread ½ of batter in greased and floured Bundt or tube pan. Top with apple slices, and sprinkle with ½ of almond mixture. Pour in remaining batter, and top with remaining almond mixture. Bake at 375° for about 45 minutes. Cool 30 minutes in pan.

Note: Can be baked, then wrapped in foil and frozen—reheated in foil at 350° for 50 minutes. Open foil last 10 minutes. (Can use apples which are no longer good eating, but haven't turned brown.)

With Lots of Love (Wyoming)

Raspberry Cream French Toast

Simply delicious!

½ cup powdered sugar
2 teaspoons vanilla extract
½ cup milk
1 cup heavy cream
2 cups raspberries, fresh or frozen
6 eggs, beaten

12 slices day-old French bread (1 inch thick)
Vegetable oil as needed
Sifted powdered sugar (optional)
Fresh raspberries (optional)

Preheat oven to 400°. Place powdered sugar, vanilla, milk, heavy cream, and raspberries in a blender and blend until smooth. Pour mixture into a large bowl and whisk in beaten eggs. Place bread slices in a large shallow pan. Pour egg mixture over the bread and turn to coat both sides. Let sit 5 minutes.

Meanwhile, heat a nonstick skillet or griddle over medium-low heat. When hot, add 1 tablespoon of oil and heat for 1 minute. Add several soaked bread slices and cook for 5–6 minutes, until golden brown, then flip and cook on the other side until golden brown, 4–5 minutes more. Remove bread from skillet and place on a baking sheet in the preheated oven for 3–5 minutes, or until crisp.

While the first batch is crisping in the oven, cook the next batch of bread in the same manner, 5–6 minutes on the first side and 4 or more minutes on the other side. Finish in the oven for an additional 3–5 minutes. Sprinkle with powdered sugar and fresh raspberries, if desired. Serve with warm maple syrup. Makes 4–5 servings.

Recipe from Rusty Parrot Lodge, Jackson, Wyoming
The Cool Mountain Cookbook (Wyoming)

Old-Fashioned Potato Pancakes

We serve these with a heap of rustic bacon, grilled tart apples, and a fruity syrup, sometimes our own homemade chokecherry compote.

4 cups peeled, diced, raw
  baking potatoes, divided
2 tablespoons all-purpose flour
½ teaspoon baking powder
¼ teaspoon baking soda

½ teaspoon salt
2 eggs
2 tablespoons Butter Flavor
  Crisco

Using blender or food processor, liquefy 3½ cups of potatoes. Blend in the dry ingredients and eggs. Add the remaining ½ cup potatoes, blending or processing until chunks are quite small. Cook in Crisco on 375° griddle until crispy outside, tender inside, turning once. Serves 6 big appetites.

Recipe from Charley Montana Bed & Breakfast, Glendive, Montana
A Taste of Montana (Montana)

Homemade Maple Syrup

1 cup brown sugar
1 cup white sugar
1 cup light corn syrup
1 cup water

Few grains salt
½ teaspoon maple flavoring,
  or to taste

Combine all ingredients except flavoring. Boil 1–2 minutes. Remove from heat; stir in flavoring. This will not sugar. Store in refrigerator.

Favorite Recipes of Montana (Montana)

INTERNATIONAL PANCAKE HALL OF FAME

In Liberal, Kansas, the day before Lent means just one thing . . . it's Pancake Day. The friendly little competition between Liberal, Kansas, and Olney, England, with women running down the streets of each town flipping pancakes, has been going on for more than 50 years, and is still the only race of its kind. Racers must wear a head scarf and apron and must flip their pancake at the starting signal, and again after crossing the finish line, to prove they still have their pancake.

Waffles Supreme

5¼ cups biscuit mix	3 cups club soda
1 cup oil	1 teaspoon vanilla
2 large eggs	½ cup chopped pecans

Put biscuit mix in large bowl. Add oil, eggs, and small amount of club soda. Mix. Add vanilla and pecans. Add rest of club soda in small amounts and mix. Heat waffle iron and cook as per instructions for your waffle iron. May freeze and reheat in toaster.

90th Anniversary Trinity Lutheran Church Cookbook (Kansas)

Sinfully Chocolate Waffles

My craving for chocolate brings this absolutely fabulous recipe to my best of friends (and probably a few "unfriendlies," too). When I received the recipe from a friend, I thought chocolate waffles were going a bit far . . . wrong— they are the BEST waffles I have ever had the privilege to savor. Need I tell you more!!!?

2 cups all-purpose flour	2 eggs, separated
4 teaspoons baking powder	1½ cups low-fat milk
1 teaspoon salt	1 teaspoon maple flavoring
3 tablespoons sugar	4 tablespoons vegetable oil
3 teaspoons cocoa	

In a large mixing bowl, add the dry ingredients and stir to mix well. Add egg yolks, milk, maple flavoring, and oil. Mix well. Beat egg whites until soft peaks form; add to batter mixture. Bake in waffle iron as you would any other waffle.

Serve with Mapeline Syrup or syrup of your choice. I spoon fresh fruit on top, then a little Mapeline Syrup on top of the fruit. Yields 6–8 waffles.

MAPELINE SYRUP:

2 cups granulated sugar	½ teaspoon maple flavoring
1 cup water	

Mix together and bring to boil. Serve warm with waffles.

Best-of-Friends, Festive Occasions Cookbook (Montana)

Huckleberry Waffles

1½ cups cake flour
¼ cup oat bran
2 teaspoons baking powder
1 tablespoon sugar

3 eggs, separated
¼ cup butter, melted
1½ cups milk
1½ cups huckleberries

Sift together flour, bran, baking powder, and sugar. Beat egg yolks. Add to butter. Stir into dry ingredients until dry particles are just moistened. Beat egg whites stiff. Fold into batter along with huckleberries. Bake on preheated waffle iron. Serves 4.

The Rocky Mountain Wild Foods Cookbook (Idaho)

Cream Cheese Brunch Bars

2 tubes crescent rolls
2 (8-ounce) packages cream
  cheese, softened
1 cup sugar

1 egg, separated
½ cup sugar
1–2 teaspoons cinnamon

Spread one tube of crescent rolls in 9x13x2-inch pan, patting edges together to form crust. Meanwhile, whip softened cream cheese, one cup sugar, and egg yolk together. Spread on layer of rolls. Top with other tube of rolls. Glaze with beaten egg white. Mix together ½ cup sugar and cinnamon. Sprinkle over egg white. Bake at 350° for 20 minutes. Makes 24 bars.

Recipe from Candlelight Bed and Breakfast, Belle Fourche, South Dakota.
South Dakota Sunrise (South Dakota)

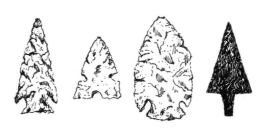

Sunrise Enchiladas

8 whole green chiles
(about 2 [4-ounce] cans)
8 (7-inch) flour tortillas
2 cups cooked sausage,
crumbled, or chopped ham
or bacon
½ cup sliced green onions
½ cup finely chopped green
bell pepper
2½ cups shredded Cheddar,
divided

4 eggs
2 cups light cream
1 tablespoon flour
¼ teaspoon salt
1 clove garlic, minced
Tabasco
Avocado slices (optional)
Salsa for garnish
Sour cream for garnish
Cilantro for garnish

Place opened green chile on one end of tortilla. Combine meat, green onions, pepper, and ⅓ cup plus 3 tablespoons cheese. Spoon over green chile. Roll up and arrange in greased casserole dish, seam-side-down. Combine eggs, cream, flour, salt, garlic, and Tabasco, and pour over tortillas. Cover and refrigerate overnight. Uncover, and bake in 350° oven for 45–50 minutes. Sprinkle with remaining cheese and bake 3 minutes. Serve with avocado, salsa, sour cream, and cilantro. Makes 8 enchiladas.

Breakfast and More (Wyoming)

Breakfast Pizza

1 pound sausage
1 package crescent rolls
1 cup frozen hash browns,
thawed
1 cup sharp Cheddar cheese,
shredded

5 eggs
½ cup milk
½ teaspoon salt
⅛ teaspoon pepper
2 tablespoons grated Parmesan
cheese

Cook sausage; drain off fat. Separate crescent rolls. Place in ungreased pizza pan with points toward center. Press over bottom and up sides to form crust. Seal edges. Spoon sausage over crust. Sprinkle with hash browns. Top with Cheddar cheese.

In bowl, beat eggs, milk, salt, and pepper. Pour over crust. Sprinkle with Parmesan cheese. Bake at 375° for 25–30 minutes. Yields 8–10 servings.

Centerville Community Centennial Cookbook (Kansas)

Deviled Egg Bake

8 hard-boiled eggs, peeled
¼ cup butter, melted
½ teaspoon Worcestershire
1 teaspoon dried parsley

1 tablespoon grated onion
¼ teaspoon dry mustard
1 cup shredded Cheddar
  cheese

Cut hard-boiled eggs in half; remove yolks. To the yolks add melted butter, Worcestershire, parsley, onion, and dry mustard. Mash and mix together. Fill egg whites and put into greased baking dish.

WHITE SAUCE:
2 tablespoons melted butter
¼ cup flour
1 cup hot water

Salt and pepper, to taste
¾ cup cream

Melt butter and blend in flour. Add hot water to flour mixture. Season with salt and pepper. Add cream. Mix well and cook over low heat until thick. Pour white sauce over eggs and sprinkle with cheese. Cover dish and bake at 350° for 25 minutes. Makes 4–6 servings.

Recipe from Willow Springs Cabins Bed & Breakfast, Rapid City, South Dakota.

South Dakota Sunrise (South Dakota)

Scrumptious Eggs

1½ pounds Monterey Jack
  cheese, shredded
¾ pound fresh mushrooms,
  sliced (or 1 can)
½ onion, chopped
¼ cup margarine
1 or 2 cups cubed ham

7 eggs
1¾ cups milk
½ cup flour
1 tablespoon parsley or
  freeze-dried chives
1 teaspoon seasoned salt

Place half of cheese in buttered 9x13-inch pan. Sauté mushrooms and onions in margarine until tender. Spread ham over mushrooms and top with rest of cheese. Cover and refrigerate till ready to bake. When ready to bake, beat eggs, milk, flour, parsley, and seasoning. Pour evenly over casserole. Bake 45 minutes at 350°. Serves 7.

Home at the Range III (Kansas)

Glacier Breakfast Bake

2 cups fully cooked diced
  ham
1 (12-ounce) package frozen
  hashbrown potatoes
½ cup sliced fresh
  mushrooms
1 cup chopped green bell
  peppers

1 tablespoon instant minced
  onion
2 cups shredded Cheddar
  cheese, divided
3 cups milk
1 cup baking mix (Bisquick)
½ teaspoon salt
4 eggs

Grease a 9x13-inch pan. Mix ham, potatoes, mushrooms, green peppers, onion, and 1 cup cheese. Spread in pan. Stir milk, baking mix, salt, and eggs together until blended. Pour over potato mixture. Sprinkle with remaining 1 cup cheese. Cover and refrigerate for at least 4 hours, but no longer than 24 hours. Preheat oven to 375°. Bake uncovered for 30–35 minutes. Let stand for 10 minutes before serving. Makes 10–12 servings.

Recipe from La Villa Montana, Whitefish, Montana
Recipes from Big Sky Country (Montana)

Beartooth Highway, a National Forest Scenic Byway in Montana, has been described by the late CBS correspondent Charles Kuralt as "the most beautiful road in America." From its beginning at the border of the Custer National Forest to its terminus near the northeast entrance to Yellowstone National Park, this 69-mile stretch of paradise will take you to the top of the world at 12,000 feet, and through the Custer, Shoshone, and Gallatin national forests. Glaciers are found on the north flank of nearly every mountain peak over 11,500 feet in these mountains.

Editor Gwen McKee, roadside on Beartooth Highway.

Breakfast in One

12 eggs, beaten
2 cups milk
6 slices bread, cubed
1 cup grated American cheese
½ cup shredded pepper
   cheese
1½ pounds cooked sausage,
   or 1 pound cubed ham

1 (4-ounce) can chopped green
   chiles
½ teaspoon salt
Dash Worcestershire
½ teaspoon dry mustard

Combine all ingredients well; place in greased baking dish. Cover; leave in refrigerator overnight.

Bake in 350° oven for 1 hour or until golden brown on top.

Cooking with Cops, Too (Idaho)

Breakfast in the Skillet

6 bacon slices
2 tomatoes, diced
½ cup grated cheese
6 eggs, beaten

1 tablespoon snipped chives
1 tablespoon snipped parsley
1 tablespoon Worcestershire
Salt and pepper

In large skillet, cook bacon until crisp, then drain on paper towels. To bacon fat, add tomatoes; sauté 3 minutes. With a wooden spoon, blend in grated cheese, then pour eggs into skillet. Cook mixture over low heat, lifting it occasionally from bottom of skillet with pancake turner, until eggs are set but still very soft. Break bacon into small pieces and add to eggs along with chives, parsley, Worcestershire, and salt and pepper. Toss lightly. Makes 2 generous servings.

Mackay Heritage Cookbook (Idaho)

Spinach and Feta Scramble

12 eggs
½ cup milk
Dash salt and pepper
2 tablespoons butter
½ cup frozen chopped spinach,
   thawed and squeezed

1 cup shredded Monterey Jack
   cheese
½ cup crumbled feta cheese
½ cup chopped mushrooms

Beat together the eggs, milk, salt and pepper. Heat butter in large skillet and scramble eggs until partially set. Fold in spinach, cheeses, and mushrooms until cheese melts. Serves 4.

Recipes Tried and True (Idaho)

Basque Baked Eggs

1 cup Basque chorizo, cut in
   ½-inch cubes
10 eggs
3 cups milk
Dashes of oregano, dry
   mustard, cayenne, pepper,
   and salt

1 (10¾-ounce) can nacho
   cheese soup
1–2 tablespoons milk
3 cups shredded hash browns,
   cooked until browned

Layer chorizo, eggs beaten with milk, oregano, dry mustard, cayenne, pepper, and salt in greased baking dish. Thin cheese soup with 1–2 tablespoons milk and add to dish. Layer browned hash browns last. Bake at 350° for 40 minutes. Serve with toasted bread triangles and fruit of choice. Yields 6–8 servings.

Note: Basque chorizo is an authentic Spanish chorizo made with beef and pork, usually with a slight flavor of oregano and smoke.

A Century of Recipes (Idaho)

 In the late 1800s, a large number of Basque immigrants (people from a small region that straddles the border of Spain and France) came to Idaho from Spain to work mainly as sheepherders. Today, Boise, Idaho's capital, has the largest Basque community in the United States as well as the country's only Basque Museum.

Copper King
Cheese and Bacon Quiche

CRUST:

2 cups flour
½ teaspoon salt

⅓ cup margarine
4–5 tablespoons water

In medium bowl, sift flour and salt; cut in margarine until crumbly. Gather into ball using water to make crumbly dough stick together. Roll between 2 squares of waxed paper to a round that will line a pie pan completely, or line a spring form pan within ½ inch of edge.

FILLING:

1 pound bacon, fried and crumbled
1 pound shredded Swiss cheese
⅓ cup finely chopped onion

4 eggs
2 cups whipping cream
¾ teaspoon salt
¼ teaspoon pepper
½ teaspoon ground red pepper

Combine bacon, cheese, and onion; place in pastry-lined pie pan or spring form pan. Beat eggs lightly and add remaining ingredients. Beat until well blended. Pour egg mixture over other contents. Bake at 350° for 1 hour; test. If quiche is still soft in middle, add 15 minutes baking time, or bake until tester comes out clean. Let stand for 10 minutes and cut into wedges. Serve with fruit.

Recipe from Copper King Mansion, Butte, Montana
Montana Bed & Breakfast Guide & Cookbook, 2nd Edition
(Montana)

As telephone, telegraph, and electrical wire was strewn throughout the country at the end of the 19th century, huge copper mines in the area around Anaconda, Montana (near Butte), provided the necessary materials to build these lines. Marcus Daly, founder of Anaconda, built his own copper smelter just outside of town, which attracted thousands of workers from around the world. The Anaconda Stack, over 585 feet high and 75 feet interior diameter, is one of the tallest freestanding brick structures in the world and the only remnant of the huge copper smelting plant. The site is listed in the National Register of Historic Places.

Egg Blossoms

2 sheets filo pastry
Fresh Parmesan, grated
Fresh spinach leaves
Eggs
Salt
Pepper
Minced green onion
Hollandaise sauce

Preheat oven to 350°. Cut filo into 6- to 6½-inch squares. Using 3 squares, stack askew, brushing melted butter between each layer. Gently push into prepared (sprayed) custard cups. Place spoon of fresh Parmesan in each cup, then fresh spinach. Break egg in each cup; salt and pepper as desired and top with minced onion. Place custard cups on cookie sheet. Bake 25 minutes. Remove blossoms from cups. Before serving, place dollop of hollandaise sauce on top of each blossom.

Variation: You may serve egg on top of a buttered and toasted English muffin instead of baked in the filo blossom.

Editor's Extra: Easy to buy packaged powdered mix for Hollandaise sauce if you're not inclined to make your own.

Breakfast and More (Wyoming)

Oven Apple Butter

5 quarts unsweetened
   applesauce
10 cups sugar
1 cup vinegar
2 teaspoons cinnamon
1 teaspoon ground cloves

Mix all ingredients together. Put in a large roasting pan. Bake at 350° for 3 hours or until thick. Stir every 20 minutes. Pour into jars and seal. Makes approximately 10–12 pints.

Cookin' in Paradise (Idaho)

Deluxe Crockpot Oatmeal

Prepare this at night, then have a delicious, nutritious breakfast waiting for you in the morning.

2 cups milk
¼ cup brown sugar
1 tablespoon butter, melted
¼ teaspoon salt
½ teaspoon cinnamon

1 cup old-fashioned oats
  (Quaker Oats)
1 cup chopped apples
½ cup raisins
½ cup chopped almonds

Grease or spray Pam inside of crockpot. Put above ingredients inside crockpot and mix well. Cover and turn on low heat. Cook overnight or 8–9 hours. Stir before serving. Yields 6–8 servings.

Sharing Our Best (Wyoming)

SOUPS, CHILIS, and STEWS

South of Buhl, Idaho, in the Salmon Falls Creek Canyon stands the world-famous Balanced Rock. Over 48 feet tall and weighing 40 tons, the wind-carved rock balances precariously on a pedestal only 3 feet by 17 inches.

Baked Potato Soup

⅔ cup butter or margarine
⅔ cup flour
7 cups milk
4 large baking potatoes,
  baked, cooled, peeled
  and cubed (about 4 cups)
4 green onions, sliced

12 bacon strips, cooked and
  crumbled
1¼ cups Cheddar cheese
1 cup (8 ounces) sour cream
¾ teaspoon salt
½ teaspoon pepper

In a large soup kettle, melt the butter. Stir in flour; heat and stir until smooth. Gradually add milk, stirring constantly until thickened. Add potatoes and onions. Bring to a boil, stirring constantly. Reduce heat; simmer for 10 minutes. Add remaining ingredients. Stir until cheese is melted. Serve immediately. Yields 8–10 servings.

Amana Lutheran Church 125th Anniversary Cookbook (Kansas)

Potato Soup

12 potatoes, peeled and diced
2 stalks celery, chopped
2 carrots, chopped
2 onions, chopped
½ pound bacon, cooked and
  crumbled

1 (12-ounce) can evaporated
  milk
Salt and pepper to taste
Grated cheese for garnish
Chopped green onions for
  garnish

Cook the potatoes, celery, carrots, and onions in a little water until tender. Add crumbled bacon along with drippings to the potato mixture. Add evaporated milk, salt and pepper to taste. Heat thoroughly. Serve garnished with grated cheese and chopped green onions.

Spragg Family Cookbook (Idaho)

To be sure you're getting genuine, top-quality Idaho potatoes, look for the "Grown in Idaho" seal, which features a silhouette of the state of Idaho, and for the registered certification mark, "Idaho Potatoes." Small Idaho potatoes are ideal for use in salads. Medium-sized Idaho potatoes can be used baked, mashed, or fried. Large potatoes are ideal for french fries or the "meal-in-itself" baked potato.

Cheesy Potato Soup

4–6 strips bacon
4 potatoes, cubed
Water
½ teaspoon garlic powder
   (optional)
Salt and pepper to taste
1 tablespoon chopped onion
   (or more)

1 (10½-ounce) can cream of
   chicken soup or broth
2 tablespoons cornstarch
3 cups milk
1 cup shredded American or
   Velveeta cheese

Fry bacon crisp; crumble and set aside. Cook potatoes in small amount of water (to cover potatoes). Add seasonings and onion. Add bacon. Cook until potatoes are done. Add soup or broth. Dissolve cornstarch in a little water. Add milk and cornstarch to potatoes. Stir in cheese. Heat until cheese is melted.

Note: Ham can be used instead of bacon. May omit cheese.

Simac Family Favorites (Montana)

Broccoli Cheese Soup #3

2 tablespoons butter or
   margarine
¾ cup onion, chopped finely
6 cups water
6 chicken bouillon cubes
1 (8-ounce) package fine egg
   noodles (4 cups)

1 teaspoon salt
⅛ teaspoon garlic powder
2 (10-ounce) packages frozen,
   chopped broccoli
6 cups milk
1 pound Velveeta cheese
Pepper to taste

Heat butter in large saucepan. Add onion and sauté over medium heat for 3 minutes. Add water and bouillon cubes. Heat to boiling, stirring occasionally until bouillon is dissolved. Gradually add noodles and salt so that bouillon mixture continues to boil. Cook, uncovered, for 3 minutes, stirring occasionally. Stir in garlic powder and broccoli. Cook one minute more. Add milk, cheese, and pepper, and continue cooking until cheese melts. Stir constantly and closely watch temperature of soup. As soon as it is hot, remove from heat, as this will curdle if it boils. Reheat leftovers in double boiler or LOW crockpot. Serves 12.

Home at the Range IV (Kansas)

Zuppa Tortellini
(Tortellini Soup)

Freezes well—the taste of Italy.

1 smoked ham hock, split
4 cans chicken broth
1 quart water
2 tablespoons margarine
1 large onion, sliced
2 ribs celery, sliced
1 green pepper, diced
3 carrots, peeled and diced
1 clove garlic, minced
1 box fresh mushrooms, sliced
1 (28-ounce) can tomatoes
1 pound hot Italian sausage
1 package fresh tortellini (from deli section)
1 zucchini, sliced
Parmesan cheese
Parsley

Simmer ham hock in chicken broth and water until meat begins to fall off the bone. Remove, discarding fat and bone. Dice meat. In margarine, sauté onion, celery, green pepper, carrots, and garlic until onion begins to turn golden. Add vegetables to pot. Sauté mushrooms in remainder of margarine. Add to pot. Add tomatoes and simmer ¾ hour. Skim off fat. In the meantime, cook Italian sausage and slice when warm enough to handle. Add to pot. Ten minutes before serving, add tortellini. Five minutes before serving, add zucchini. Garnish with Parmesan cheese mixed with parsley.

If It Tastes Good, Who Cares? II (North Dakota)

Hamburger Soup

1 pound hamburger, browned and drained
2 (14-ounce) cans beef broth
1 (14-ounce) can tomatoes, diced
1 cup chopped onions
⅔–1 cup quick barley
2 cups frozen mixed vegetables
1 (4-ounce) can mushrooms
2 cans golden mushroom soup
1 cup chopped green pepper
Salt and pepper

Mix all ingredients in large saucepan. Bring to a slow boil. Simmer 15–20 minutes, or till barley is tender.

Cookin' with Farmers Union Friends (North Dakota)

Wagon Master Soup

1 large or 2 small cloves of garlic
2 ounces Parmesan cheese, cut into 2 or 3 pieces
4 ounces lean beef, cut into 1-inch cubes
4 ounces lean pork, cut into 1-inch cubes
4 ounces lean turkey, cut into 1-inch cubes
1½ slices white bread, broken into bite-size pieces
¾ cup sliced onion, divided
⅓ cup milk
1 cup sliced carrots
1 cup sliced zucchini
1 (46-ounce) can chicken broth
2 cups cheese-filled tortellini
1 tablespoon basil

Place garlic, Parmesan cheese, beef, pork, turkey, bread, ¼ cup onion, and milk in food processor container with food processor running. Process until evenly ground. Shape into 1-inch meatballs. Place in stockpot. Add ½ cup onion, carrots, zucchini, broth, tortellini, and basil. Bring to a boil. Reduce heat. Simmer slowly for 30–40 minutes or until vegetables are tender. Yields 10 servings.

Cheyenne Frontier Days "Daddy of 'em All" Cookbook (Wyoming)

PHOTO ©PHIL KONSTANTIN

Worn two to six feet into an eroded sandstone ridge by wagon wheels, the Oregon Trail Ruts provide moving testimony of the route followed by thousands of Americans in their migration westward across the Plains during the mid-1800s. The Oregon Trail Ruts National Historic Landmark is located on the south side of the North Platte River about one-half mile south of the town of Guernsey, Wyoming.

Hearty Hamburger Soup

2 tablespoons butter
1 pound hamburger
1 cup chopped onion
1 cup sliced carrots
2 cups tomato juice
1½ teaspoons salt

¼ teaspoon pepper
½ cup chopped bell pepper
1 cup diced potatoes
1 teaspoon seasoned salt
¼ cup flour
4 cups milk, divided

Melt butter in saucepan; brown meat, then add onion and cook until transparent. Stir in remaining ingredients, except flour and milk. Cover and cook over low heat until vegetables are tender, about 20–25 minutes. Combine flour with 1 cup milk. Stir into soup mixture. Boil. Add remaining milk. This makes quite a large amount.

Amish Country Cooking

Spanish Rice and Beef Soup

1 pound beef cube steaks
2 tablespoons butter
1 clove garlic, minced, divided
1 (6.8-ounce) package Spanish rice mix

5 cups water
1 (14½-ounce) can chili-seasoned diced tomatoes, undrained
Chopped fresh cilantro (optional)

Stack beef steaks; cut lengthwise into 1-inch-wide strips, then crosswise into 1-inch pieces. Heat butter in Dutch oven over medium-high heat until melted. Add ½ of beef and ½ of garlic; stir-fry 2–3 minutes or until outside surface of beef is no longer pink. (Do not overcook.) Remove from Dutch oven. Repeat with remaining beef and garlic. Season with 2 teaspoons seasoning mixture from rice mix.

Combine rice mix, remaining seasoning mixture, water, and tomatoes in Dutch oven; bring to a boil. Reduce heat to medium-low; cover tightly and simmer 15–17 minutes or until rice is tender. Return beef to Dutch oven; heat through. Stir in cilantro, if desired. Serve immediately. Makes 4 servings.

Ranch Recipe Roundup IV (Wyoming)

Dorothy's Taco Soup

If you're a taco lover, you'll love this soup!

2 pounds ground beef
1 onion, chopped
2 (15-ounce) cans kidney
   beans with liquid
2 (15-ounce) cans white
   kernel corn with liquid

2 (10½-ounce) cans tomatoes
   with green peppers and
   onions
2 (15-ounce) cans tomato sauce
1 package taco seasoning

Brown ground beef and onion. Add remaining ingredients; cook for 1 hour or so. Serve with corn chips, olives, sour cream, and grated cheese. If too thick, add canned beef broth.

Soup's On at Quilting in the Country (Montana)

Country Chicken and Barley Soup

4 chicken thighs, skinned
½ cup barley
5½ cups chicken stock
1 stalk celery, chopped
3 small carrots, diced
1 large tomato, peeled and
   chopped
2 cloves garlic, minced

1 tablespoon tamari or soy
   sauce
½ teaspoon basil
Dashes of oregano, thyme, and
   cayenne pepper
2 tablespoons minced fresh
   parsley

Place all ingredients, except parsley, in a large saucepan. Bring to a boil, then cover and reduce heat. Simmer for 1¼ hours, stirring occasionally. Remove thighs; when they have cooled slightly, remove meat from bones; cut into bite-size pieces and return the meat to the soup. Simmer for an additional 15–20 minutes; stir in the parsley and serve. Makes 4 servings.

Wolf Point, Montana 75th Jubilee Cookbook (Montana)

Red and Gold Split Pea Soup

It's lucky nasturtiums are in flower right into fall because no one wants to cook split pea soup in summer, and besides, the bright red and gold of the nasturtium blossoms fit so splendidly on a fall table. Nasturtium flowers contain vitamin C, so you are feeding your health and your eyes at the same time.

Don't be surprised to find a pungent taste. Nasturtium is in the same general family as watercress. But the smooth richness of split pea soup asks for an exotic garnish.

If you are out of nasturtiums in your garden, you can use marigold petals. Marigolds are also edible and the colors are the same—red-orange, yellow-gold. If you are out of flowers entirely, a dash of paprika will do nicely.

2 tablespoons chopped onion
1 clove garlic, minced
2 tablespoons oil
1 cup dried split peas
4 cups water
1 teaspoon salt
¼ cup chopped celery leaves
Pinch of summer savory
1 potato, diced

½ cup grated carrot
1 rib celery, chopped
1 tablespoon chopped sweet red pepper
¼ cup chopped parsley
1 cup yogurt
¼ cup nasturtium flowers (petals only)

Sauté the onion and garlic in oil in a large, heavy pot. Add washed split peas, water, salt, celery leaves, and summer savory. Bring to a boil; cover, then simmer 45 minutes or until the peas are tender. Add potato, carrot, celery, red pepper, and parsley. Simmer 25 minutes. Serve hot with a dollop of yogurt and a sprinkling of nasturtium petals. Serves 4.

The Kim Williams Cookbook and Commentary (Montana)

 Between 1861 and 1866, Idaho's gold output totaled about $52 million—or about 19% of the total discovery for the United States at that time.

Pen's Lentil Soup

Lentils abound here in North Central Idaho. The Palouse region, which encompasses parts of Idaho and eastern Washington, is billed the "Lentil Capitol of the World." Whether that's actually true or not, I don't know. What I do know is this: we enjoy a great variety of locally produced lentils. My wife created this recipe one winter day, and it's become a favorite, especially on those cool, gloomy days when fog banks hang halfway down the timbered ridges, and the best spot in the house is being backed up to the woodstove.

1 cup brown lentils
6 slices bacon, diced into
  ¼-inch pieces
4–6 cloves garlic, minced
1 large onion, minced
4–6 ribs celery, diced or
  chopped fine
1 (15-ounce) can garlic and
  herb tomato sauce
2 cups chopped fresh spinach

1½ teaspoons coarsely ground
  pepper
¾ teaspoon garlic salt
4 teaspoons sun-dried tomato
  mustard, if available, or
  3 teaspoons ketchup
1 teaspoon yellow mustard
1½ teaspoons horseradish or
  creamed horseradish

Soak lentils for several hours or overnight, then rinse thoroughly. Bring soaked lentils to a boil in Dutch oven with twice the water to cover; add remaining ingredients. Add water to cover ingredients, and simmer until all fresh vegetables are cooked.

More Cee Dub's Dutch Oven and Other Camp Cookin' (Idaho)

"Eat Your Carrots" Soup

Your mother will be glad that you ate your carrots, and just think how good it is for your eyes!

1 tablespoon margarine
1 large onion, chopped
2 stalks celery, chopped
2 pounds carrots, chopped
6 cups chicken broth

½ teaspoon salt
Ground pepper to taste
Tabasco to taste
¼ cup fresh dill; reserve a few
  sprigs for garnish

In stock pot, melt margarine. Lightly sauté onions and celery. Add carrots, broth, salt, pepper, Tabasco, and dill. Boil 40 minutes. Purée in food processor. Serve immediately. Garnish with fresh dill sprigs. Enjoy!

Soup's On at Quilting in the Country (Montana)

Fresh Cream of Tomato Soup

2 medium-size onions, thinly
 sliced
4 tablespoons butter, divided
5 (14½-ounce) cans diced
 tomatoes, or comparable
 amount of fresh, diced,
 divided
1 bay leaf
4 whole allspice

3 sprigs parsley
1 teaspoon sugar
1 teaspoon salt
¼ teaspoon black pepper
½ teaspoon baking soda
3 cups half-and-half
½ cup flour
1 cup milk

Sauté onions in 2 tablespoons butter for 3–4 minutes. Add 3 cans of the tomatoes, bay leaf, allspice, parsley, sugar, salt, and pepper. Simmer for 8–10 minutes. Put into blender or processor and purée; return to pan. Add soda and half-and-half to the purée.

In a stockpot, melt 2 tablespoons butter. Blend in flour and cook over low heat until smooth and bubbly. Stir in milk; bring to a simmer, stirring constantly. Stir in purée and the remaining 2 cans tomatoes. This gives a chunky consistency. Bring to a simmer. Serve hot.

From the High Country of Wyoming (Wyoming)

Cheatin' Chicken Chowder

2 boneless chicken breasts
 or thighs
2 tablespoons vegetable oil
4 tablespoons soy sauce
6 medium potatoes

3 (10¾-ounce) cans cream of
 mushroom soup
1 (10¾-ounce) can cream of
 chicken soup
1 cup milk

Cut chicken into ½-inch cubes; stir-fry in oil and soy sauce until solid white inside. Cut potatoes into ½-inch cubes; boil for 10 minutes; drain. Mix soups, milk, chicken, and potatoes in soup pot. Cook on low heat for ½ hour, stirring frequently.

Tastes from the Country (Idaho)

All American Clam Chowder

3 slices bacon
½ cup minced onions
1 (7½-ounce) can minced
   clams (save clam liquor)
1 cup cubed potatoes
1 can cream of celery soup
1½ cups milk
Dash of pepper

Cook bacon in frying pan until crisp. Remove and break into 1-inch pieces. Brown onion in bacon fat. Add clam liquor and potatoes. Cover and cook over low heat until potatoes are done, about 15 minutes. Blend in bacon pieces, minced clams, and other ingredients. Heat, but do not boil. Bacon may be used for garnish.

Recipe by Former First Lady Barbara Bush
First Ladies' Cookbook (Montana)

Thunder Mountain Turkey Soup

4 quarts water
1 turkey carcass with some
   meat still attached
1 cup butter
3 onions, finely chopped
1 cup flour
2 (3½-ounce) packages
   boil-in-bag rice
2 large carrots, shredded
2 teaspoons salt
¾ teaspoon coarsely ground
   black pepper

Bring water and turkey carcass to boil in very large stockpot, then reduce heat, cover, and simmer for 3 hours or more. Cool; remove carcass and pick off all the meat, returning it to the broth. Heat butter and sauté onions for 5 minutes. Add flour to the onion and cook 2 minutes more. Add some broth and stir to make a smooth medium paste, then add more to make roux runny. Add roux to the turkey stock and stir until well mixed. Add rice, carrots, and salt and pepper. Bring to boil, then reduce heat and simmer until rice is tender and soup is somewhat thickened. Serve hot.

Note: You may need to add more water to the stock at some point to make texture right, but end product should be thick and stew-like. I call it "Stoup."

Recipes Tried and True (Idaho)

Turkey Gumbo

1 turkey carcass
8 cups water
½ cup butter or margarine
1 cup chopped onion
1 cup chopped celery
⅓ cup flour
1 (28-ounce) can tomatoes
3 cups sliced okra
4–5 bay leaves
⅛ teaspoon thyme
⅛ teaspoon marjoram
2 tablespoons chopped parsley
2 teaspoons gumbo filé
Salt and pepper
Steamed rice

Boil turkey carcass in water until meat falls from the bones, about 2–3 hours. Remove meat from bones and set aside. Reserve broth.

In a large soup kettle, melt butter or margarine and sauté onion and celery. Add flour and stir mixture over medium heat until golden, the color of caramel. Stir in reserved broth, then add tomatoes, okra, bay leaves, thyme, marjoram, parsley, gumbo filé, and reserved turkey meat. Heat to boiling and simmer 30 minutes. Add salt and pepper to taste. To serve, put ½ cup rice in each bowl. Ladle gumbo over rice. Makes 10–12 servings.

Bound to Please (Idaho)

Chili and Cornbread

CHILI:

2 pounds ground beef
2 (10¾-ounce) cans tomato
  soup
1 large onion, chopped
1 (2-pound) can red kidney
  beans, undrained
4 cloves garlic, minced

½–1 red Fresno pepper,
  chopped
1–2 jalapeño peppers, chopped
1–2 green peppers, chopped
At least 2 tablespoons chili
  powder
Salt and pepper to taste

In the bottom of the 14-inch Dutch oven, brown ground beef. Then add all of the other ingredients into the Dutch oven and mix.

CORNBREAD:

2 boxes corn muffin mix
  (Jiffy)

2 eggs
⅔ cup milk

Mix corn muffin mix with eggs and milk, then add to the top of the chili mix. Cook 25–30 minutes at 400°.

Potatoes Are Not the Only Vegetable! (Idaho)

Cow Punching Chili and Dumplings

CHILI:

1 pound ground beef, browned
1 cup chopped onion
1 (28-ounce) can tomatoes
2 8-ounce) cans tomato sauce

1 tablespoon chili powder
2 teaspoons salt
1 (15-ounce) beans (optional)

DUMPLINGS:

1 cup all-purpose flour
1 cup mashed potato flakes
2 teaspoons baking powder
½ teaspoon salt

1 cup milk
1 egg
2 tablespoons oil

Combine all chili ingredients in a pot and simmer until right before serving time. For dumplings, combine flour, flakes, baking powder, and salt. Mix milk with egg and oil and add to above. Stir to moisten. Let stand several minutes. Place spoonfuls on chili, cover tightly and cook 15 minutes.

The Best Little Cookbook in the West (South Dakota)

Northwest Chili

At the core of this chili are the Northwest's chickpeas and lentils.

1 cup chopped onion
2 large garlic cloves, minced
1½ tablespoons canola oil
1 cup dry lentils, rinsed
1 cup diced potatoes
½ cup shredded carrots
1 green bell pepper, seeded
  and chopped
1 tablespoon chili powder,
  or to taste
2½ cups water

2 teaspoons beef bouillon
  granules, or 2 cubes
1 (14½-ounce) can tomatoes
1 (8-ounce) can tomato sauce
1 (15-ounce) can chickpeas,
  drained and rinsed, or about
  2 cups boiled
¼ teaspoon crushed red
  pepper, or to taste
Salt and freshly ground black
  pepper to taste

In a large, heavy saucepan, cook onion and garlic in oil for 3–4 minutes. Add lentils, and stir to coat them with oil. Add potatoes, carrots, bell pepper, chili powder, water, and bouillon. Bring to a boil. Reduce heat, cover, and simmer about 25 minutes, or until lentils are tender.

Add tomatoes, breaking them up as you do, and tomato sauce, chickpeas, and red pepper. Simmer for another 15 minutes. Season to taste with red pepper, salt, and black pepper. Serves 6–8.

The Pea & Lentil Cookbook (Idaho)

Gunsmoke Chili

4 pounds venison, elk or beef,
  ground
2 large onions, minced
1½ teaspoons salt
1 teaspoon coarsely ground
  black pepper
2 tablespoons parsley flakes

1 teaspoon seasoned salt
1½ teaspoons basil
1½ teaspoons oregano
1 teaspoon cayenne pepper
4 tablespoons chili powder
4 cups strong beef bouillon
4 cups tomato sauce

Brown meat and onions together; add remaining ingredients and simmer 2½–3 hours. Serve with cornbread. Serves 10.

Recipes Tried and True (Idaho)

Chili for a Crowd

1 large onion, chopped
1 green pepper, chopped
2 garlic cloves, minced
2 tablespoons butter or
  margarine
2 pounds lean ground beef
½–1 pound bacon, cut into
  ½-inch pieces
½ pound pinto beans,
  cooked till tender
1 pint tomato juice

1 (16- to 20-ounce) can
  chopped tomatoes
1½ tablespoons salt
1 teaspoon cumin
½ tablespoon sugar
2 quarts water from beans
2 tablespoons flour
2 tablespoons chili powder
1 tablespoon Worcestershire
¼ cup water

Sauté onion, green pepper, and garlic cloves in butter. Add ground beef and bacon pieces and sauté till cooked thoroughly. Add beans, tomato juice, chopped tomatoes, salt, cumin, sugar, and water from beans. Cook ingredients together on medium heat till hot; reduce heat; cook for at least 2 hours. Mix together flour, chili powder, and Worcestershire with water; add to chili; stir well. Simmer till ready to serve. Serves 10–12.

The Joy of Sharing (Nebraska)

Drovers' Stew

2 tablespoons olive oil
4 boneless, skinless chicken
  breast halves (1 pound),
  cut into 1-inch pieces
1 cup chopped onion
½ medium green bell pepper,
  chopped
½ medium yellow bell
  pepper, chopped
1 teaspoon chopped garlic

2 (14½-ounce) cans stewed
  tomatoes
1 (15-ounce) can pinto beans,
  drained and rinsed
¾ cup picante sauce
1 tablespoon chili powder
1 tablespoon ground cumin
½ cup shredded Cheddar
  cheese
6 tablespoons sour cream

In large stockpot, heat olive oil over medium heat. Add chicken, onion, bell peppers, and garlic; cook until chicken is no longer pink. Add tomatoes, beans, picante sauce, chili powder, and cumin. Reduce heat to low and simmer for 25 minutes or up to 2 hours. Place in individual serving bowls and top with cheese and sour cream.

From the High Country of Wyoming (Wyoming)

Shepherd's Stew

Back then cowboys had no time for sheep or sheepherders. But more than one cowboy sat down at a sheep camp to fill his belly. I'm sure they wouldn't have ever admitted it in front of anyone. It is also said that a few cooks stole a sheep or two to feed the cowhands so they wouldn't have to use any of their own beef. So it only seemed right to throw in a lamb recipe.

2 pounds lamb shoulder, cubed in 1-inch pieces	**4–5 carrots, sliced**
2 tablespoons fat or butter	**4–5 potatoes, cubed**
Flour	**1 onion, chopped**
2 quarts water	**3–4 ears of corn, cut off**
Garlic, parsley, salt, pepper, and bay leaf to taste	**1 cup green peas**
	2 tablespoons flour

In a Dutch oven, brown the meat in hot fat after it has been dredged in flour. Add the water and seasonings and simmer about 2 hours. Add carrots, potatoes, onion, and corn, and cook another 30 minutes. Add the peas and cook for 15 minutes. Thicken stew with flour and water.

Sowbelly and Sourdough (Idaho)

PHOTO ©RANGE MAGAZINE.

Youngsters with linked arms lead the way through downtown Ketchum, Idaho, during the annual October Trailing of the Sheep Festival.

From 1881 to 1917, the sheep ranching industry boomed in Ketchum, Idaho. Many say it was second only to Sydney, Australia, as the sheep shipping capital of the world. Over the years, several million sheep have trailed through the valley and have been shipped from various points along the railway. The sheep driveway, which parallels the railroad in many places, is still maintained. Sheepherders today still trail their sheep through the Wood River Valley during their annual migrations to and from summer pastures in the northern mountains, and in October 1997, the first annual "Trailing of the Sheep" celebration was held.

Basque Bean Stew

1 pound Idaho Great
  Northern beans
5 cups water
Meaty ham bone or ham hocks
3 bay leaves, divided
1 large onion, quartered
4 potatoes
4 carrots
2 cloves garlic, minced
1 teaspoon thyme
½ pound fully cooked sausage
Salt and pepper
Chopped parsley

Soak beans overnight in water. Or, for quick-soak method, add beans to boiling water, boil 2 minutes and let stand 1 hour. Measure soaking liquid and add water to make 4 cups. Cook beans, ham bone or hocks, 2 bay leaves, and onion in reserved liquid about 2 hours or until beans are tender. Drain, reserving liquid. Peel and coarsely dice potatoes and carrots. Cook in bean liquid with garlic, thyme, and 1 bay leaf until tender.

Add beans, meat from ham bone, and sausages, thickly sliced. Cook just until heated through. Add salt and pepper to taste. Remove bay leaf. Before serving, sprinkle with chopped parsley.

Idaho's Favorite Bean Recipes (Idaho)

Rattlesnake Stew

For the less adventurous, substitute stew meat or cubed steak for rattlesnake.

1 large rattlesnake, skinned,
  cooled and cubed
⅓+ cup flour, divided
1 tablespoon oil
1 large onion, chopped
5 cups water, divided
1 teaspoon seasoned salt
½ teaspoon pepper
2–3 teaspoons salt, or to taste
6 medium potatoes, peeled and
  cubed
2 carrots, peeled and sliced
1 cup sliced celery
2 teaspoons browning sauce

Coat meat lightly with flour (reserve ⅓ cup) and brown in oil in a large pan. Cover with 4 cups water and add chopped onion and seasonings. Bring to a boil and turn down to simmer until meat is tender (1–2 hours), then add vegetables. Bring to a boil and turn down to simmer until the vegetables are tender, about 30 minutes. Combine ⅓ cup flour, 1 cup cold water, and browning sauce until smooth. Stir into the stew, stirring until stew thickens slightly.

Sharing Our Best (Idaho)

Christmas Eve Beef Stew

1 (4-pound) beef brisket
  (or any sturdy beef cut)
Flour
3 tablespoons margarine or
  butter
3 tablespoons vegetable oil
3 garlic cloves, finely chopped
2 tablespoons chopped fresh
  parsley
2 (1-inch pieces) orange peel
1 bay leaf

2 cups warm Burgundy wine
1/4 teaspoon nutmeg
4 carrots, sliced
6 ribs of celery (cut into strips)
12 small white onions
1 teaspoon each salt and
  pepper, or to taste
1 pound fresh mushrooms,
  quartered
1 (10-ounce) package frozen
  peas

Remove fat from brisket and cut into 2-inch cubes. Flour cubes (I throw flour and beef in paper bag and shake). Brown very well in a large heavy Dutch oven on stove in butter and oil. Add garlic, parsley, orange peel, bay leaf, wine, and nutmeg. (Add water if wine doesn't cover beef.) Bring to boil and reduce heat. Cover and simmer on low heat for 1½–2 hours, until meat is tender. Add carrots, celery, onions, salt, and pepper. Cook until meat is thoroughly tender. Add mushrooms and peas the last ½ hour. Serve over noodles or potatoes. Serves 4–6.

The Hole Thing Volume II (Wyoming)

SALADS

Chimney Rock, the slender spire soaring some 500 feet up from the valley floor, signaled to Oregon Trail travelers the end of the prairie and the beginning of the rugged high plains. Bayard, Nebraska.

Country Coleslaw

1 medium head cabbage,
  shredded (8 cups)
1–2 medium onions, diced
  (2 cups)
3 tablespoons chopped canned
  pimento, drained
6 tablespoons chopped green
  bell pepper
¾ cup white vinegar
1 cup sugar
½ teaspoon celery salt
1 heaping tablespoon salt
1 teaspoon celery seed
Salt to taste

Combine all ingredients except salt, blend well, and barely cover with boiling water. Let stand for one hour. Pack into jars and refrigerate overnight. Drain and salt lightly before serving. Serves 6.

All About Bar-B-Q Kansas City Style (Kansas)

Crispy Oriental Salad

DRESSING:
¾ cup canola oil
½ cup sugar
¼ cup red wine vinegar
2 tablespoons soy sauce

Ingredients can be made 3 days in advance and refrigerated.

SALAD:
½ cup margarine or liquid
  butter
1 (1-ounce) bottle sesame
  seeds
2 packages Ramen noodles,
  broken up (do not use
  seasoning)
1 (½-cup) package slivered
  almonds
2 tablespoons sugar
2 pounds bok choy (or Nappa
  cabbage)
5 green onions with tops,
  sliced

In a large skillet melt margarine over medium heat. Add sesame seeds, noodles, almonds, and sugar. Cook until lightly browned. Set aside, cool to room temperature. Meanwhile coarsely chop bok choy using both stalks and leaves. Combine with green onions and chill. Combine everything together just prior to serving. Serves 8–12.

The Hagen Family Cookbook (North Dakota)

Spinach Salad

2 (10-ounce) packages frozen
   chopped spinach
3 boiled eggs, chopped
½ cup chopped celery

½ cup chopped onion
1 cup Longhorn cheese,
   cubed

Squeeze moisture from thawed spinach. Add chopped eggs, celery, onion, and cheese. Add dressing. Best if stored overnight.

DRESSING:

1 cup Miracle Whip
½ teaspoon salt

½ teaspoon Tabasco
2 tablespoons vinegar

Eastman Family Cookbook (Kansas)

Spinach-Avocado-Orange Toss

DRESSING:

½ teaspoon grated orange
   peel
¼ cup orange juice
½ cup oil

2 tablespoons wine vinegar
¼ teaspoon salt
2 tablespoons sugar
1 tablespoon lemon juice

Combine ingredients in a jar and shake until thoroughly blended. Chill.

SALAD:

6 cups washed and torn fresh
   spinach
1 avocado, peeled and sliced
1 small cucumber, thinly
   sliced

2 tablespoons sliced green
   onions
1 (11-ounce) can Mandarin
   oranges, drained

Mix Salad ingredients in bowl and chill. To serve, pour Dressing over Salad and toss lightly.

Cooking with the Ladies (Wyoming)

Avocado Citrus Toss

6 cups torn salad greens
2 medium grapefruits,
   peeled and sectioned
3 oranges, peeled and
   sectioned

1 ripe avocado, peeled and
   sliced
¼ cup slivered almonds,
   toasted

In a large salad bowl, toss the salad greens, grapefruits, oranges, avocado, and almonds.

DRESSING:

½ cup vegetable oil
⅓ cup sugar
3 tablespoons vinegar
2 teaspoons poppy seeds

1 teaspoon finely chopped
   onion
½ teaspoon dry mustard
½ teaspoon salt

In a jar with a tight-fitting lid, combine the Dressing ingredients; shake well. Pour over salad and toss. Serve. Makes 6 servings.

Another Cookbook (Idaho)

Mount Rushmore is a national treasure. The 60-feet tall faces of presidents Washington, Jefferson, Teddy Roosevelt, and Lincoln were originally carved at a cost of $989,992.32. The sculptor, Gutzon Borglum, was born near Bear Lake, Idaho. Borglum spent 14 years working on the massive sculpture (from 1927 until his death in 1941), removing more than 400,000 tons of granite from the 6,200-foot cliff.

Six "S" Salad

Splendid, Summertime, Sports Season, Sunflower Seed salad.

2 (11-ounce) cans Mandarin
  oranges, well drained
½–1 head bibb lettuce, or 1
  head red leaf or combination
1 bunch or more spinach
Chinese pea pods, blanched
  (optional)
Broccoli florets, fresh,
  cut small
½ cup chopped fresh parsley

1 large red onion, or 1 bunch
  green onions, sliced thin
1 (7½-ounce) jar sunflower
  seeds, dry-roasted
1 (6- to 8-ounce) carton frozen
  orange juice concentrate
½ cup (or more) mayonnaise
Seasoned cooked chicken
  strips, heated

Place Mandarin oranges in bottom of large salad bowl; add torn lettuce, spinach, pea pods, broccoli, parsley, onions, and sunflower nuts. Cover. Chill.

Whisk orange juice concentrate and mayonnaise until smooth; adjust mayonnaise to keep tart taste. Pour dressing to coat, but not drench salad, just before serving. Toss. Serve remaining dressing on the side. Serve topped with 3–4 hot seasoned chicken strips for each serving.

Optional additions: May add one or more or substitute, hard-cooked eggs, sprouts/bamboo shoots, cauliflower florets, olives/water chestnuts, cherry tomatoes/radishes, jicama, sliced thin; bacon, shrimp, nuts.

Variation for Dressing: Pineapple chunks and pineapple juice with mayonnaise and orange juice concentrate.

Recipe submitted by Bob Wilson, President/General Manager, Billings Mustangs
Montana Celebrity Cookbook (Montana)

Autumn Salad

SALAD:

2 heads butter lettuce
½ red onion, diced
1 (4-ounce) package blue cheese, crumbled

1 Granny Smith apple, diced
½ cup chopped pecans or walnuts
½ cup dried cranberries

RASPBERRY VINAIGRETTE:

⅓ cup raspberry jam
¼ cup olive or canola oil
4 teaspoons rice vinegar
4 teaspoons cider vinegar, or 8 ounces raspberry vinegar

1 teaspoon coarse-grind mustard, or ½ teaspoon dry mustard

Toss all Salad ingredients. Pour blended Raspberry Vinaigrette over salad.

Salad Sampler from Quilting in the Country (Montana)

Strawberry & Romaine Salad

A wonderful salad. The combination of strawberries and onion is simply delicious—everyone's favorite.

Romaine, washed and torn
Red onion, sliced

Fresh strawberries, sliced
Slivered almonds for garnish

DRESSING:

2 cups mayonnaise
⅔ cup sugar
⅓ cup light cream

⅓ cup raspberry vinegar
2 tablespoons poppy seeds
2–3 tablespoons raspberry jam

Combine dressing ingredients. Toss romaine, onion, and strawberries. Just before serving, drizzle dressing over salad. Dressing can be kept at least a week in refrigerator. Good on fruit, too.

If It Tastes Good, Who Cares? I (North Dakota)

Zesty New Potato Salad

A tangy, light, side dish. Serve either hot or cold. Especially complimentary to ham on the grill.

**1 pound small new potatoes,
  preferably red**
2 ribs celery
3 green onions

**¼ cup prepared Good Seasons
  Salad Dressing**
**2 tablespoons chopped fresh
  parsley**

Peel a ¼-inch ribbon around the middle of each potato. Steam or boil potatoes until barely tender when pierced with a fork (about 15 minutes); drain and quarter. Place in medium bowl. Chop celery and onions, and add to potatoes. Add salad dressing and toss lightly. (Add dressing while potatoes are still warm so the dressing flavor seeps into the potatoes.) Chop parsley and sprinkle on top. Serve warm or chilled. Serves 4–6.

VARIATION:

To add color, toss in other vegetables like yellow squash, red onions, peas, tomatoes, roasted red bell peppers, or pimentos. Or add capers and fresh mint.

Hall's Potato Harvest Cookbook (North Dakota)

Easy German Potato Salad

**1 (24-ounce) package frozen
  hash brown potatoes**
4 slices bacon
1 small onion, chopped
2 teaspoons sugar
1 teaspoon flour

**1 teaspoon instant beef
  bouillon**
1 teaspoon salt
¼ cup vinegar
½ cup water
1 teaspoon chopped chives

Thaw potatoes in a large skillet. Fry bacon until crisp; remove. Add onion to drippings. Cook until tender and golden. Stir in sugar, flour, bouillon, and salt. Cook over medium heat, stirring until bubbly. Remove from heat; stir in vinegar and water. Heat to boiling, stirring constantly. Crumble bacon; carefully stir bacon, potatoes, and chives into hot mixture. Heat thoroughly, stirring lightly to cover potatoes. Yields 5–6 servings.

The Kearney 125th Anniversary Community Cookbook (Nebraska)

Sweet-Sour Green Beans

3 pounds green beans
3 onions, thinly sliced and
  separated into rings
1⅓ cups vinegar
1⅔ cups sugar

⅔ cup water
3 tablespoons salad oil
1½ teaspoons salt
½ teaspoon pepper

Cut off tips of beans; leave whole. Cook in boiling salted water until tender; drain. Combine beans and onion rings in large bowl. Stir together remaining ingredients; pour over bean mixture. Refrigerate at least 24 hours, stirring occasionally. Makes about 3½ quarts.

Note: If fresh beans are not available, use 3 (1-pound) cans whole green beans.

Blew Centennial Bon-Appetit (Kansas)

Bean Salad

1 (20-ounce) can red beans
1 (20-ounce) can green beans
1 (20-ounce) can wax beans
1 (20-ounce) can garbanzo
  beans
1 medium onion, chopped

3 tablespoons olive oil
2 tablespoons Dijon mustard
2 teaspoons red wine vinegar
1 tablespoon lemon juice
1 teaspoon Louisiana hot sauce
1 clove of garlic, minced

Drain and rinse beans. Combine beans and onion in bowl; mix well. Pour mixture of olive oil, Dijon mustard, wine vinegar, lemon juice, hot sauce, and garlic over bean mixture, stirring to coat. Chill, covered, for 2–8 hours before serving. Yield: 12 servings.

The Kansas City Barbeque Society Cookbook (Kansas)

WWW.CITYOFLIBERAL.COM

The Wizard of Oz house, located at the Coronado Museum in Liberal, Kansas, is an exact replica of Auntie Em's house, complete with ruby slippers and a stuffed replica of Toto, too.

Mexicali Chicken Bean Salad

1 (16-ounce) can black beans
1 (16-ounce) can kidney beans
1 (16-ounce) can white beans
2 cups cubed, cooked chicken
1½ cups cubed Cheddar
   cheese
3 medium green peppers,
   chopped
2 cups chunky salsa, medium
½ cup chopped red onion
¼ cup chopped fresh cilantro
2 tablespoons lime juice

Rinse and drain beans. Add rest of ingredients and stir until well combined; refrigerate. Makes a great appetizer with chips or a side dish.

Recipe from The Horned Toad Bed & Breakfast, Ten Sleep, Wyoming
Tastes & Tours of Wyoming (Wyoming)

Marinated Onion-Tomato Salad

2 large onions
   (Idaho-Eastern Oregon)
2 large, ripe tomatoes
2 tablespoons chopped
   parsley
½ cup olive oil
2 tablespoons red wine
   vinegar
1 clove garlic, minced
1½ teaspoons crushed basil
   leaves
1 teaspoon sugar
½ teaspoon each salt and
   black pepper

Cut onions and tomatoes in ¼-inch slices. Combine remaining ingredients except parsley to make marinade. Make a layer of onions and tomatoes and parsley on a platter; drizzle with half of marinade; repeat layers. Cover tightly with plastic wrap and refrigerate overnight. Serves 8.

Onions Make the Meal Cookbook (Idaho)

Smoked Turkey Salad

Delicious served on fresh salad greens, in half a cantaloupe, or on good-quality bread as a sandwich filling, this recipe makes plain old chicken salad taste pretty tame.

2¼ cups bite-sized pieces of
   smoked turkey
1 cup chopped red onion
4 hard-boiled eggs, chopped
   fine
2 cups mayonnaise

2 tablespoons Dijon mustard
1 teaspoon celery salt
1 jalapeño pepper, diced
1 teaspoon white pepper
1 teaspoon black pepper
1 teaspoon ground cumin

Combine turkey, onion, and eggs. In a separate bowl, combine mayonnaise with remaining ingredients. Add mayonnaise mixture to turkey mixture and blend well. Refrigerate until ready to serve. Serves 6–8.

All About Bar-B-Q Kansas City Style (Kansas)

More Than Chicken Salad

MARINADE:

2 tablespoons lemon juice
1 teaspoon prepared mustard
¼ cup oil
¼ teaspoon salt
¼ teaspoon pepper

¼ teaspoon tarragon
¼ teaspoon basil
¼ teaspoon thyme
¼ teaspoon marjoram

Combine ingredients in a cruet and shake.

SALAD:

2 cups cooked and diced
   chicken
1½ cups halved seedless
   green grapes
1 cup mayonnaise

½ cup chopped celery
½ cup slivered almonds,
   toasted
1 teaspoon lemon juice

Toss chicken with Marinade and refrigerate 2 hours. Add remaining ingredients and toss to blend. Serve on lettuce bed or with tomato slices. Serves 6.

The Great Entertainer Cookbook (Wyoming)

Cranberry Chicken Salad

1 (3-ounce) package lemon
  Jell-O
1½ cups hot water
2 cups diced, cooked chicken
2 hard-boiled eggs, chopped
2 teaspoons minced onion

¼ cups chopped, stuffed
  olives
½ cup diced celery
½ cup salad dressing
1 cup cranberry sauce
2 teaspoons orange juice

Dissolve Jell-O in hot water. Mix chicken, eggs, onion, olives, celery, and dressing. Add ½ of Jell-O mixture to chicken mixture. Put this chicken/Jell-O mixture in an 8x8-inch pan. Chill. Meanwhile, mix cranberry sauce until smooth. Add orange juice and remaining Jell-O. Chill before pouring over the chicken layer. Refrigerate until all has set. Cut in squares and serve on a lettuce leaf.

North Dakota: Where Food is Love (North Dakota)

Garden Fresh Chicken Pasta Salad

When you're grilling chicken breasts for another recipe, do three to four extra and try this dish for a change of pace. It makes a quick dish when you want a "lite" dinner or lunch.

1 (12-ounce) package
  vegetable rotini
½ (15-ounce) can black
  olives, sliced
½ cup green olives, sliced
  (optional)
½ small purple onion, diced
1 cucumber or zucchini,
  diced into ½-inch cubes
3–4 large mushrooms, sliced

2 Roma tomatoes, diced
½ green or red bell pepper,
  diced
1 teaspoon salt
4–6 tablespoons olive oil
½ cup vinegar
Ground black pepper to taste
3–4 chicken breasts, grilled and
  seasoned to taste, cut into
  1-inch squares

Cook pasta according to package directions; rinse, and chill in fridge or cooler. Put veggies in a bowl, add salt, and toss. Let veggies rest for 15–20 minutes. Add oil, vinegar, pasta, pepper, and chicken. Gently toss. Let salad rest for about 30 minutes, stirring occasionally. Serve with a side of garlic or French bread.

More Cee Dub's Dutch Oven and Other Camp Cookin' (Idaho)

Gwen's Macaroni Salad

1 (16-ounce) package elbow
   macaroni, cooked
1 slice ham, cut ½ inch
   thick, cubed
1 cup cubed Cheddar cheese
½ cup sliced carrots
½ cup sliced celery
¼ cup diced onion
½ cup diced sweet pickles

1 (4-ounce) can sliced black
   olives
1½ cups mayonnaise
⅓ cup milk
¼ cup sweet pickle juice
½ teaspoon salt
¼ teaspoon pepper
⅛ teaspoon chili powder

In a large bowl, mix macaroni, ham, cheese, carrots, celery, onion, sweet pickles, and olives. In a medium bowl, mix mayonnaise, milk, pickle juice, salt, pepper, and chili powder. Pour mayonnaise mixture over macaroni and vegetable mixture. Stir well until all macaroni and vegetables are well coated. Refrigerate for 1 hour.

The Miracle Cookbook (Idaho)

Greek Feta Salad

DRESSING:
1 cup heavy mayonnaise
1 tablespoon dried oregano
   leaves

1 teaspoon black pepper
¾ cup Italian salad dressing

Whisk Dressing ingredients together in a small bowl; set aside.

SALAD:
1 pound medium-size pasta
   shells
1 cup chopped celery
½ pound Greek feta cheese,
   crumbled

¾ cup sliced black olives
½ cup shredded Parmesan
   cheese
2 ripe tomatoes

Cook pasta in plenty of water, al dente. Drain, and rinse well with cold water. Toss Dressing with pasta and remaining ingredients (except tomatoes). Chop tomatoes coarsely, and gently fold them into the salad. Serves 8.

Salad Sampler from Quilting in the Country (Montana)

Fettuccine Heaven Salad

This recipe is fantastic at the height of tomato season!

DRESSING:

½ cup extra virgin olive oil
1 medium garlic clove, minced
2 tablespoons balsamic vinegar
1 teaspoon salt
Freshly ground pepper to taste

Shake Dressing ingredients together.

SALAD:

1 pound fettuccine, fresh if available
1 medium red onion, diced
1 (3½-ounce) jar capers, drained
1 cup pitted and sliced Greek olives
1 bunch basil leaves, sliced
1 bunch fresh spinach, coarsely chopped (leaves only)
3 pounds ripe tomatoes, diced

Cook fettuccine al dente; drain and toss with Dressing. Add onion, capers, olives, and basil. Just before serving, toss with spinach and transfer to a serving bowl lined with extra spinach leaves. Top with tomatoes and serve at room temperature.

Salad Sampler from Quilting in the Country (Montana)

Hidden Pear Salad

1 (16-ounce) can pears (liquid drained and reserved)
1 (3-ounce) package lime flavored gelatin
1 (3-ounce) package cream cheese, softened
¼ teaspoon lemon juice
1 envelope whipped topping mix
Lettuce leaves

In a saucepan, bring pear liquid to a boil. Stir in gelatin until dissolved. Remove from the heat and cool at room temperature until syrupy. Meanwhile, purée pears in a blender. In a mixing bowl, beat cream cheese and lemon juice until fluffy and smooth. Add puréed pears and mix well. Prepare whipped topping according to package directions; fold into pear mixture. Fold in cooled gelatin. Pour into an oiled 4½-cup mold. Chill overnight. Just before serving, unmold salad onto a lettuce-lined platter. Yield: 6–8 servings.

Rainbow's Roundup of Recipes (South Dakota)

Pear and Walnut Salad

½ cup oil
3 tablespoons vinegar
¼ cup sugar
½ teaspoon celery seeds
¼ teaspoon salt
¼ cup walnut halves
4 cups torn lettuce
1 pear, sliced or chopped
2 ounces bleu cheese, crumbled

Combine oil, vinegar, sugar, celery seeds, and salt in jar with tight-fitting lid; shake to dissolve sugar and mix well. Chill in refrigerator. Spread walnuts in baking dish. Bake at 375° for 3–5 minutes or microwave on HIGH for 3–4 minutes or until golden brown, stirring occasionally. Combine walnuts with lettuce, pear, and bleu cheese in salad bowl. Add dressing at serving time; toss lightly to coat well. Yields 4 servings.

Y Cook? (North Dakota)

Festive Cranberry Salad

Also a quick and easy dessert.

1 can sweetened condensed
  milk
¼ cup lemon juice
1 (20-ounce) can crushed
  pineapple, drained

1 (16-ounce) can whole
  cranberry sauce
½ cup nuts, chopped
1 (9-ounce) carton whipped
  topping

Thoroughly mix all ingredients except topping. Fold in whipped topping. Freeze. Remove from freezer about 5 minutes before serving. Serves 12.

Note: Can be frozen in a large pan, or in individual servings.

Recipes 1978–1998 (Kansas)

Overnight Layered Fruit Salad

2 cups shredded lettuce
2 Golden Delicious apples
2 navel oranges
2 cups seedless grapes

⅓ cup mayonnaise
⅓ cup sour cream
1 cup shredded mild Cheddar
  cheese

Spread lettuce on bottom of a 2-quart dish. Core, quarter and thinly slice apples; spread over lettuce. Peel and section oranges; squeeze teaspoon or so of orange juice over apples, and arrange orange sections over top of apples. Layer grapes next. Combine mayonnaise and sour cream; spread over grapes. Sprinkle cheese over all of it. Cover tightly with plastic wrap and refrigerate overnight.

Fire Hall Cookbook #2 (Montana)

Lemon Jell-O Salad

1 (6-ounce) package lemon
  Jell-O
3 cups boiling water
1½ cups miniature
  marshmallows

1 cup crushed pineapple,
  drained (save juice)
4 bananas, sliced

Dissolve Jell-O in boiling water. Add marshmallows and let melt. Allow to cool, but not set. Add crushed pineapple and bananas. Let this set before adding Topping.

TOPPING:
Reserved pineapple juice
1½ cups sugar
2 tablespoons flour
2 tablespoons butter

2 eggs, beaten
1 cup Cool Whip
Sliced almonds

Cook pineapple juice, sugar, flour, butter, and eggs till thick. Let cool to room temperature; add Cool Whip. Spread on Jell-O; garnish with almonds.

Heavenly Recipes and Burnt Offerings (Montana)

Cucumber Sauce

Excellent served with cold poached salmon or as a topping for a crisp salad.

1 cup sour cream
2 teaspoons fresh lemon juice
1 teaspoon prepared mustard
½ teaspoon dill weed

1 teaspoon finely minced onion
1 large cucumber, peeled,
  seeded, and finely chopped
3 drops Tabasco

Combine all ingredients in a small bowl. Blend well; cover and refrigerate overnight. Makes 2 cups.

Bound to Please (Idaho)

Hot Bacon Dressing

4–5 slices bacon
1 large egg
1 tablespoon flour (heaping)
3 tablespoons granulated
    sugar

¼ teaspoon salt
Dash black pepper
Cider vinegar to taste
1½ cups cold water

Cut bacon in pieces and fry until crisp. Remove from pan and drain. Mix egg, flour, granulated sugar, salt, pepper, vinegar (add by the tablespoon to taste) and water. Pour mixture into the frying pan. With heat set at medium, stir the mixture constantly until it thickens and begins to boil slowly.

Remove from heat when thick. Add drained bacon and ladle over salad greens; toss lightly. Makes 15 servings.

Reader's Favorite Recipes (Kansas)

Raspberry Vinaigrette

The color alone is enough to make you swoon. Try this on a number of salads . . . I promise you'll never want bottled dressing again.

¼ cup fresh or frozen
    raspberries
1 tablespoon chopped red
    onion
¼ teaspoon finely chopped
    garlic
¼ teaspoon pink peppercorns
    (optional)

¼ teaspoon minced fresh
    thyme leaves
2 tablespoons raspberry
    vinegar
2 tablespoons rice wine vinegar
2 tablespoons red wine vinegar
½ cup olive oil
¼ cup honey

Blend raspberries, red onion, garlic, pink peppercorns (optional), thyme and all 3 vinegars in a blender. With the blender on medium speed, slowly drizzle in olive oil, then honey, blending until creamy. Strain through a small-holed sieve to trap raspberry seeds. Chill. Makes 1 cup.

The Cool Mountain Cookbook (Montana)

Grandmother's Mayonnaise

This was my great-grandmother's recipe from about 1905. My mother made this and kept a jar in the refrigerator for salads with fresh lettuce from the garden, and to go with fruits as well.

2 cups sugar	1½ cups hot water
2 tablespoons flour	2 eggs
1 teaspoon dry mustard	1 cup vinegar
½ teaspoon white pepper	1 tablespoon melted butter
(optional)	1 cup milk
1 teaspoon salt	

In the top of a double boiler, mix together sugar, flour, mustard, pepper, and salt. Add hot water and cook till smooth. Beat eggs and add half of the cooked mixture. Beat, then add the other half and mix well. Add vinegar, butter, and milk. Heat through and pour in jar with good cover and keep in the refrigerator.

A Century of Recipes (Idaho)

VEGETABLES

PHOTO © WILLIAM H. MULLINS OUTDOOR PHOTOGRAPHY

Idaho's higher elevations, ideal climate, and light, volcanic soil tend to produce superior potatoes. It is no surprise that Idaho leads the nation in potato production with more than 30% of potatoes grown. Washington ranks second.

Roasted Potatoes

A must-try recipe! You can use this recipe as the base for many of your own creative variations.

4 pounds potatoes
8 cloves garlic
4 tablespoons chopped fresh
  parsley
2 teaspoons dried basil

2 teaspoons dried oregano
Ground black pepper to taste
8–12 tablespoons light olive or
  vegetable oil
Salt to taste

Preheat oven to 350°. Peel potatoes (or leave skins, if you wish), and cut each potato in 2-inch chunks. Mince garlic. In large bowl, combine all ingredients except salt, and toss so potatoes are covered with oil. Spread potatoes in single layer in 9x13-inch (or larger) pan. Bake uncovered for one hour—turning once—or until golden brown and cooked through. Season potatoes with salt before serving. Serves 4–6.

Hall's Potato Harvest Cookbook (North Dakota)

Ruth's Smashed Potato Bites

A perfect treat for unexpected guests because you can make them in advance, freeze them, and pop them in the oven when friends drop by.

1½ pounds potatoes,
  preferably red
2 slices bacon
1 small onion (¼ cup finely
  chopped)

1 cup crushed barbecue potato
  chips
¼ cup grated Parmesan
  Cheese
1 egg, beaten

Preheat oven to 400°. Peel potatoes, and cut in half. Boil until tender when pierced with a fork (about 20 minutes); drain. Cook bacon in microwave until crisp; crumble into fine pieces. Finely chop onion. Mash potatoes with bacon and onion. Form into 1-inch balls. Combine cheese and chips. Roll balls in egg, and then in cheese/chip mixture. Bake 8–10 minutes, or until hot throughout. Serves 24.

Note: If you are in a hurry, use instant dry potato flakes to make the mashed potatoes.

Hall's Potato Harvest Cookbook (North Dakota)

Heavenly Sour Cream Potatoes

2 cups mashed Idaho potatoes
1½ cups creamed cottage
  cheese
½ cup sour cream
¾ tablespoon grated onion

1¼ teaspoons salt
Pepper to taste
2 tablespoons butter, melted
¼ cup chopped almonds

Mix potatoes and cottage cheese. Add sour cream, onion, salt, and pepper. Spoon into a buttered 1-quart casserole. Brush surface with melted butter. Bake at 350° for 30 minutes. Sprinkle with almonds. Place under broiler to brown lightly. Makes 6 servings.

Bound to Please (Idaho)

Flathead Lake Monster Potatoes

2 pounds frozen hashbrown
  potatoes
1 can cream of mushroom
  soup
2 cups grated Cheddar cheese

2 cups sour cream
½ cup chopped onion
½ stick butter, melted
1 cup cooked elk sausage or
  summer sausage (optional)

Combine hashbrowns, soup, cheese, sour cream, onion, melted butter, and elk meat, if desired. Turn into greased 9x13-inch pan.

TOPPING:
2 cups crushed cornflakes   ¼ cup butter, melted

Stir Topping ingredients together. Sprinkle over potato mixture. Bake at 350° for 30 minutes. (May add ½ cup green or red bell pepper for added zest.) Makes 8 side dishes.

Recipe from Outlook Inn B&B, Somers, Montana
A Taste of Montana (Montana)

WWW.GONORTHWEST.COM.

Montana's Flathead Lake is the largest natural freshwater lake in the western United States. It covers an area of 191.5 square miles. The lake is one of the cleanest in the world for its size and type. The lake is inhabited by the native bull trout and cutthroat trout, as well as the non-native lake trout, yellow perch, and lake whitefish. It is also reportedly inhabited by the infamous Flathead Lake Monster.

Microwave Scalloped Potatoes

1 pound potatoes, peeled and
  cut in ¼-inch slices
½ teaspoon salt
¾ teaspoon Italian herb
  seasoning
⅛ teaspoon pepper
2 tablespoons butter
½ cup water

½ teaspoon instant beef
  bouillon
½ cup shredded Cheddar
  cheese
2 tablespoons grated Parmesan
  cheese
¼ teaspoon paprika

Place all ingredients, except cheese and paprika into a 8-inch round baking dish. Cover loosely with plastic wrap. Microwave on HIGH 4 minutes, remove, stir, cover and cook 4 minutes more. Combine cheeses and paprika. Sprinkle over potatoes. Cook, uncovered for 2 minutes more. Let stand 5 minutes before serving. Makes 6 servings.

Silver Celebration Cookbook (Kansas)

Easy au Gratin Potatoes

A nice compliment to ham or roast beef.

1½ pounds (24 ounces) frozen
  hash browns (with onions
  and/or green pepper,
  optional)
1 (8-ounce) carton sour cream
1 can cream of potato soup,
  undiluted

1–2 cups (4–8 ounces)
  grated Cheddar cheese
  (either sharp or mild)
Dash of salt or pepper
2 tablespoons butter or
  margarine
Paprika (optional)

Microwave frozen potatoes in a 2-quart covered microwave-safe casserole for 5 minutes at HIGH (100%). Stir in sour cream, soup, cheese, salt, and pepper. Dot with butter. Microwave, covered, for 10 minutes at HIGH (100%). Stir. Sprinkle with paprika, if desired. Microwave, covered, again for 10–12 minutes at medium (50%). Let stand 5 minutes. Yields 4 servings.

Easy Livin' Microwave Cooking for the Holidays (Nebraska)

Puffy Coated Onion Rings

2 large onions
  (Idaho-Eastern Oregon)
2 eggs, separated
1¼ cups buttermilk

1½ tablespoons oil
1¼ cups all-purpose flour
1 teaspoon salt
1¼ teaspoons baking powder

Peel and slice onions ¼ inch thick. Separate into rings. Beat egg yolks. Add buttermilk, oil, and sifted dry ingredients. Beat egg whites until stiff. Fold into buttermilk mixture. Dip onion rings into batter. Fry, a few at a time, in deep fat (375°). Drain thoroughly on paper towels and sprinkle with salt. Keep in warm oven. Serves 4.

Note: May be frozen. When ready to serve, place frozen onion rings on baking sheet and heat at 450° for 5 minutes.

Onions Make the Meal Cookbook (Idaho)

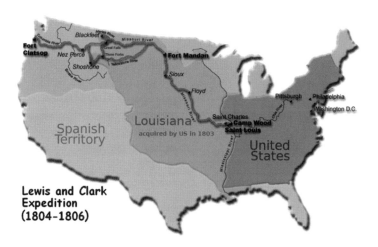

**Lewis and Clark
Expedition
(1804-1806)**

In their quest for an overland route to the Pacific Ocean, explorers in the Lewis and Clark expedition formed a camp with the Shoshone Indians a few miles south of present-day Dillon, Montana, which they named "Camp Fortunate." Here, Sacagawea, the expedition's Indian guide and translator, learned that her brother, Cameahwait, was now chief of the Shoshone tribe. (She had been kidnapped by Plains Indians five years previously.) It was an emotional scene when brother and sister were reunited. The Lewis and Clark Expedition explored the land that would become the state of Montana for the first time on April 25, 1805. The group rested and celebrated their arrival at the junction of the Yellowstone and Missouri rivers near the future site of Fort Union.

Caramelized Onion Tarts
with Gorgonzola Sauce

ONION FILLING:

6 Vidalia or other sweet
  yellow onions
½ cup butter (1 stick)

2 tablespoons fresh thyme
Salt and pepper

Thinly slice the onions. In a large sauté pan, melt the butter and cook the onions until caramelized (deep golden brown color), about 25–35 minutes. Stir in fresh thyme and season with salt and pepper.

TART SHELLS:

1 sheet puff pastry, or 6 puff
  pastry circles

½ cup water
1 egg

I bought the package of puff pastry circles. There were 6 to a box and they were 3 inches in diameter, which is what you need for this recipe. If you buy the sheet, cut out 6 circles with a 3-inch cookie cutter. Mix water and egg together to make a wash. Brush circles with the egg wash and place on a lightly greased sheet pan. Bake until golden brown, about 20–25 minutes. Cool and then hollow a 2-inch circle out of the center. Set aside.

GORGONZOLA SAUCE:

1½ cups heavy cream
1 cup crumbled Gorgonzola
  cheese (blue cheese)

1 tablespoon chopped fresh
  thyme
Salt and pepper

Bring cream to a boil. Reduce heat and add cheese. Add thyme and season with salt and pepper. Cook another 2–4 minutes, until the consistency is thick enough to coat the back of a spoon.

Putting it all together: Place a puff pastry shell on a plate. Place about ¼ cup of caramelized onions on the inside and spread a few around the outside of the shell. Drizzle 2–3 tablespoons of sauce all over plate making sure a good portion is on the tart shell. Garnish with a sprig of fresh thyme. Makes 6 servings.

Recipe from Crescent H Ranch, Wilson, Wyoming
The Great Ranch Cookbook (Wyoming)

Honeyed Onions

6 medium onions
2 tablespoons chili sauce
½ teaspoon salt
2 tablespoons butter or
  margarine, melted

2 tablespoons honey
⅛ teaspoon pepper
1 teaspoon paprika

Peel onions and cut in half crosswise. Place them in 8x12x2-inch baking dish, cut-side-up. In small bowl, stir together other ingredients and brush over onion halves. Bake covered for an hour at 350°, or until fork-tender.

Wolf Point, Montana 75th Jubilee Cookbook (Montana)

Microwave Creamed Onions

2 medium onions
  (Idaho-Eastern Oregon)
2 tablespoons water
2 tablespoons flour
½ teaspoon salt
½ teaspoon dill weed

⅛ teaspoon ground white
  pepper
½ cup skimmed milk
½ cup chicken broth
2 tablespoons minced parsley

Peel and slice onions ¼ inch thick. Combine onions and water in a 1½-quart casserole. Microwave on HIGH, 3½ minutes. Stir and microwave 3½ minutes more, or until onions are tender; drain off liquid. Combine remaining ingredients in a microwave bowl and mix well. Microwave on HIGH for 1½ minutes; stir and microwave 1½ minutes more or until thickened. Pour sauce over onions, toss to coat, and microwave on medium 2–3 minutes or until thoroughly heated. Serves 4.

Onions Make the Meal Cookbook (Idaho)

Jackson Hole, Wyoming, was originally named Jackson's Hole for Davey Jackson, a mountain man who trapped in this area during the late 1800s. "Hole" was a term used at that time to describe a high mountain valley. The Jackson Hole Ski Area in Wyoming has the longest continuous vertical rise of any ski area in the United States. From the valley floor to the top of Rendezvous Mountain is 4,139 feet.

Spinach Casserole

2 (10-ounce) packages frozen
  chopped spinach
1 (16-ounce) carton cottage
  cheese
2½ cups grated sharp cheese
3 eggs, beaten

3 tablespoons flour
1 stick margarine, melted
¼ teaspoon garlic salt
¼ teaspoon pepper
¼ teaspoon onion salt

Defrost spinach; squeeze out water. Mix spinach with remaining ingredients and place in greased 9x13-inch pan. Bake uncovered for 1 hour at 325°. Can be made in advance and refrigerated prior to baking.

Cooking with the Ladies (Montana)

Spinach and Feta Pie

2 pounds fresh spinach
7 ounces olive oil, divided
2 large onions, finely chopped
9 ounces feta cheese,
  crumbled
2 eggs, beaten

2 tablespoons finely chopped
  fresh parsley
1 tablespoon finely chopped
  fresh dill
Salt and pepper to taste
10 sheets filo pastry dough

Preheat 12-inch Dutch oven to 350°. Pick through the spinach, removing any large stalks, then wash, drain, and roughly chop. Heat 2 tablespoons olive oil in a pan, and fry the onions until soft and golden. Add spinach and cook for 5 minutes, or until tender. Remove from pan, drain thoroughly in a colander, then place in a large bowl with the feta, eggs, parsley, and dill. Mix well; season and let cool.

Brush the Dutch oven with olive oil. Line with 1 sheet of filo dough, brush with oil, and continue with 4 more sheets of dough, covering the last sheet with the spinach mixture. Add the remaining filo dough in the same way and score the top of the pie with a sharp knife. Bake for 40 minutes until golden brown. Serve hot or cold.

Bacon is not a Vegetable (Idaho)

Zucchini Pie

4 cups thinly sliced zucchini
1 cup chopped onion
½ cup margarine
½ cup chopped parsley, or
   2 tablespoons parsley flakes
½ teaspoon salt
½ teaspoon pepper
¼ teaspoon garlic powder
¼ teaspoon basil
¼ teaspoon oregano leaves
2 eggs, beaten
4 ounces (1 cup) shredded
   mozzarella cheese
4 ounces (1 cup) shredded
   sharp Cheddar cheese
1 (8-ounce) can crescent rolls
2 teaspoons prepared mustard

Cook and stir zucchini and onion in margarine for 10 minutes. Stir in parsley (or flakes), salt, pepper, garlic powder, basil, and oregano. Combine eggs and cheeses; stir into zucchini mixture. Separate crescent rolls into 8 triangles. Place in ungreased 10-inch pie pan (or 12x8-inch pan; just separate rolls into rectangles to form crust). Press over bottom and up sides to form crust. Spread crust with mustard. Pour vegetable mixture into crust. Bake at 375° for 18–20 minutes, or until center is set. Cover crust with foil last 10 minutes. Let stand a few minutes before slicing. Serves 6.

Cookin' in Paradise (Idaho)

Impossible Garden Pie

2 cups chopped or thinly
   sliced zucchini
1 cup chopped tomato
⅓ cup chopped onion
1 cup shredded Swiss or
   Jack cheese
2 cups milk
4 eggs, beaten
1 cup Bisquick
⅓ cup Parmesan cheese
¼ teaspoon salt
⅛ teaspoon pepper

Grease a 10-inch pie plate, or 10x7-inch Pyrex casserole dish. Layer all vegetables in pan. Sprinkle cheese over vegetables. Beat milk, eggs, Bisquick, cheese, and spices. Pour over all and bake at 375° for 35–40 minutes or until a knife inserted comes out clean.

Note: You may also add a layer of cooked ground beef and a few green pepper rings. (Use a slightly deeper casserole dish.) Garnish with zucchini and tomato slices, if desired.

Rainbow's Roundup of Recipes (South Dakota)

Bountiful Stuffed Squash

2 (1¼-pound) acorn squash
½ cup chopped onion
1 tablespoon or more
   vegetable oil
¾ cup ground turkey
1 cup finely chopped red
   cooking apple

1 tablespoon flour
1 tablespoon low sodium, light
   soy sauce
¼ cup raisins

Cut acorn squash in halves; remove fiber and seeds. Place cut-side-down in microwave dish and cover with plastic wrap. Microwave on HIGH 14 minutes or until tender yet firm. Turn dish once during baking.

Meanwhile, sauté onion in hot oil in large skillet over high heat until translucent. Add turkey and apple; cook and stir over medium heat, about 5 minutes, or until turkey is no longer pink. Sprinkle flour evenly over meat mixture; stir to blend. Gradually stir in light soy sauce; cook and stir until slightly thickened. Stir in raisins. Remove from heat. Fill each squash with the turkey mixture. Microwave on HIGH 1–2 minutes until heated through. Makes 4 servings.

Pumpkin, Winter Squash and Carrot Cookbook (North Dakota)

Baked Cabbage

1 medium head cabbage,
   shredded or cut in ½-inch
   pieces
10 slices bacon
2 tablespoons flour

1 teaspoon salt
¼ teaspoon pepper
2 teaspoons brown sugar
1 cup light cream

Preheat oven to 350°. Spray 2-quart casserole with vegetable spray. Place cabbage in casserole. Brown bacon until almost crisp; drain. Combine flour, salt, pepper, sugar, and cream. Stir and pour over cabbage. Sprinkle bacon over surface. Bake, covered, for 35 minutes. Remove cover and bake 10 minutes longer until bacon is browned.

Regent Alumni Association Cookbook (North Dakota)

Nebraska Corn Pie

6 strips bacon
1½ cups fine bread crumbs
2 fresh tomatoes
1 green pepper, minced
1 teaspoon salt

¼ teaspoon pepper
1 teaspoon sugar
3 cups fresh uncooked corn
2 tablespoons butter

Place 3 strips of slightly cooked bacon in the bottom of a baking dish. Place the other strips around the sides. Add a layer of bread crumbs, and then a layer of peeled, sliced tomatoes and green pepper. Sprinkle with salt, pepper, and sugar. Over this, place a layer of corn, and continue with alternate layers until the dish is filled. Cover with bread crumbs and dot with butter. Bake at 375° for 35 minutes. Serves 6.

Taste the Good Life! Nebraska Cookbook (Nebraska)

Triple Corn Casserole

1 egg, slightly beaten
1 cup sour cream
½ cup butter or margarine, melted
1 (15-ounce) can cream-style corn

1 (15-ounce) can whole-kernel corn, undrained
1 small package cornbread mix

Put into mixing bowl in order given; mix well. Pour into greased casserole dish. Bake at 350°, uncovered, for 1 hour.

Quilter's Delight, Busy Day Recipes (Idaho)

Corn Casserole

Good with Mexican meal.

1 cube butter (2 tablespoons)
2 (3-ounce) packages cream cheese

1 can chopped green chiles
Dash garlic salt
2 cans white shoepeg corn

Melt butter and cream cheese. Add chiles, garlic salt, and corn. Bake in casserole at 350° until heated through, about 20 minutes.

Home at the Range III (Kansas)

Fresh Vegetable Medley with Parmesan-Lemon Sauce

VEGETABLE MEDLEY:

1 (1-pound) head cauliflower
(about 1½ cups), cut into
1-inch pieces

1 pound fresh broccoli
(about 2 cups), cut into
1-inch flowerets

1 large carrot, cleaned and cut
into sticks

1 small zucchini and/or small
yellow squash, peeled and
thinly sliced

Using a 10-inch glass pie plate or microwave-safe serving dish, arrange cauliflower around the outer edge. Arrange broccoli inside the cauliflower ring, with the stems pointing toward outer edge of plate. Place carrot sticks between broccoli stems. Pile zucchini slices in the center.

PARMESAN-LEMON SAUCE:

½ stick (¼ cup) reduced-
calorie margarine, melted

2 teaspoons lemon juice

¼ teaspoon garlic powder

¼ teaspoon onion powder

1 teaspoon dried basil

¼ cup grated Parmesan
cheese

Mix ingredients except for the grated cheese in a small bowl. Pour over vegetables. Sprinkle with Parmesan cheese. Cover loosely with plastic wrap. Microwave for 8–10 minutes at HIGH (100%). Let stand 3 minutes. Yields 8 servings.

Easy Livin' Low-Calorie Microwave Cooking (Nebraska)

Zippy Glazed Carrots

No one will know that you did not take the time to peel, slice, and cook these delicious carrots.

1 tablespoon butter

1 tablespoon brown sugar

1 teaspoon mustard

¼ teaspoon salt

1 (15-ounce) can sliced carrots,
drained

Combine butter, brown sugar, mustard, and salt in a 12-inch non-stick skillet. Cook until blended. Add carrots. Fry until carrots are heated and glazed. Yields 1½ cups or 4 servings.

Mom's Camper Cooking (Kansas)

Fun Lady's Tomato Pie

Rich and delicious.

CRUST:

1 (9- or 10-inch) deep dish pie crust

Bake in preheated 350° oven for 10 minutes. Cool completely.

FILLING:

3 cups (10 ounces) shredded mozzarella cheese
1 pound cooked, crumbled bacon
1½ cups chopped green pepper
2 sliced avocados
2 large or 4 medium sliced, seeded tomatoes
Oregano
Basil
1 cup mayonnaise
1 cup freshly grated Parmesan cheese
⅛ teaspoon bottled hot pepper sauce
½ teaspoon Worcestershire
¼ cup chopped fresh parsley

In pre-baked, cooled crust, layer in order: one cup mozzarella cheese and half each of the bacon, green pepper, avocados, and tomatoes. Sprinkle with oregano and basil. Repeat. Put the third cup of mozzarella cheese over the second layer.

Mix the mayonnaise, Parmesan, hot pepper sauce, and Worcestershire, and spread it over the top. Sprinkle with chopped parsley. Bake at 350° for 30 minutes or until golden. Let stand 10–15 minutes. Serve warm or cool. Store in refrigerator. Serves 6.

Presentations (North Dakota)

Asparagus Casserole

1 sleeve saltine crackers
1 cup grated Cheddar cheese
½ cup butter or margarine,
  melted
1 (14½-ounce) can cut
  asparagus

1 (10¾-ounce) can cream of
  mushroom soup
½ cup chopped pecans

Crush crackers and mix together with grated cheese and melted butter. In a separate bowl mix together asparagus and soup. In a 9x13-inch baking dish, layer soup and asparagus mixture with cheese mixture, ending with cheese mixture on top. Sprinkle pecans over the casserole. Bake at 350° for 20 minutes. Serves 6–8.

Be Our Guest (Idaho)

Pop's Pepper Poppers

Great as an appetizer, too!

Hot banana peppers, or your
  choice
Cream cheese

Sharp Cheddar cheese
Bacon or bacon bits

Wash and cut stem end off peppers; remove seeds and cut in half lengthwise. Lay on foil-lined pan (for easy cleanup) and stuff with cream cheese or Cheddar cheese (or mixture). Put in 350° oven for 20 minutes. Meanwhile, fry bacon and crumble. Sprinkle on peppers and serve while hot.

Note: Because hot peppers contain oils that can burn your eyes, lips and skin, protect yourself when working with the peppers by covering one or both hands with plastic gloves or plastic bags. Be sure to wash your hands thoroughly before touching your eyes or face.

Sisters Two II (Kansas)

SOUTH DAKOTA TOURISM.

De Smet, South Dakota, was the childhood home of author Laura Ingalls Wilder and the setting for her *Little House* series of pioneer adventure books. The books were adapted into a popular American television series, "Little House on the Prairie," which aired from 1974 to 1983, and is now syndicated worldwide. The Ingalls Homestead, built in 1887, the church (shown here), and the Surveyor's Shanty, where the Ingalls family spent their first Dakota winter, are open to the public.

Garlicky Green Beans with Mushrooms

1 pound fresh green beans
1 tablespoon margarine
1 cup quartered fresh
  mushrooms
2 cloves garlic, minced
¼ tablespoon onion powder
¼ tablespoon salt
⅛ teaspoon pepper

Wash beans, trim ends, and remove strings. Arrange in a vegetable steamer, and place over boiling water. Cover and steam 5 minutes. Drain and plunge into cold water; drain again. Melt margarine in a nonstick skillet coated with cooking spray. Add mushrooms and garlic; sauté 3 minutes or until mushrooms are tender. Add beans, onion powder, salt, and pepper. Stir well. Cook 3 minutes or until thoroughly heated.

Rare Collection Recipes (Montana)

Barbecued Green Beans

4 strips bacon
½ cup diced onion
½ cup ketchup
½ cup brown sugar, packed
1 tablespoon Worcestershire
3 cans French-style green
  beans, well-drained

Place bacon in baking dish, cover with waxed paper, and microwave on HIGH for 5 minutes or until crisp. Remove bacon and drain on paper towels. Sauté onion in bacon grease for 3 minutes. Add ketchup, brown sugar, and Worcestershire to the sautéed onions and mix. Add drained green beans and stir gently. Top with crumbled bacon. Cover. Bake at 325° for 2 hours. Makes 8 servings.

Recipe from Country Dreams, Marion, Kansas
Savor the Inns of Kansas (Kansas)

Baked Bean Casserole

1½ pounds ground beef, browned
½ pound bacon, cut up and browned
1 large can pork and beans
1 can kidney beans, drained
1 can pinto beans, drained
1 can lima beans, drained
1 onion, diced
¼ cup brown sugar
1 teaspoon dry mustard
¼ teaspoon ginger
¼ cup vinegar
1 cup ketchup
3 tablespoons liquid smoke
Salt and pepper

Mix all together. Bake in a 300° oven for 2 hours.

Homemade Memories (Kansas)

Chuck Wagon Bean Pot

This savory "stew" featuring ham and beans borrows its robust seasonings from the chuck wagon cooks of the old western cattle ranges. The secret is long, slow cooking, and your electric slow-cooker is ideal for the job. Just follow the directions that come with your particular model. If you don't have one, slow-cook the mixture on top of the stove in a heavy pot with lid.

1 pound (any variety) dried beans
1 ham hock or shank
1 large onion, chopped
6 cups water
1 teaspoon salt
1 (7- to 10-ounce) can green chile salsa, or 1 (8-ounce) can tomato sauce, or 2 cups canned or stewed tomatoes

Rinse and sort beans. If using an electric slow-cooker, put in all ingredients, cover, set temperature at LOW, and forget for at least 10 hours. If you have only ½ day, cook the mixture 5 or more hours on HIGH.

For top-of-stove cooking, heat all ingredients to boiling with pot uncovered. Turn down heat, cover, and simmer gently, adding enough boiling water to keep beans well covered. Most varieties will be done in 2–3 hours.

When beans are done, take out ham bone, cut meat off the bone, and put meat back into pot. Serve hot with cornbread or muffins.

Idaho's Favorite Bean Recipes (Idaho)

Cowboy Beans

Great with grilled hamburgers or hot dogs and fresh corn on the cob.

1 pound ground beef
1 (16-ounce) can baked beans
1 (16-ounce) can kidney beans
2 cups chopped onions
¾ cup brown sugar

1 cup ketchup
2 tablespoons dry mustard
¼ teaspoon salt
2 teaspoons vinegar

Brown and drain meat. Mix all of the ingredients together in a crockpot. Cook on HIGH 1–2 hours or until thoroughly heated.

Down Home Country Cookin' (Idaho)

Firehole Beans

Firehole Beans was given its name by cowboys up in the northern range when the cook prepared the dark ones more or less in the Boston-baked manner. "Firehole" in this case was not related to pit roasting, although this method was sometimes used, but was a corruption of frijoles, the name for beans in Spanish.

1 quart black beans
1 rounded tablespoon salt
3 quarts water
½ pound salt pork

⅔ cup blackstrap molasses
1 teaspoon dry mustard
1 can tomatoes

Using a galvanized pail, soak the beans overnight. Pour off the top water and with it any floaters, twigs, etc. Swirl the beans for a time. This will allow any rocks to go to the bottom just like nuggets in a miner's pan. Lift the beans using the fingers of the two hands as a strainer. Transfer to a heavy iron pot, or Dutch oven, equipped with a well-fitting lid. Add salt and cold water. Bring slowly to a boil and keep boiling for 3 hours, adding water if the level drops beyond what appears to be a safe point. Slice the salt pork into 1-inch-wide strips and cut crosswise, forming squares of fat attached to rind. Add the pork, molasses, mustard, and tomatoes. Cover and bake at 350° about 2 hours, checking water level periodically.

Cow Country Cookbook (Montana)

Idaho Buckaroo Beans

1 pound (2 cups) pink, red,
or pinto beans, soaked
overnight in 6 cups water
½ pound smoked ham, salt
pork, or slab bacon, cut up
1 large onion, coarsely
chopped
2 garlic cloves, sliced
1 small bay leaf

2 cups solid-pack or fresh-
peeled tomatoes
½ cup chopped green pepper
2 teaspoons chili powder
2 tablespoons brown sugar
½ teaspoon dry mustard
¼ teaspoon crushed oregano
leaves
Salt (optional)

Drain beans and add fresh water to 2 inches above beans. Add meat, onion, garlic, and bay leaf. Heat to boiling and cover tightly. Cook over low heat for 1½ hours or until beans are almost tender.

Add all remaining ingredients, except salt, and more water if necessary. Simmer, uncovered, for 2 hours, stirring once or twice. Taste and add salt, if necessary. There should be enough liquid left on the beans to resemble a medium-thick gravy.

If desired, the beans may be baked, covered, at 325° after the first step is completed. Makes 8–10 servings.

Note: Long, slow cooking helps to give a rich, full flavor. May be made ahead and refrigerated, then reheated, even on a barbecue grill.

Bound to Please (Idaho)

PASTA, RICE, ETC.

PHOTO BY CHAD COPPESS, SOUTH DAKOTA DEPARTMENT OF TOURISM

Sculpted by 75 million years of sedimentation and erosion, the Badlands' 243,000 acres are crammed full of cones, ridges, buttes, gorges, gulches, pinnacles, and precipices in an eerily sparse yet breathtakingly beautiful landscape, some rising more than 1,000 feet into the sky. North and South Dakota.

Creamy Garden Spaghetti

½ pound fresh broccoli, broken into florets
1½ cups sliced zucchini
1½ cups sliced fresh mushrooms
1 large carrot, sliced
1 tablespoon olive or vegetable oil
8 ounces uncooked spaghetti
¼ cup chopped onion
3 garlic cloves, minced
2 tablespoons butter or margarine
3 tablespoons flour
2 teaspoons chicken bouillon granules
½ teaspoon dried thyme
2 cups milk
¼ cup white wine, or ¼ cup more milk
½ cup shredded Swiss cheese
½ cup shredded mozzarella cheese

In a large skillet, sauté the broccoli, zucchini, mushrooms, and carrot in oil until crisp-tender. Remove from heat and set aside.

Cook spaghetti according to package directions. In another saucepan, sauté onion and garlic in butter until tender. Stir in the flour, bouillon and thyme until blended. Gradually add the milk and wine. Bring to a boil; cook and stir for 2 minutes or until thickened.

Reduce heat to low; stir in cheeses until melted. Do not boil. Add vegetables; heat through. Drain spaghetti; toss with vegetable mixture. Serves 4.

Another Cookbook (Idaho)

In search of adventure as a young man, Teddy Roosevelt returned to the Dakota Territory again and again to live the life of a cowboy, explore, invigorate his body, and renew his spirit. He later wrote: "I would not have been president had it not been for my experiences in North Dakota." Today, the colorful North Dakota badlands provides the scenic backdrop to the Theodore Roosevelt National Park which memorializes the 26th president for his enduring contributions to the conservation of our nation's resources. The area was first established as a Memorial Park in 1947. It gained National Park status in 1978.

Mock Lasagna Rolls
with Cheese Filling

Low-calorie eggplant substitutes for the pasta.

1 large eggplant, peeled
  and sliced lengthwise
  into 6-inch by ¼-inch-
  long thin slices
1 small onion (⅔ cup), finely
  chopped
2 cloves garlic, minced
1 teaspoon olive oil
2 teaspoons water
¼ cup grated Parmesan
  cheese
½ cup grated mozzarella
  cheese (optional)

1¼ cups low-fat cottage
  cheese, drained
1 teaspoon Italian seasoning
1 teaspoon dried chives
1 large egg white
1 (16-ounce) jar sugar-free
  spaghetti sauce with
  mushrooms*
Parmesan cheese and chives to
  garnish (optional)

Place eggplant slices in a 10-inch or 12x8-inch flat microwave-safe casserole. Cover with lid or vented plastic wrap. Microwave for 10–11 minutes at HIGH (100%), or until tender, rearranging once. Drain and set aside. Combine onion, garlic, olive oil, and water in a small microwave-safe dish. Microwave uncovered for 2–3 minutes at HIGH (100%), or until tender-crisp. Stir in cheeses, Italian seasoning, chives, and egg white until mixed. Place 2 spoonfuls of cheese mixture on each slice, distributing more toward one end. Start at that end and roll up. Place rolls seam-side-down in the flat casserole. Pour spaghetti sauce over rolls. Cover with vented plastic wrap or lid. Microwave for 12–13 minutes at HIGH (100%), rearranging rolls halfway through cooking. Sprinkle each roll with a dash of Parmesan cheese and chives to garnish, if desired. Let stand 2 minutes. Yields 6 servings.

*Use no-salt-added variety for lowest sodium values, if desired.

Variation: For Mock Lasagna Rolls with Meat Filling, add ½ pound cooked ground turkey, veal, or lean ground beef with cheese filling.

Easy Livin' Low-Calorie Microwave Cooking (Nebraska)

Chicken Lasagna

2 cups cubed chicken breasts
3 cups sliced mushrooms
2 cloves garlic, minced
1 large onion, chopped
1 teaspoon dried oregano
1 teaspoon dried basil
1 teaspoon dried thyme
2 tablespoons olive oil
1 (28-ounce) can Italian
  tomatoes
1 (15-ounce) can tomato
  sauce
3 tablespoons freshly ground
  Romano cheese
2 cups grated carrots
½ teaspoon salt
1 teaspoon freshly ground
  black pepper
1 (8-ounce) package lasagna
  noodles, cooked and drained
½ cup freshly ground Romano
  cheese
6–8 slices mozzarella cheese

Sauté chicken, mushrooms, garlic, onion, oregano, basil, and thyme in olive oil until chicken loses its pink color. Stir in tomatoes and tomato sauce, 3 tablespoons Romano cheese, carrots, salt, and pepper. Simmer 10–15 minutes. In oiled 9x13-inch baking dish, place half lasagna noodles, top with half the sauce mixture, Romano, and mozzarella cheeses. Repeat layers. Cover and bake at 350° for 20 minutes. Uncover and bake 10 minutes or until bubbly. Let rest 5 minutes in pan before serving.

To Tayla with TLC (South Dakota)

Sundance Ziti

1 (16-ounce) package ziti (or rigatoni) noodles
4 quarts water
4 tablespoons olive oil, divided
1 onion, diced
½ green pepper, diced
10 mushrooms, quartered
4 cloves garlic, crushed
Oregano, basil, and pepper to taste
1 yellow squash, quartered and sliced
2 (15-ounce) cans tomato sauce
½ block tofu, drained and squeezed
1 (8-ounce) carton ricotta
1 (8-ounce) package grated mozzarella, divided
4 ounces grated Cheddar
1 tomato, sliced

Boil noodles in water and 1 tablespoon olive oil until tender. Drain. In pan, sauté onion, green pepper, mushrooms, and garlic in 3 tablespoons olive oil. Spice to taste with oregano, basil, and pepper. Sauté until onions are tender. Add yellow squash and tomato sauce. Reduce heat and simmer.

In a large bowl, combine tofu, ricotta, and ½ the mozzarella. Add sauce mixture and noodles. Pour into 12-inch Dutch oven and sprinkle with remaining mozzarella and Cheddar. Top with tomato slices and sprinkle with additional oregano and basil. Bake in 350° oven for 45 minutes to 1 hour.

Bacon is not a Vegetable (Idaho)

Butch Cassidy, a.k.a. George Leroy Parker, purchased a ranch near Dubois, Wyoming, in 1890. This location is close to the notorious Hole-in-the-Wall, a natural geological formation that afforded outlaws much welcomed protection and cover, and so the suspicion has always existed that Parker's ranching, at which he was never economically successful, was in fact a façade that operated to conceal more clandestine activities. Cassidy, perhaps in conjunction with Hole-in-the-Wall outlaws, robbed the bank in Montpelier, Idaho, on August 13, 1896. He got away with $7,165, allegedly to hire a lawyer for his mentor Matt Warner, who was awaiting trial for murder in Ogden, Utah.

Pasta Primavera

1 sweet onion, thinly sliced
6 garlic cloves, minced, or
  to taste
1 tablespoon olive oil
¼ cup pine nuts
2 cups sliced mushrooms
8 basil leaves, chopped
¼ cup white wine or
  vegetable broth
4 Roma tomatoes, cut in
  bite-size wedges
Salt and pepper to taste
1 pound fresh linguine
½ cup Parmesan

Sauté garlic and onions in olive oil until onions become slightly translucent. Toast pine nuts until golden brown. Set aside. Add mushrooms, basil, and wine to garlic-onion mixture. Sauté until mushrooms are tender.

Gently stir in tomatoes and toasted pine nuts. Season with salt and pepper. Meanwhile, add separate strands of linguine to lightly salted boiling water and cook 7–10 minutes, or until al dente. Do not overcook. Drain.

Add linguine to sauté pan and gently toss with vegetables. Toss with Parmesan. Serve immediately. Serves 4.

Northern Lites: Contemporary Cooking with a Twist (Idaho)

Pasta with the Works

4 cups cooked corkscrew
  macaroni (about 3 cups dry)
½ cup thinly sliced
  pepperoni (2 ounces)
1 medium green pepper, cut
  into strips
2 cups spaghetti sauce with
  mushrooms
⅓ cup pitted ripe olives,
  cut in half
1 cup shredded mozzarella
  cheese (4 ounces)
Grated Parmesan cheese

Boil macaroni and drain. In skillet over medium heat, cook pepperoni and pepper until pepper is tender-crisp, stirring often. Stir in spaghetti sauce and olives over medium to high heat; heat to boiling. Reduce heat to low. Cover; cook 10 minutes, stirring occasionally. Remove from heat. Add macaroni and mozzarella cheese. Toss to coat. Serve with Parmesan cheese. Makes 4 main-dish servings.

Norman Lutheran Church 125th Anniversary Cookbook
(North Dakota)

Pizza Hot Dish

2 pounds ground beef
½ onion, chopped
½ green pepper, chopped
  (optional)
1 (10-ounce) can pizza sauce
½ cup ketchup
2 (10¾-ounce) cans Cheddar
  cheese soup
1 (8-ounce) can mushrooms
¾ (1-pound) package noodles,
  cooked
1 (8-ounce) package mozzarella
  cheese
1 (3½-ounce) package
  pepperoni slices

Brown hamburger, onions, and green pepper, if desired. Then mix together with pizza sauce, ketchup, soup, mushrooms, and cooked noodles. Pour mixture into a greased 10x13-inch casserole, or 2 or 3 smaller casseroles. Sprinkle with mozzarella cheese and arrange pepperoni slices on top. Bake at 350° for 1 hour. Can be frozen and baked as needed.

Wolf Point, Montana 75th Jubilee Cookbook (Montana)

Speedy Overnight Casserole

3 cups chopped cooked
  chicken or turkey
2 cups large elbow macaroni,
  uncooked
1 can cream of mushroom
  soup
1 can cream of chicken soup
1 soup can milk
1 soup can chicken broth
1 small onion, chopped
1 small can water chestnuts,
  sliced
½ teaspoon salt
½ pound grated cheese (save
  some for topping)
1 cup crushed potato chips

Mix all ingredients except chips. Put in 9x13-inch pan. Sprinkle reserved cheese and potato chips on top. Cover with foil. Refrigerate overnight. Bake, covered, for 1½ hours at 350°. This freezes well.

Home at the Range III (Kansas)

Mrs. Annie Krug's Goulash

1–2 tablespoons Crisco or
   bacon grease
2½ pounds ground beef
3 teaspoons salt
1 teaspoon chili powder
5 small onions, chopped
1 red pepper, chopped
1 green pepper, chopped
2 large bunches celery, finely
   chopped

1 (28-ounce) can tomatoes
1 (10¾-ounce) can tomato soup
2 pimientos, chopped
¼ pound (1 stick) butter
2 (15-ounce) cans red kidney
   beans
3 tablespoons crushed,
   uncooked spaghetti
1 (4-ounce) can sliced
   mushrooms (optional)

Melt Crisco or bacon grease in large frying pan. Add meat and
seasonings and cook 15 minutes, adding onions last 5 minutes.
Add pepper to suit. Add celery, canned tomatoes, tomato soup,
and pimientos. Add butter and cook slowly for 2½ hours. Last
20–30 minutes of cooking time, add red kidney beans and
uncooked spaghetti. If desired, add mushrooms during the last
5–10 minutes. Serves 20.

Recipe from Charley Montana Bed and Breakfast, Glendive, Montana
Montana Bed & Breakfast Guide & Cookbook, 2nd Edition
(Montana)

Castle Geyser eruption

Basque Style Paella

4 whole chicken breasts,
  halved
Salt and freshly ground
  pepper
¼ cup butter, melted
¼ teaspoon ground
  coriander seed
⅓ cup cooking sherry
4 cloves garlic, minced
1 medium onion, chopped
1½ cups long-grain white
  rice
⅓ cup Spanish olive oil
1 green pepper, cut in ½-inch
  strips

2 cups clam broth
1 cup chicken broth
1 pound ripe tomatoes,
  chopped
½ teaspoon salt
1½ teaspoons sugar
1 pound medium-size shrimp,
  shelled and deveined
1 dozen clams
Dash of cayenne pepper
¾ cup pimento-stuffed green
  olives

Place chicken breasts, skin-side-up, in greased 9x13x2-inch baking pan. Season with salt and pepper. Brush with melted butter. Sprinkle with coriander, cover with foil, and bake at 350° for 40 minutes. Uncover, sprinkle with sherry, and bake 20 minutes longer, basting occasionally with pan drippings.

Cook garlic, onion, and rice in hot olive oil in large skillet until golden. Add green pepper, broths, tomatoes, salt, and sugar. Cover and simmer gently for 25 minutes. Stir occasionally.

Stir in chicken, shrimp, clams, cayenne, and olives. Cover and continue cooking 5 minutes, or until clams pop open and liquid is absorbed. Serves 6–8.

Basque Cooking and Lore (Idaho)

Established on March 1, 1872, Yellowstone National Park is the first and oldest national park in the world. Found within its 3,472 square miles is the world's most extensive area of geyser activity. There are more than 10,000 thermal features including geysers, hot springs, mudpots, and fumaroles (a hole in a volcanic area from which hot smoke and gases escape). Yellowstone National Park is located 96% in Wyoming, 3% in Montana, and 1% in Idaho.

Turkey and Brown Rice Casserole

3 cups cooked turkey or
  chicken, cut in large chunks
3½ cups cooked brown rice
1 cup chopped onion
1 cup sliced celery
1 cup chopped green pepper
3 tablespoons margarine,
  divided
1 (10¾-ounce) cream of
  mushroom soup
½ cup dry white wine or
  chicken broth

1 (4-ounce) can sliced
  mushrooms, undrained
1 teaspoon dried sage leaves,
  crumbled
¼ teaspoon dried thyme leaves
½ teaspoon salt
Dash pepper
1 (4-ounce) can pimientos,
  drained and chopped
1 cup herb-seasoned croutons

Combine turkey and rice in Dutch oven or a 2½-quart casserole. Set aside.

Sauté onion, celery, and green pepper in 2 tablespoons of the margarine for 8 minutes, stirring frequently, until tender-crisp. Stir in soup, wine or broth, mushrooms, sage, thyme, salt, pepper, and pimientos. Pour mushroom-vegetable mixture over turkey and rice in casserole or Dutch oven. Stir with large spoon to combine.

Heat remaining 1 tablespoon margarine until melted. Toss croutons in melted margarine. Spoon around edge of Dutch oven. Bake with coals on top and underneath Dutch oven for 35–40 minutes, or in 350° conventional oven for 40–45 minutes, until bubbly. Yields 8 servings.

The Outdoor Dutch Oven Cookbook (Idaho)

Rice with Ham and Shrimp

½ cup Spanish olive oil
¼ pound chorizo, thinly
  sliced
2 medium onions, finely
  chopped
4 cloves garlic, minced
3 cups chicken broth
3 medium tomatoes, finely
  chopped
2 medium green bell peppers,
  seeded and cut into strips
3 tablespoons chopped Italian
  parsley

2 teaspoons sugar
½ teaspoon salt
1 teaspoon ground cumin
½ teaspoon freshly ground
  pepper
2 cups uncooked short-grain
  white rice
1 pound medium shrimp,
  cleaned
½ pound lean ham, cut into
  1½-inch cubes

Heat oil in Dutch oven until light haze forms. Add chorizo, onion, and garlic, and cook until chorizo is browned and onions are soft (approximately 5 minutes). Stir in remaining ingredients except rice, shrimp, and ham. Cook, covered, over medium heat until almost tender (approximately 12 minutes). Stir in rice, shrimp, and ham. Cook for 8–10 minutes, or until all liquid has been absorbed. Serve as an entrée with a hearty loaf of bread. Serves 6.

Basque Cooking and Lore (Idaho)

Wild Rice Casserole

1 cup wild rice, uncooked
1 chopped onion
1½ cups chopped celery
1 teaspoon seasoned salt
¾ cup white wine

2 tablespoons butter
1 quart chicken broth
Salt and pepper to taste
1 pound sliced fresh
  mushrooms

Combine wild rice, onion, celery, seasoned salt, wine, butter, and broth. Add salt and pepper to taste. Gently mix in the sliced mushrooms. Place in a casserole and bake at 325° for 1½–2 hours.

Incredible Edibles (North Dakota)

Feta-Crab Quiche

1 (9-inch) pie crust
1 cup imitation crab, crumbled
¼ cup crumbled feta cheese
4 ounces mozzarella cheese,
    shredded
1 green onion, chopped fine
4 eggs
1 cup milk
¼ teaspoon pepper
½ cup grated Parmesan

Preheat oven to 350°. In pie shell, layer crab, feta, mozzarella, and onion. Beat together eggs, milk, and pepper, and pour gently into pie crust. Sprinkle with Parmesan. Bake 40–50 minutes. Let set 5 minutes before slicing. Garnish with cherry tomatoes and chopped green onions. Delicious!

Idaho Cook Book (Idaho)

Crustless Quiche

1¼ cups milk
½ cup biscuit mix
3 tablespoons butter
3 eggs
Dash salt and pepper
Dash garlic powder (optional)
Dash cayenne pepper
1 cup diced ham, bacon, or
    shrimp
2 green onions, chopped
4 ounces sliced mushrooms
1 cup grated sharp cheese

Preheat oven to 350°. Combine the first 7 ingredients in food processor and mix well. Turn into greased 9- or 10-inch deep-dish pie plate. Mix together meat, onions, mushrooms, and cheese. Sprinkle over egg mixture, poking the meat mixture down into the egg mixture with a knife. Bake until the top is golden, about 45 minutes. Let stand for 10 minutes before serving. Makes 8 servings.

Recipe from The Timbers B&B, Ronan, Montana
A Taste of Montana (Montana)

Hash Brown Quiche

3 cups frozen hash browns,
  thawed and pressed
  between paper towels
⅓ cup melted margarine
4 ounces hot pepper cheese

4 ounces Swiss cheese
6 ounces ham
Salt to taste
2 eggs
½ cup cream

Put well-dried hash browns in 9-inch pie plate, pressing some up sides. Drizzle with melted margarine. Bake 10 minutes at 400°.

Process balance of ingredients in food processor. Pour over hash brown crust. Bake 35–45 minutes at 350° or until knife comes out clean. Let stand 10 minutes before serving. Can be served hot, cold, or at room temperature for lunch, brunch or an appetizer.

If It Tastes Good, Who Cares? II (North Dakota)

Tomato, Basil and Cheese Pie

2 large tomatoes, sliced
  ½ inch thick and drained
1 (9-inch) pastry shell,
  slightly baked
¾ cup grated provolone
  cheese

¼ cup Parmesan cheese
3 eggs
¼ cup heavy whipping cream
2 tablespoons Pesto
¼ teaspoon each salt and
  coarsely ground pepper

Arrange tomatoes in pastry shell and sprinkle with cheeses. Beat eggs, cream, Pesto, salt and pepper together, and pour over tomatoes and cheese. Bake in a 375° oven for 30–40 minutes. Allow pie to stand 5 minutes before slicing and serving. Serves 4.

PESTO:

2 bunches basil
3 cloves garlic, minced
½ cup pine nuts (or almonds)

2 teaspoons olive oil
Pinch each salt and pepper

Combine and run in food processor with metal blade until paste-like in consistency. Store in refrigerator or freeze for later use.

Recipes Tried and True (Idaho)

Super Stuffed Pizza

½ pound Italian sausage,
 casing removed
½ pound fresh mushrooms,
 sliced
1 small green bell pepper,
 chopped

1 small onion, chopped
2 (17-ounce) frozen thin pizza
 crusts, thawed
1 cup shredded mozzarella
1 tablespoon olive oil

In a skillet, brown and drain sausage. Sauté fresh vegetables in drippings. Place one pizza crust right-side-up in bottom of 14-inch Dutch oven. Spread vegetable/sausage mixture over pizza. Top with second pizza crust upside-down and bake 20 minutes (in 350° oven) till heated through. Brush top with olive oil, sprinkle cheese on top, and bake again till cheese is golden.

Note: Any meat, chicken, or vegetable can be used. Frozen pre-made pizza or plain fresh precooked pizza can be used with your own pizza sauce or spaghetti sauce.

Hey Ma! Come Quick! The Hog's in the Garden Again!! (Idaho)

MEATS

PHOTO © THOMAS BÖTTGER

The Old West is alive and well in both Montana and Wyoming, where traditional cattle drives are still commonplace. You can even vacation on a working cattle ranch and participate in a cattle drive just like the real cowboys.

Peppery T-Bone Steaks & Chili Corn

4 ears fresh sweet corn, in
　husks
1–2 garlic cloves, minced
½ teaspoon coarse ground
　black pepper

2 well-trimmed beef T-bone
　steaks, cut 1–1½ inches thick
2 tablespoons butter
½ teaspoon chili powder
¼ teaspoon ground cumin

Pull back corn husks from each ear of corn leaving husks attached to base. Remove corn silk. Fold husks back around corn; tie at the end of each ear with string or a strip of one of the outside corn leaves. Soak corn in cold water 3–4 hours. Remove from water and place on grill over medium coals. Cook 20 minutes, turning often. Combine garlic and pepper; rub into both sides of beef T-bone steaks.

Place steaks on grill with corn; continue cooking, turning steaks once, and corn often. Grill 1-inch thick steaks 16–20 minutes for rare (140°) to medium (160°) or to desired doneness. Grill 1½-inch thick steaks 22–30 minutes (rare to medium) or to desired doneness. Remove corn when tender. Meanwhile, melt butter; add chili powder and cumin. Carve steaks into thick slices and serve with corn and seasoned butter.

Taste the Good Life! Nebraska Cookbook (Nebraska)

Barbecued Steak

1 cup ketchup
½ cup water
¼ cup vinegar
¼ cup chopped green pepper
¼ cup chopped onion
1½ tablespoons
  Worcestershire

1 tablespoon prepared mustard
2 tablespoons brown sugar
½ teaspoon salt
⅛ teaspoon pepper
4 pounds round steak, cut
  ½-inch thick

Combine all ingredients except steak in a saucepan. Bring to a boil, then simmer for about 5 minutes over low heat. Keep barbecue sauce hot. Cut steak into serving-size portions. Place pieces in a large roasting pan. Pour hot barbecue sauce over meat. Cover and bake at 325° for 1½–2 hours. Makes 8–10 servings.

Recipes & Remembrances /Courtland Covenant Church (Kansas)

Pepper Steak

1 pound round (or sirloin)
  steak, cut in ½-inch-thick
  strips
1 tablespoon paprika
2 tablespoons butter or
  margarine
2 cloves garlic, crushed
1½ cups beef broth
1 cup sliced green onions,
  including tops

2 green peppers, cut in strips
2 tablespoons cornstarch
¼ cup water
¼ cup soy sauce
2 large fresh tomatoes, cut in
  eighths
3 cups hot cooked rice

Sprinkle strips of beef with paprika, and allow to stand while preparing other ingredients. Using a large skillet, brown meat in butter. Add garlic and broth. Cover and simmer for 30 minutes. Stir in onions and green peppers. Cover and cook for 5 minutes more. Blend cornstarch, water, and soy sauce. Stir into meat mixture. Cook, stirring until clear and thickened, about 2 minutes. Add tomatoes and stir gently. Serve over beds of fluffy rice. Makes 6 servings.

Our Daily Bread (Kansas)

Chicken-Fried Steak

A western mainstay that shows hints of southern cookery. Great numbers of Southerners homesteaded land or established ranches throughout Texas and Oklahoma. Their method of cooking round steak spread to every corner of the West.

2 pounds top round steak   **Shortening or cooking oil**
Salt and pepper   **2 tablespoons water**
2 cups flour

Slice steak ⅓ inch thick and cut into serving pieces. Pound pieces on both sides with a meat hammer until about ¼ inch thick. Salt and pepper pieces and thoroughly dredge both sides in flour. (A modern variation is to first dip the steak slices in well-beaten egg and then dredge in flour.)

Heat ¼ inch of shortening or cooking oil in a black skillet. Shortening is hot enough when a pinch of flour will sizzle when dropped into the skillet. Place steak in skillet and allow to slowly brown; do not turn until flour has browned to the point where it won't stick to skillet. Then turn the pieces and brown on other side. Cover skillet with tight-fitting lid, turn heat to low, and cook 10 minutes. Add 2 tablespoons water, cover with lid, and cook another 10 minutes. Remove to serving plate and place in low-heat oven to keep warm. Serves 4–6.

True chicken-fried steak must always be served with Cream Gravy. At the table, generously ladle gravy over homemade biscuits and even certain vegetables, such as green beans. Try it and see how you like it!

CREAM GRAVY:
3 tablespoons pan drippings   **Salt**
2 tablespoons flour   **Freshly ground pepper**
2 cups milk

Scrape up brown bits in skillet and heat the pan drippings. Stir in flour and blend thoroughly, cooking over low heat until lightly browned. Slowly add milk, stirring constantly until smooth. Add salt and pepper to taste, and cook 5–7 minutes, depending on desired thickness.

Matt Braun's Western Cooking (Idaho)

Beef Pineapple Fantasy

1½ pounds top round steak (½ inch thick)
2 medium green peppers
1 medium white or yellow onion
1 (2½-ounce) jar sliced mushrooms, drained
1 (15½-ounce) can pineapple chunks, drained; reserve juice

2 tablespoons soy sauce
1½ tablespoons cornstarch
1 (6-ounce) box frozen pea pods
2 tablespoons cooking oil
¼ teaspoon salt
¼ teaspoon pepper
1 beef bouillon cube
1 cup boiling water
½ cup English walnuts, quartered

Trim excess fat from meat and slice in thin strips, 1–1½ inches long. Slice peppers and onions into 1½-inch strips and put aside. Drain mushrooms; put aside. Mix ½ cup pineapple juice, soy sauce, and cornstarch; put aside. Place frozen pea pods in boiling water for 1 minute to separate. Drain; put aside.

Heat oil in frying pan or Chinese wok over medium-high heat. Add meat and sprinkle with salt and pepper. Stir frequently while cooking. Drain excessive liquid from meat after it has cooked 5 minutes. Return to stove and continue cooking 10 minutes, until brown. Dissolve bouillon cube in boiling water; add to meat. Continue cooking for 5 additional minutes. Add peppers, onion, mushrooms, pineapple chunks, and pea pods; cook 5 minutes more, stirring frequently. Add cornstarch mixture and walnuts. Stir continually while cooking for 10 minutes. Turn heat to warm and serve. Serves 4–6.

The Fine Art of Cooking (Montana)

Where's the beef? A good guess is Nebraska. In 2007, Nebraska produced 7.22 billion pounds of red meat—more than any other state in the country—according to a report from the U.S. Department of Agriculture. Besides the prestige of beating out Iowa and Kansas, Nebraska's high cattle and livestock production is a source of economic strength. About one out of every five to seven jobs in Nebraska is related to cattle production. The cattle industry provides jobs in farming and ranch production, meat processing, meat packing, and other positions.

My Favorite Beef Stroganoff

2 round steaks, cut into cubes
Flour
1 small onion, finely chopped
1¼ cups water, divided
¼ cup butter or margarine
2 beef bouillon cubes
1 (4-ounce) can mushrooms,
    undrained
1 (10¾-ounce) can mushroom
    soup
1 cup sour cream
1 (8-ounce) package noodles,
    cooked

In frying pan, brown floured cubes of beef. Add onion, ¼ cup water, butter or margarine, and bouillon cubes. Simmer until onion is tender. Remove from frying pan, removing all brown particles, too. Put meat and onion with juice in roasting pan, adding mushrooms, mushroom soup, and remaining 1 cup water. Simmer 1½ hours. Add sour cream and noodles, cooked according to package directions. Cook 10 minutes longer. Serve hot.

Editor's Extra: This can be done in one pot—a Dutch oven or large deep pan.

Horse Prairie Favorites (Montana)

LANDER, WYOMING, CHAMBER OF COMMERCE

Lander, Wyoming, claims to have held the first rodeo where cowboys were paid. Lander's first rodeo was held in 1893, and the annual "Pioneer Days Rodeo" has been held on the Fourth of July ever since.

Six-Shooter Steak

Some camp cooks cut tough steaks very thin and fried them quickly. A better method was to cut them thick and pound them. There were many preferences for pounding—a dull butcher knife, the back of a cleaver, a chain flail, even the side of a dish. But the favorite among old-time cooks was the six-shooter—the barrel fit the hand, and the butt ending in a wedge of steel was shaped to bruise the meat, to pulp and tenderize it, without punching holes all the way through.

1 teaspoon whole peppercorns   **1 cup lard**
1 cup flour   **Salt to taste**
2 full-cut round steaks

Pulverize the peppercorns. Don't grind them, just crush them on a slab of hardwood. Brush them into the flour; any fragments left will be picked up when the steak is pounded. Cut the round steaks into the desired sizes. Do not trim off the fat. Using the butt of a six-shooter, pound them while sprinkling them lightly with flour and pepper. Don't hammer. Merely lift the gun and let if fall. Its weight will be sufficient. Don't work them down too thin. They are best reduced to about ⅔ of their original thickness.

Heat a heavy iron skillet or griddle. Melt the lard, and when it is hot enough to smoke, fry the steaks a few at a time, browning on both sides and setting aside in a warm pan while they are still red in the middle. Salt them. Cover the pan and keep it hot but not sizzling. The redness will fade after 3 or 4 minutes, and your genuine, old-time six-shooter steaks will go to the table done through, tender and delicious.

Editor's Extra: We suggest using an alternate method of tenderizing the steak rather than using a gun, but wanted to preserve this authentic recipe.

Cow Country Cookbook (Montana)

Chili on a Stick

Summertime and the kitchen is hot—too hot to make chili. Unless you make chili on a stick! And use that randy old whitetail that doesn't taste very good, if that's all you have. The marinade will soothe all but the most gamy flavors.

2 pounds shoulder steaks	2 cloves garlic, minced
¾ cup red wine vinegar	½ teaspoon chili powder
½ cup apple juice	½ teaspoon salt
½ cup vegetable oil	1 teaspoon black pepper
¼ cup minced onion	½ cup mesquite wood chips
1 teaspoon dried leaf cilantro, or 1 tablespoon chopped fresh cilantro	6 fresh, whole jalapeño peppers
	12 large-bulbed green onions
	1 pound cherry tomatoes

Trim the steaks of all fat and sinewy material, then pat dry with paper towels. In a glass bowl or resealable plastic bag, combine the marinade ingredients: vinegar, apple juice, oil, onion, cilantro, garlic, chili powder, salt, and black pepper. Stir, then add the steaks. Place the marinating steaks in the refrigerator, covered or sealed, for 2–4 hours.

When the first hour is up, put the mesquite wood chips in a pail of water, and prepare the vegetables for the skewers. Wearing rubber gloves, cut off the tops of the jalapeños and core and seed them. Cut them in half lengthwise. Trim the tops and bottoms of the onions, leaving about 3 inches of green tops. Drain the meat, cut it up into 1- to 2-inch chunks, and alternate the meat, onion, jalapeños, and tomatoes on the skewers. Begin and end with the meat to secure the stringer.

For a propane barbecue: Drain the wood chips and place them in a wood box. Set it on one side of the coal grate. Preheat the unit for 10 minutes, then turn down to medium-high heat. For charcoal: Start 40 charcoal briquettes on one side of the grill, wait 25 minutes, then spread them out in a single layer, leaving room in the middle to nestle the wood box among the coals.

Place the kabobs over the hot coals, and not directly over the wood chips. Cover the grill and cook 8–10 minutes, basting often and turning once. Serve with lots of chips and Mexican beer in well-chilled glasses. Yields 6 servings.

Game on the Grill (Montana)

Southwestern Beef Brisket

1 (3-pound) fresh beef brisket
1¼ teaspoons salt, divided
½ teaspoon pepper, divided
2 tablespoons cooking oil
1½ cups water
1 (8-ounce) can tomato sauce
1 small onion, chopped
2 tablespoons red wine
   vinegar
1 tablespoon chili powder
1 teaspoon dried oregano
¾ teaspoon ground cumin
½ teaspoon garlic powder
⅛ teaspoon ground red pepper
3 sweet red peppers, cut into
   strips
1½ cups sliced carrots

Season beef with 1 teaspoon salt and ¼ teaspoon pepper. In a Dutch oven, heat oil; brown the beef on both sides. Combine water, tomato sauce, onion, vinegar, chili powder, oregano, cumin, garlic powder, red pepper, and remaining salt and pepper. Pour over meat. Cover and bake at 325° for 2 hours. Add red peppers and carrots; bake 1 hour longer or until meat is tender. Remove meat; let stand 15 minutes before cutting. Thicken juices with a little flour, or cook over high heat to reduce and thicken.

Feeding the Herd (Wyoming)

Working Man's Roast

1 (3-pound) rump roast
¼ teaspoon garlic powder
¼ teaspoon seasoned salt
⅛ teaspoon salt
⅛ teaspoon pepper
1 package onion soup mix
2 tablespoons Worcestershire
1 can cream of mushroom soup

Put foil in a cake pan and place roast in pan. Mix together garlic powder, seasoned salt, salt, pepper, onion soup mix, Worcestershire, and soup. Pour over roast. Seal foil and bake at 200° from 7:00 a.m. to 5:00 p.m. or for 10 hours.

Recipes from the Heart / Epsilon Omega Sorority (Nebraska)

French Dip

½ cup soy sauce
1 beef bouillon
1 bay leaf
1 teaspoon thyme
1 teaspoon garlic powder

3–4 peppercorns
Water
1 (3-pound) rump roast
French bread rolls

Put soy sauce, bouillon, bay leaf, thyme, garlic powder, and peppercorns in crockpot. Mix with 1 cup water. Put rump roast in and cover with water. Cook on LOW 8–10 hours; put sliced meat on rolls and use juice for dipping.

St. Joseph's Table (South Dakota)

Tenderloin with Shiitake Sauce

1 tablespoon cracked black
  pepper
4 (6-ounce) beef tenderloins
2 cups fresh shiitake
  mushrooms, washed and
  sliced
1 tablespoon flour

½ cup nonfat beef broth
½ cup red wine
1 tablespoon Worcestershire
½ teaspoon salt
6 fresh parsley sprigs for
  garnish

Press cracked pepper into both sides of tenderloins. Set aside. Cook mushrooms in nonstick pan until soft. Stir flour into mushrooms until all slices are coated. Add broth, red wine, Worcestershire, and salt. Stir until thickened. Heat nonstick pan to medium high. Add tenderloins; sear quickly on each side. Lower heat and add mushroom sauce. Cook over low heat until tenderloins are cooked as desired. Remove tenderloins to warm plates and top with sauce. Garnish with parsley. Serves 4.

Note: If you like your meat cooked rare, the internal temperature would be 130°, medium rare, 135°–140°, medium, 145°–150°, and well-done, 160°. Or test doneness by making small slit in middle of steak and twisting knife to give a look at inside. Tenderloin will be medium rare if center is pink.

Northern Lites: Contemporary Cooking with a Twist (Idaho)

Beef Tenderloin
with Pepper Jelly Sauce

1 (4-pound) center-cut beef
  tenderloin
1½ teaspoons salt
¾ teaspoon chili powder
½ teaspoon coarsely ground
  black pepper

¼ teaspoon ground cumin
¼ teaspoon dried oregano
  leaves
1½ cups beef stock
¾ cup balsamic wine vinegar
⅓ cup jalapeño pepper jelly

Preheat oven to 450°. Trim fat from tenderloin. Tie at equal intervals in 4 places around tenderloin. Combine salt, chili powder, pepper, cumin, and oregano in small bowl. Rub mixture over tenderloin. Place tenderloin on rack in roasting pan in middle of oven. Roast for 30 minutes or to 120° on meat thermometer. Transfer to heated platter. Let stand at room temperature for 10 minutes before serving.

Pour off fat. Add stock, vinegar, and jelly to pan. Cook for 5 minutes or until slightly thickened, stirring occasionally. Serve in 1-inch-thick slices with sauce spooned over each serving. Yields 8 servings.

Cheyenne Frontier Days "Daddy of 'em All" Cookbook (Wyoming)

PHOTO COURTESY OF IDAHO DEPARTMENT OF COMMERCE

Southern Idaho near Bruneau is home to a unique desert formed in the middle of a natural basin. The Bruneau dunes contain the largest single sand dune in North America. The two most prominent dunes cover about 600 acres.

Roast Beef Pastries

1 (4-ounce) can chopped
  mushrooms
1 onion, chopped
1 medium carrot, grated
1 celery stalk, chopped
2 tablespoons butter
½ teaspoon salt
4 tablespoons Dijon mustard

1 (10-ounce) package frozen
  patty shells (6), thawed
1 pound rare roast beef, sliced
  thin or shaved
½ cup grated Monterey Jack
  or Swiss cheese
1 egg, beaten with a teaspoon
  of water

Sauté mushrooms, onion, carrot, and celery in butter over medium heat, about 10 minutes, stirring occasionally. Remove from heat; stir in salt and one tablespoon mustard. On lightly floured surface, roll each patty shell into 7-inch circle; spread each circle with mustard to within one inch of edge. Cover mustard with sliced roast beef, dividing evenly. Spoon vegetable mixture over beef; sprinkle with cheese. Brush edge of each pastry circle with egg wash mixture. Bring 2 sides of pastry up and over filling to form package. Press edges firmly to seal. Brush with egg wash; place on ungreased pan. Bake at 425° for 15 minutes.

Recipes & Remembrances / Buffalo Lake (South Dakota)

WWW.WIKIPEDIA.ORG

With no foothills to mar the view, the Teton Mountain Range is considered the most photogenic of America's mountains. Rising 7,000-plus feet from the floor of Wyoming's Jackson Hole Valley, the Tetons are the youngest mountains in the Rockies. The Teton Range has more than twelve peaks at elevations greater than 12,000 feet, with it's highest peak, Grand Teton, reaching 13,770 feet.

Montana Pasty

The pasty was a favorite in Butte, a gift from the Cornish miners who were among the first of the European immigrants to arrive in the copper-mining city. It is still the cherished staple among the real people of Butte.

THE PASTY:

3 cups flour	2 eggs
1 teaspoon salt	1 cup water
½ pound Crisco (although the Cousin Jacks say lard is best)	

THE STUFFING:

6 potatoes, diced	1 teaspoon salt
1 medium onion, chopped	1 teaspoon pepper
½ stick margarine or butter, melted	A good round steak or pork, diced

Mix flour, salt, and Crisco with egg beater until like cornmeal. Add 2 eggs and a cup of cold water. Put all this on a table, with a thin layer of flour; sprinkle water on slightly; and then knead into a roll. Put all this into the refrigerator to chill for awhile.

Take your pasty roll out of the refrigerator and make 10 round things with your rolling pin. Then fold them over with the Stuffing in the middle and make neat half-moon shapes, poking arty stab holes in them to let the steam out (pierce with a fork). Roll up the edges and press with the fork aesthetically. You can paint them with milk or egg white to make them brown, if you want. This enhances their natural beauty. Bake them in an oven for 1 hour at 425°. Serve with gravy or ketchup on a plate—or munch hand-held cold. A 10-pasty recipe.

Potluck (Montana)

Potato Pepperoni Hot Dish

This hot dish brings many compliments.

1½–2 pounds hamburger
1 small onion, diced
1 can Cheddar cheese soup
1 can tomato soup
1 cup milk
½ teaspoon oregano
¼ teaspoon pepper

1 teaspoon sugar
6–8 potatoes, sliced
1 package pepperoni slices
½ cup Parmesan cheese
1 cup shredded mozzarella
  cheese

Brown hamburger and onion. Mix the soups, milk, and seasonings. Mix together the hamburger, potatoes, and soup mixture. Place in a 9x13-inch pan. Bake at 350° for one hour, or until potatoes are tender. Top with pepperoni slices. Bake for 5 minutes. Top with Parmesan and mozzarella cheese. Bake until cheese melts.

North Dakota: Where Food is Love (North Dakota)

Hobo Dinners

1 pound ground beef
Worcestershire
Salt and pepper
4 medium potatoes

2 large carrots
2 medium onions
1 (16-ounce) package frozen
  peas

Divide ground beef into 4 equal portions. Make patties and place each on an 18-inch piece of heavy-duty aluminum foil. Season each patty with Worcestershire and salt and pepper to taste. Pull sides of foil up around patties to form a bowl.

Wash, but do not peel potatoes. Cut into ¼-inch rounds and place potato slices on each patty. Slice carrots into ¼-inch rounds and add to each dinner. Slice onions and add to each. Top each with 4 ounces frozen peas. Seal each Hobo Dinner by crimping the foil as tightly as possible at the opening. Place on a cookie sheet and bake at 375° for 1 hour.

Cooking with the Ladies (Wyoming)

Hobo Delight

Each person assembles his own meal, starting with Fritos, and building up.

2 pounds ground beef	5 cans water
1 teaspoon chili powder	1 cup Minute Rice
2 teaspoons oregano	1 large package Fritos
4 tablespoons sugar	1 pound shredded cheese
1 teaspoon salt	1 head lettuce, cut up
2 teaspoons cumin seed	3 cups tomatoes, cut up
1 tablespoon minced onion	1 cup sliced dark olives
2 cloves garlic	1 cup chopped green onion
3 (6-ounce) cans tomato paste	1 pint sour cream
2 (8-ounce) cans tomato sauce	Picante sauce

Fry ground beef; drain off fat. Add chili powder, oregano, sugar, salt, cumin seed, minced onion, minced garlic, tomato paste and sauce, water, and rice. Bring to a boil. Simmer for 40 minutes.

To serve, put in separate dishes in this order: Fritos, meat mixture, cheese, lettuce, tomatoes, olives, green onions, sour cream, and picante sauce.

Cooking with Iola (Nebraska)

Sweet and Sour Meatballs

3 pounds hamburger
1½ cups quick oatmeal
2 (10-ounce) cans water
  chestnuts, chopped
1 teaspoon onion salt
1 teaspoon garlic salt
2 tablespoons soy sauce
2 eggs, beaten
1 cup milk

2 (15-ounce) cans crushed
  pineapple
2 cups light brown sugar
1 cup white vinegar
4 tablespoons soy sauce
2 cubes beef bouillon
6 tablespoons cornstarch
⅔ cup chopped green pepper

Mix together hamburger, oatmeal, chopped chestnuts, onion and garlic salts, soy sauce, eggs, and milk. Form into meatballs. Fry or broil, turning occasionally until done. Drain pineapple into saucepan. Add brown sugar, vinegar, soy sauce, and bouillon. Bring to low boil. Thicken with cornstarch. Stir in green peppers and pineapple. Heat through but leave peppers crisp-tender. Serves 20.

St. Joseph's Table (South Dakota)

Swedish Meatballs with Red Wine Sauce

1 cup fine dry bread crumbs
1 teaspoon cornstarch
1 teaspoon salt
¼ teaspoon pepper
Dash of allspice or mace
1 egg, beaten
1 cup rich milk or cream
1 pound twice-ground beef

1 small onion, minced
Fat or oil
3 tablespoons flour
2 cups water
⅔ cup burgundy or any red
  wine
Salt and pepper

Add bread crumbs, cornstarch, salt, pepper, allspice or mace, beaten egg, and milk to the ground beef. Sauté onion lightly in fat or oil. Mix with ground meat mixture. Blend ingredients thoroughly. Shape into tiny balls—40 to 42 in all. Brown lightly in a little oil or fat. Remove meatballs from pan.

Make gravy by slowly blending the flour into the fat in pan, and then slowly adding water and wine. Add salt and pepper to gravy, to taste. Return meatballs to pan; simmer 20 minutes.

Sharing Our Best (Idaho)

Border Burgers

2 pounds lean ground beef
1 (4-ounce) can diced green
   chiles
1½ cup finely shredded
   Cheddar cheese (divided)
½ teaspoon salt
½ teaspoon pepper
½ teaspoon cumin
4 hamburger buns, separated
2 (15-ounce) cans chili with
   beans, heated
1 cup chopped red onion

Combine ground beef, green chiles, ¾ cup Cheddar cheese, salt, pepper, and cumin in bowl; mix well. Shape into eight ¾-inch thick patties. Grill 4–6 inches above hot coals for 8 minutes for rare, 12 minutes for medium and 15 minutes for well-done, turning once or twice. Move patties to edge of grill. Place buns cut-side-down on grill. Grill for one minute or until light brown. Remove from grill. Arrange patties on buns on serving platter. Top with chili; sprinkle with cheese and onion. Yields 8 servings.

The Kansas City Barbeque Society Cookbook (Kansas)

Green Chile Cheese Burgers
by Denise

1 pound ground beef
½ cup finely sliced green
   onions
1 teaspoon Mrs. Dash
   Seasoning Blend
1 teaspoon minced fresh
   cilantro
2 cloves garlic, minced
2 teaspoons taco seasoning
   mix
1 (7-ounce) can chopped green
   chiles
Shredded lettuce
1 cup grated Monterey Jack
   cheese
1 cup finely chopped white
   onion
6 tablespoons salsa
Avocado slices for garnish

Combine beef, green onions, Mrs. Dash, cilantro, garlic, and taco seasoning. Shape into 6 patties and broil or grill. Heat green chiles. To serve, place meat patty on bed of shredded lettuce; mix heated chiles, cheese, and onion together and pour over meat, then top with salsa. Garnish with avocado slices. Makes 6 burgers.

You're Hot Stuff, Flo! (Wyoming)

Shepherd's Pie

1 pound ground beef
2 tablespoons fat
1 cup chopped onion
½ cup diced green pepper
1 (10¾-ounce) can cream of
    mushroom soup

2 cups cooked or canned peas
    and carrots
2 cups seasoned hot mashed
    potatoes
Melted butter
Parsley (optional)

Brown beef in hot fat; add onion and green pepper; cook until tender, but not brown. Stir in soup; place in greased 1½-quart casserole; sprinkle peas and carrots over soup. Arrange mashed potatoes in ring on top; drizzle melted butter over top. Bake uncovered in a 350° oven for 25 minutes or until heated through. Serves 6.

Note: String beans may be substituted for peas and carrots.

Feeding the Herd (Wyoming)

Cheese-Filled Meat Loaf

1½ pounds ground beef
¾ cup quick rolled oats
¼ cup chopped onion
1 egg
½ teaspoon salt

½–1 teaspoon oregano
¼ teaspoon pepper
1 (8-ounce) package mozzarella
    cheese (large slices)
1 (8-ounce) can tomato sauce

Mix beef, oats, onion, egg, salt, oregano, and pepper. Divide meat mixture in 3 parts. In bread loaf pan (approximately 9x5x3 inches), layer ⅓ of meat mixture, ½ of cheese, ⅓ meat mixture, rest of cheese and top with last ⅓ of meat mixture. Seal edges as you put in layers. Top with tomato sauce. Bake at 350° for one hour.

Yesterday and Today Friendly Circle Cookbook (North Dakota)

Summer Sausage

2 pounds hamburger
½ teaspoon garlic powder
⅛ teaspoon mustard seed
2½ teaspoons liquid smoke
1 cup water

¼ teaspoon onion powder
¼ teaspoon black pepper
2½ tablespoons Morton Tender
  Quick

Mix well; make into long rolls. Wrap in foil, shiny side in. Refrigerate 24 hours. Poke holes in bottom of foil. Place on rack of broiler pan with a little water in bottom of pan. Bake at 325° for 90 minutes. Unwrap to cool.

Fire Hall Cookbook (Montana)

Stuffed Cabbage Rolls

1 egg, beaten
½ cup milk
¼ cup finely chopped onion
1 teaspoon Worcestershire
¾ teaspoon salt
Dash of pepper
1 pound ground beef, or ½
  beef and ½ pork, cooked

¾ cup cooked rice
6 large or 12 medium cabbage
  leaves
1 (10¾-ounce) can condensed
  tomato soup
1 tablespoon brown sugar
1 tablespoon lemon juice

In mixing bowl, combine egg, milk, onion, Worcestershire salt, and pepper. Mix well. Add cooked meat and cooked rice. Mix thoroughly. Remove center vein of cabbage leaves, keeping each leaf in one piece. Immerse each leaf in boiling water until limp (3 minutes). Drain. Put cabbage leaf on waxed paper. Place ¼–½ cup mixture on each cabbage leaf. Make sure you fold in sides of each leaf, then roll. Arrange each roll in a 7½x12x2-inch baking pan or dish.

Stir together tomato soup, brown sugar, and lemon juice. Pour sauce over cabbage rolls. Bake, uncovered, at 350° for 1¼ hours, basting once or twice with sauce. Makes 6–8 servings.

Generations "Coming Home" (Idaho)

Quick Crescent Taco Pie

1 pound ground beef
1 package taco seasoning mix
½ cup water
½ cup chunky salsa
1 (8-ounce) can crescent
   dinner rolls
1½ cups crushed corn chips,
   divided

1 (8-ounce) carton dairy sour
   cream
6 slices American cheese
Shredded lettuce
Sliced black olives
Diced tomatoes

Brown meat in skillet; drain. Add seasoning mix, water, and salsa; simmer for 5 minutes. Spread crescent roll dough in 10-inch pie plate to form crust; press edges together at seams. Sprinkle 1 cup corn chips on crust bottom; keep remaining ½ cup. Spoon on meat mixture. Spread sour cream over meat. Cover with cheese slices; sprinkle on remaining ½ cup corn chips. Bake at 375° for 20 minutes, until crust is golden brown. Top with lettuce, olives, and tomatoes.

Wolf Point, Montana 75th Jubilee Cookbook (Montana)

Walking Taco

1½ pounds hamburger
1 small onion, chopped
1 teaspoon garlic salt
Salt and pepper to taste
10 (2¾-ounce) bags Fritos or
   nacho cheese Doritos chips
2 cups lettuce, shredded

1 cup tomatoes, chopped
1 cup shredded Cheddar
   cheese
1 cup sour cream
1 can black olives, drained
Taco sauce to taste

Brown hamburger, onion, garlic salt, salt and pepper. Cut ¼-inch top off chip bags. Crush chips slightly. Fill bags with cooked hamburger mixture. Top with lettuce, tomatoes, cheese, sour cream, and olives. Stick fork in bag and serve. Offer taco sauce.

Recipes from the Heart /Epsilon Omega Sorority (Nebraska)

Tamale Pie

1 medium onion, chopped
1 clove garlic, minced
2 tablespoons peanut oil
1½ pounds ground beef
1½ cups canned tomatoes
2 teaspoons salt

¼ teaspoon pepper
1 teaspoon ground cumin
4 teaspoons chili powder
3 cups cornmeal mush (per
   package directions)
Shredded cheese

Sauté onion and garlic in hot oil until browned. Add ground beef and cook until brown. Add tomatoes, salt, pepper, and spices; simmer on low heat for 10 minutes. Remove and set aside.

Follow package directions and mix 3 cups cornmeal mush. Line bottom and sides of casserole dish with cornmeal mixture, reserving about ⅓. Pour cooked meat filling into casserole. Spread remainder of cornmeal mixture over top of pie. Preheat oven and bake for 30 minutes at 425°. Sprinkle with shredded cheese and serve hot. Serves 6–8.

Matt Braun's Western Cooking (Idaho)

Veal Parmigiana

1 pound thin veal scallopini
2 eggs, beaten
1 cup seasoned bread crumbs
¼ cup olive or salad oil
½ cup chopped onion
1 clove garlic, crushed
1 cup tomatoes
2 teaspoons sugar

¾ teaspoon salt
½ teaspoon dried oregano
¼ teaspoon dried basil
¼ teaspoon pepper
1 package sliced mozzarella
   cheese, divided
¼ cup grated Parmesan
   cheese, divided

Preheat oven to 350°. Dip veal in eggs, then crumbs, coating lightly. In skillet, heat oil. Add veal and cook until brown; remove from skillet. Sauté onion in hot oil (add more if necessary); add garlic. Add tomatoes (smash tomatoes if using whole tomatoes). Add sugar and spices. Bring to boil, then reduce heat and simmer, covered, for 10 minutes. Place veal in baking dish. Add half sauce and half cheeses. Repeat layers, ending with Parmesan cheese. Cover with foil and bake 30 minutes. Serve over rice.

Sharing Our Best (Wyoming)

Liver and Onions

½ pound bacon
1 pound sliced onions

1 pound baby beef liver
1 cup flour

Preheat oven to lowest temperature. Fry bacon and drain on paper towels. Place on oven-proof plate in warm oven to maintain temperature. Pour bacon grease from skillet and set aside; return 2 tablespoons to skillet, and return skillet to medium-high heat. Place onions in skillet; fry until golden brown, stirring occasionally and adding bacon grease 1 tablespoon at a time, if needed. Place onions on heat-proof platter and set in oven to keep warm. Return remaining bacon grease to skillet and heat to medium high. Dredge liver in flour and place in skillet; watch carefully. As soon as liquid seeps through top of meat, turn over and cook 2 more minutes. To serve, arrange liver over onions and bacon on top of liver. Discard any remaining flour, or use for gravy for this recipe only.

GRAVY:

1½ cups beef broth

Remaining flour

Have beef broth ready and sitting close at hand. Sprinkle remaining flour into hot skillet, stirring constantly with long-handled meat fork. As soon as flour begins to turn brown, add broth. (Do this very carefully, as steam will rise, and can burn you. This is the reason for using a long-handled fork.) Bring to a boil for 1 minute, then reduce heat and simmer for 1 minute longer.

Elegant Cooking Made Simple (Idaho)

Western Barbecued Ribs

RIBS:

½ cup firmly packed brown
  sugar
¼ cup country-style Dijon
  mustard

3 cups apple juice
1 teaspoon hot pepper sauce
3 pounds beef, pork loin, or
  country-style ribs

In Dutch oven, stir together all ingredients, except ribs; add ribs. Cook over high heat until mixture comes to a full boil. Cover; reduce heat to low. Continue cooking, turning ribs occasionally, until ribs are fork-tender, 40–50 minutes. Prepare grill.

BARBECUE SAUCE:

¼ cup firmly packed brown
  sugar
¼ cup chopped onion
1 cup ketchup
½ cup Worcestershire

¼ cup lemon juice
½ teaspoon coarsely ground
  pepper
¼ teaspoon salt
¼ teaspoon cayenne pepper

In 1-quart saucepan stir together all Barbecue Sauce ingredients. Place ribs on grill. Brush ribs with Barbecue Sauce. Grill, brushing with Sauce and turning occasionally, until ribs are done, 12–15 minutes. Cook remaining Barbecue Sauce over medium heat, stirring occasionally, until it just comes to a boil. Serve with ribs. Serves 4.

Favorite Recipes (Wyoming)

More pronghorn can be found in Wyoming than anywhere else in the world. As a matter of fact, with 416,000 pronghorn, Wyoming has 70% of the world's population. Often called "antelope," the pronghorn is actually a relative of the African gazelle. Capable of reaching speeds up to 70 miles per hour, the pronghorn is North America's fastest land animal.

Jerry's Superb Short Ribs

4–5 pounds lean short ribs
1 teaspoon salt
¼ teaspoon sugar
⅛ teaspoon turmeric
⅛ teaspoon paprika
⅛ teaspoon celery salt
⅛ teaspoon black pepper
1 cup ketchup
¾ cup water
½ cup finely chopped onion
½ cup finely chopped green
  pepper
⅓ cup cider vinegar
¼ cup firmly packed brown
  sugar
1 tablespoon Worcestershire
1½ teaspoons minced garlic
1 teaspoon dry mustard
½ teaspoon hot pepper sauce
½ teaspoon salt
¼ teaspoon basil
¼ teaspoon black pepper

Brown short ribs in oil (optional). Place in a roaster. Combine 1 teaspoon salt, sugar, turmeric, paprika, celery salt, and ⅛ teaspoon pepper; sprinkle over ribs. Bake, covered, for 1 hour at 350°. Drain off fat.

Meanwhile, combine the remaining ingredients and spoon over the ribs. Reduce heat to 275° and bake 2–3 hours, basting every 30 minutes, until the ribs are done and very tender. Serve with rice pilaf and tossed salad.

Simac Family Favorites (Montana)

Kurt's Killer Pork Ribs

1 large package of pork ribs
1 (18-ounce) bottle barbecue
  sauce (Bull's Eye)
¾ (1-pound) package brown
  sugar

Place ribs in 14-inch Dutch oven, taking care not to stack ribs. Cook for 1½ hours in 350° oven, covered, or until the ribs are close to being done. While the ribs are cooking, pour the whole bottle of sauce in a bowl. Add ¾ package brown sugar to the sauce. Drain juice from ribs and pour sauce over the ribs. Continue to simmer for ½ hour, uncovered, so the ribs can absorb the sauce.

Hey Ma! Come Quick! The Hog's in the Garden Again!! (Idaho)

Blue Ribbon Barbecued Country Back Ribs

2 slabs country back pork ribs
Teriyaki sauce (enough to
　cover ribs)
Morton Nature's Seasons®
　Seasoning Blend, to taste

1 (12-ounce) can beer, room
　temperature
K.C. Masterpiece barbecue
　sauce (original)

Do not trim fat from ribs or parboil. Marinate overnight in the refrigerator in a mixture of teriyaki sauce and Morton's seasoning.

　Prepare coals around sides of grill and let ash down, about 45 minutes. Stack ribs, one on top of the other, in the center of the grill. Leave in this position for 10 minutes, with the lid closed, at 300°. Rotate the stack, putting top slab on the bottom, and cook for 10 minutes more. Repeat the process on the other side of each slab of ribs. (This takes 40 minutes in all.) Allow heat to lower to 225° and continue rotating slabs, occasionally basting with beer to keep ribs moist on the outside. Turn every 20–30 minutes for about 2 hours. Baste with barbecue sauce for another hour, continuing to rotate ribs and letting fire die out naturally. Serves 4–6.

All About Bar-B-Q Kansas City Style (Kansas)

Orange-Glazed Pork Butt

½ cup frozen orange juice
　concentrate
½ cup honey
2 tablespoons fresh lime juice
2 tablespoons butter
1 teaspoon ground ginger

1 (5- to 7-pound) pork butt,
　trimmed
3 tablespoons garlic salt
1 tablespoon pepper
1 tablespoon ground ginger

Bring orange juice concentrate, honey, lime juice, butter, and one teaspoon ginger to a boil in saucepan. Boil for one minute. Remove from heat. Sprinkle pork with garlic salt, pepper, and remaining one tablespoon ginger. Place pork on grill rack in covered grill with water pan. Cook with lid down at 230° for 7–9 hours or to 165° on meat thermometer. Brush pork with orange glaze 30 minutes before end of cooking process. Yields 25 servings.

The Kansas City Barbeque Society Cookbook (Kansas)

Bourbon Pork Tenderloins

A winner for a dinner party.

2 pork tenderloins	**½ cup bourbon**
½ cup soy sauce	**4 tablespoons brown sugar**

Marinate tenderloins in remaining ingredients for up to 2 hours before baking. Bake 1–1½ hours at 325°; cool to room temperature.

MUSTARD SAUCE:

1 tablespoon dry mustard	**2 tablespoons white wine**
Dijon mustard to taste	**vinegar**
2 tablespoons sugar	**4 egg yolks**
½ teaspoon salt	**1 cup heavy cream**

Combine ingredients in top of double boiler and cook until thick. Serve at room temperature with sliced tenderloins.

Rare Collection Recipes (Montana)

Pork Chop and Potato Bake

6 pork chops	**1 (3-ounce) package cream**
Seasoned salt	**cheese, softened**
Pepper	**2 tablespoons chopped onions**
1 (10¾-ounce) can cream of	**1 cup shredded Cheddar**
celery soup	**cheese**
½ cup milk	**1 (2.8-ounce) can French's**
½ cup sour cream	**French fried onions**
1 (24-ounce) package O'Brien	
or hash brown potatoes,	
thawed	

Brown pork chops. Sprinkle with seasoned salt and pepper. Set aside. Combine soup, milk, and sour cream. Stir in potatoes, cream cheese, and onions. Spoon mixture into a 9x13-inch pan. Arrange pork chops over potatoes. Bake in 350° oven for 40 minutes. Top with cheese and French fried onions. Bake for 5 minutes more until cheese melts.

The Best of Rural Montana Cookbook (Montana)

Pork Sauerkraut Platter

6–8 pork chops
Salt and pepper
2 (16-ounce) cans sauerkraut
1 medium onion, chopped
  (optional)
3 tablespoons brown sugar

1 (10¾-ounce) can cream of
  mushroom soup
1 (4-ounce) can sliced
  mushrooms (optional)
4 cups hot mashed potatoes

Brown chops in heavy skillet, turning once. Remove chops from skillet and season with salt and pepper. Drain off part of fat from skillet. Empty drained sauerkraut in skillet; sprinkle with chopped onion and brown sugar. Heat about 5 minutes, stirring. Empty sauerkraut into a large shallow greased baking dish and arrange chops on top. Spoon soup over chops. Sprinkle on mushrooms, if desired. Cover and bake in preheated 325° oven until chops are tender, about 1¼ hours. Remove from oven. Using a pastry tube or spoon, make a border of mashed potatoes. Brown under broiler. Makes 6 servings.

Wolf Point, Montana 75th Jubilee Cookbook (Montana)

Apple Baked Pork Chops with Sherry

6 boneless pork chops
3 large apples, peeled, cored,
  and sliced
¼ cup packed brown sugar

½ teaspoon ground cinnamon
2 tablespoons butter
1 pinch each salt and pepper
½ cup dry sherry

In a large skillet, brown chops about 2 minutes on each side. Preheat oven to 350°. Arrange apple slices in bottom of a 9x13-inch baking dish. Sprinkle with brown sugar and cinnamon. Dot with butter. Top with the browned pork chops and season with salt and pepper to taste. Pour sherry over all; cover and bake for 1 hour or until internal temperature of pork has reached 160°.

The Miracle Cookbook (Idaho)

Dutch Oven Pork Chops

Here is an old favorite of ours, good for a whole family meal—a favorite espe-cially of mine, since I have always been a pork chop man.

2 pounds pork chops
½ cup dry sherry
¼ cup soy sauce
2 tablespoons sugar
1 egg yolk
¼ teaspoon rosemary
¼ teaspoon oregano
¼ teaspoon basil
Flour
⅓ cup plus 2 tablespoons
   vegetable oil, divided
1 large onion (Texas Sweet)

1 red pepper
1 ounce mushrooms
1 cucumber
1 stalk celery
8 green onions
1 can pineapple chunks,
   drained; reserve syrup
¼ cup white vinegar
3 tablespoons tomato sauce
1 cup water
3 tablespoons cornstarch

Marinate pork chops in pot with sherry, soy sauce, sugar, egg yolk, and condiments for an hour or so. Drain pork chops and coat with flour. Heat 2 tablespoons vegetable oil in Dutch oven. Cook the pork until brown.

Slice the onion into thin slices. Cut and chop red pepper. Cut mushrooms in quarters. Slice cucumber into ¼-inch-thick pieces. Cut celery into chunks and add some of the tops along with green onions. Remove and drain pork chops.

Add ⅓ cup vegetable oil as needed, and heat over hot fire. Stir-fry vegetables 5 minutes. To drained vegetables, add pineapple syrup, vinegar, and tomato sauce. Combine water and cornstarch. Add pineapple chunks and pork chops. Cook and stir thoroughly. Serves 6.

Old-Fashioned Dutch Oven Cookbook (Idaho)

Idaho has a rich mining history. Silver Valley's Morning Star is one of the deepest mines in America at over a mile and a half deep. Bunker Hill ranks as America's largest underground mine. And the Sunshine Mine was America's richest silver mine, producing over 300 million ounces of silver, more than the entire output of Nevada's famous Comstock Lode.

Chalupa

Every bean cook has a favorite chili recipe. While not a true chili, Chalupa is a Mexican-American favorite for a hearty lunch or supper. Try it. If you like chili, you'll love chalupa. It may be made ahead and reheated, and it freezes well.

1 pound pinto beans
1 (3-pound) pork roast
7 cups water
½ cup chopped onion
2 cloves garlic, minced
1 tablespoon salt
2 tablespoons chili powder
1 tablespoon cumin
1 teaspoon oregano

1 (4-ounce) can chopped green chiles
Corn chips
Condiments: chopped tomato, chopped avocado, chopped onion, shredded lettuce, grated Cheddar cheese, taco sauce or other hot sauce

Put all ingredients, except corn chips and condiments, in Dutch oven, an electric crockery cooker or heavy kettle. Cover and simmer about 5 hours, or until roast falls apart and beans are done. Uncover and cook about ½ hour until the desired thickness. Serve over corn chips and pass condiments for choice of toppings.

Idaho's Favorite Bean Recipes (Idaho)

Ham Loaf

1¾ pounds ground cured ham
2½ pounds ground fresh pork
4 tablespoons ketchup
4 tablespoons horseradish
4 tablespoons chopped green pepper

1 cup mushrooms
1 cup cracker crumbs
2 eggs
1 cup milk
4 strips bacon

SAUCE:

½ cup prepared horseradish
½ cup mayonnaise
2 teaspoons prepared mustard

¼ cup chopped fresh parsley
2 cups dairy sour cream

Combine ingredients for ham loaf and place in a 9x13-inch baking dish with 2 strips bacon on top and bottom of loaf. Bake at 350° for 1½ hours. Serve with sauce. Serves 12.

Our Daily Bread (Kansas)

Tangy Glazed Hams

GLAZE:

1 (8-ounce) jar orange marmalade
6 ounces amaretto

½ teaspoon Tabasco or other hot pepper sauce

Mix ingredients together and let sit while you're getting the charcoal ready.

3 (2-pound) boneless canned hams
1 (15-ounce) can pineapple rings (save juice)

1 cup water
1 (4-ounce) bottle maraschino cherries (save juice)

Place hams in 12-inch Dutch oven along with juices from the cans and the water. Brush each ham with the Glaze and any other seasoning you wish to add. Place pineapple rings on each ham with a maraschino cherry in the center of each ring.

Set the Dutch oven in a firepan with 8–10 briquets underneath and 12–14 around the outside of the lid, and cook for an hour. Brush each ham with the remaining Glaze 2–3 times.

Cee Dub's Dutch Oven and Other Camp Cookin' (Idaho)

Leg of Lamb of the West

1 (5- to 6-pound) leg of lamb	Pepper to taste
1 cup dry red wine	1 teaspoon Italian seasoning
1 cup red wine vinegar and oil dressing	1 teaspoon beef bouillon granules
2–3 cloves garlic, slivered and pierced into meat at intervals	2 tablespoons Worcestershire
	Dash of Tabasco
	¼ cup soy sauce
2 onions, peeled and quartered	Dash of paprika

Place leg of lamb and all other ingredients in roasting pan. Bake at 350° for 2½–3 hours, until meat is tender, basting frequently. (The secret is in the basting!) Skim off the accumulated fat and serve juices with meat. Serves 8–10.

Wonderful Wyoming Facts and Foods (Wyoming)

Brats, Beer, and Onion Packet

2 medium onions, cut into thin wedges	5 smoked, cooked bratwurst
⅓ cup beer	5 hot dog buns, split

Heat grill. Cut 18x18-inch piece of heavy-duty foil; spray with nonstick cooking spray. Place onions in shallow layer on center of foil; sprinkle with beer. Top with bratwurst. Wrap packet securely using double-fold seals, allowing room for heat expansion. When ready to grill, place packet, seam-side-up, on gas grill over medium heat, or on a charcoal grill 4–6 inches from medium coals. Cook 30 minutes or until onions are tender. To serve, open packet carefully to allow steam to escape. Place bratwurst in buns and top with onions.

The Miracle Cookbook (Idaho)

Pepper-Style Jerky

Because jerky is virtually fat free, it makes a great snack food.

5 pounds lean meat	**1 teaspoon cayenne pepper**
4 tablespoons salt	**2 teaspoons coriander**
1 teaspoon curing salt	**2 teaspoons garlic powder**
1 teaspoon smoke flavoring	**5 cups cold water**
1 teaspoon white pepper	**Coarsely ground black pepper**
1 teaspoon chili powder	

Cut away as much fat/tallow as possible from the jerky meat. Place trimmed meat in freezer for 2–3 hours, or until meat is slightly frozen; remove from freezer. Slice the meat into ¼- to ⅜-inch-thick slabs (at this point, a protective glove is advised to help prevent accidents). Slice the meat slabs into ¼- to ⅜-inch-thick strips.

Combine meat strips and all remaining ingredients, except coarsely ground black pepper, in an ample-size, nonmetallic brining vessel; stir/mix well. Refrigerate mixture overnight (about 8 hours) to cure; continue to stir occasionally.

Next day, spread the cured jerky strips evenly on drying racks. Do not rinse strips! Sprinkle each piece generously with coarsely ground black pepper. Dry at 150°–170° in oven, smoker or dehydrator (check occasionally for doneness) until jerky reaches desired degree of dryness, 5–24 hours, depending on drying method used.

Note: Jerky is ready to eat when there is very little moisture left on the inside of the strips and slightly sticky on the outside, yet still flexible enough to bend without snapping.

Sausage & Jerky Handbook (Idaho)

POULTRY

In 1996, legislation was passed creating Tallgrass Prairie National Preserve in the Flint Hills region of Kansas, a 10,894-acre former cattle ranch, designed to educate visitors about the prairie ecosystem, Kansas' ranching heritage, and the landscape as it looked in the pioneer days. Tallgrass prairie land once covered some 400,000 square miles, from Ohio to the Rocky Mountains and from Texas up into Canada. Now, less than four percent remains, primarily in the Flint Hills of Kansas.

Mandarin Chicken with Broccoli

3 whole broiler-fryer chicken
  breasts, halved
1 teaspoon salt
¼ teaspoon pepper
¼ cup butter
½ cup minced onion
1 clove garlic, minced
2 teaspoons paprika
1 bunch fresh broccoli, cut up,
  steamed about 10 minutes

1 (11-ounce) can Mandarin
  orange sections, drained
1 cup sour cream
⅓ cup mayonnaise (NOT salad
  dressing)
⅓ cup grated Parmesan
  cheese

Sprinkle chicken meat with salt and pepper. In large frying pan, melt butter over medium heat. Add onion and garlic; sauté 3 minutes. Stir in paprika. Remove pan from heat; add chicken to mixture, turning to coat. In large shallow baking pan, place chicken in single layer, skin-side-up. Cover with foil; bake in 375° oven about 40 minutes or until fork can be inserted in chicken with ease. Remove chicken from oven; place broccoli around chicken. Add Mandarin orange sections. In medium bowl mix together sour cream and mayonnaise; spoon over chicken, broccoli, and orange segments. Sprinkle with Parmesan cheese. Return to oven; bake (uncovered) about 6 minutes longer, or until it turns golden. Serves 6.

REC Family Cookbook (North Dakota)

Real Fried Chicken

This method was handed down from a former slave who had come west following the Civil War, and had cooked for an outfit out of Texas. Folks from down south have told me that this is still the best way to do it.

2 cups flour
Salt and pepper to taste
1 (2- to 3-pound) chicken,
   cut up

Shortening or lard

Mix the flour, salt and pepper in a sack. Shake a few pieces of the chicken in the sack at a time. Starting with the largest pieces, place in a heavy cast-iron skillet in hot grease that is ½–1 inch deep. Cook 5–10 minutes, turning frequently so they don't burn. Reduce heat and continue to cook and turn until golden brown, 20–30 minutes.

   The secrets here are: grease, not oil; cast-iron cookware; and not covering chicken while cooking. The only spices are salt and pepper.

Sowbelly and Sourdough (Idaho)

Hunter's Chicken

1 pound boneless, skinless
   chicken breasts, cut in
   strips
⅓ cup cornstarch
¼ cup margarine
½ teaspoon tarragon
½ teaspoon thyme

¼ teaspoon pepper
1 cup sliced green onions
2 cups chicken broth
¾ cup white wine
1 cup sliced mushrooms
3 tomatoes, cut in eights
3 or 4 cups cooked rice

Dredge chicken in cornstarch. Brown coated chicken in margarine. Stir in seasonings and onions. Cook a few minutes longer. Add broth and wine. Cover; simmer at least 10 minutes. Gently stir in mushrooms and tomatoes. Cover; simmer 5 minutes longer. Serve over rice. Serves 6.

The Fine Art of Cooking (Montana)

Chicken Breast with Cranberry Orange Sauce

2 large onions, sliced ½-inch
   thick
6 boneless, skinless chicken
   breast halves
¼ cup frozen orange juice
   concentrate, thawed but not
   diluted
¼ cup water

Place onion slices in bottom of ungreased 9x13x2-inch baking dish. Top with chicken. Mix orange juice concentrate and water in bowl. Baste breasts with orange juice mixture. Bake one hour at 350°, until cooked through and browned. Baste occasionally with orange juice mixture. When chicken is done, transfer to serving plates. Discard onions. Spoon Cranberry-Orange Sauce over chicken. Garnish with orange slices and serve. Makes 6 servings.

CRANBERRY-ORANGE SAUCE:

1 (16-ounce) can whole-berry
   cranberry sauce
¾ cup unsweetened orange
   juice
1 teaspoon grated orange rind
2 tablespoons brown sugar
2 teaspoons cornstarch
Orange slices, for garnish

Combine all sauce ingredients in small saucepan; stir well. Bring to a boil over high heat, stirring constantly. Reduce heat to medium, and cook one minute, stirring until thickened. Serve warm.

Recipes Worth Sharing (Kansas)

William Frederick Cody, better known as Buffalo Bill Cody, founded "Buffalo Bill's Wild West" in 1883 in the area of North Platte, Nebraska. The circus-like attraction toured annually. Buffalo Bill and his performers would reenact the riding of the Pony Express, Indian attacks on wagon trains, and stagecoach robberies. The show typically ended with a melodramatic reenactment of Custer's Last Stand in which Cody himself portrayed General Custer. In 1895, Cody was instrumental in the founding of Cody, the seat of Park County in northwestern Wyoming. Cody opened the Irma Hotel in downtown Cody in November 1902, a hotel named after his daughter that is now on the National Register of Historic Places.

Blue Spruce Olive Chicken Mozzarella

4 chicken breasts
¼ cup flour
¼ teaspoon salt
¼ cup olive oil
1 clove garlic, crushed
1 medium onion, diced
1 (14-ounce) jar spaghetti
   sauce

1 (8-ounce) can sliced
   mushrooms
½ teaspoon oregano
½ cup sliced pimento-stuffed
   olives
1 (6-ounce) package sliced
   mozzarella

Skin and bone chicken breasts; cut into bite-size pieces. Combine flour and salt in a plastic bag and coat chicken. Heat oil in a skillet and brown chicken. Arrange chicken in shallow 2-quart baking dish, leaving the drippings in the skillet. Sauté garlic and onion in drippings until onion is tender. Stir in spaghetti sauce, mushrooms, oregano, and olives; pour over chicken. Cut cheese slices into strips and place on top of chicken. Bake at 350° until chicken is tender, about 30 minutes. Makes 6–8 servings.

Recipe from Blue Spruce Inn, Lander, Wyoming
Tastes & Tours of Wyoming (Wyoming)

Garlic Lovers' Chicken

½ cup dry bread crumbs
⅓ cup grated Parmesan
   cheese
2 tablespoons minced parsley
½ teaspoon salt (optional)
⅛ teaspoon pepper
¼ cup milk

6 boneless, skinless chicken
   breast halves (1½ pounds)
¼ cup butter or margarine,
   melted
1–2 garlic cloves, minced
2 tablespoons lemon juice
Paprika

In a large resealable plastic bag, combine the first 5 ingredients. Place milk in a shallow bowl. Dip chicken in milk, then shake in the crumb mixture. Place in a greased 9x13x2-inch baking dish. Combine the butter, garlic, and lemon juice; drizzle over the chicken. Sprinkle with paprika. Bake, uncovered, at 350° for 25–35 minutes or until the juices run clear. Makes 6 servings.

Cooking with the Ladies (Wyoming)

Chicken Chalupas

Best if made a day in advance.

2 (10¾-ounce) cans cream of
  chicken soup
1 pint sour cream
1 (4-ounce) can green chiles
1 (4-ounce) can chopped ripe
  olives
¼ cup chopped green onion

¾ pound grated Jack cheese
4 large chicken breasts,
  cooked, deboned, and
  chopped
12 flour tortillas
¾ pound grated Cheddar
  cheese

Combine soup, sour cream, chiles, olives, and green onion. Mix
and add Jack cheese. Remove 2 cups of mixture and set aside.
Add chopped chicken to remaining mixture; fill 12 tortillas and
roll up. Place tortillas in a 9x13-inch pan, seam-side-down. Pour
remaining mixture on tortillas. Spread evenly and top with grated Cheddar. Bake at 350° for 40 minutes.

Cooking with Cops, Too (Idaho)

Fantastic Chicken Fajitas

1 pound boneless chicken
  breast or thigh meat
1 teaspoon each garlic
  powder, oregano, ground
  cumin, and seasoned salt
2 tablespoons orange juice
2 tablespoons vinegar

½ teaspoon hot pepper sauce
1 tablespoon cooking oil
1 medium onion, peeled and
  sliced
1 green pepper, seeded and
  sliced
4 flour tortillas

Slice chicken into ¼-inch strips. Mix together garlic, oregano,
cumin, salt, orange juice, vinegar, and hot pepper sauce.
Marinate chicken strips in mixture for 10 minutes. Heat oil in
heavy skillet until hot. Stir-fry chicken strips, onion, and green
pepper until chicken is no longer pink, about 3–5 minutes. Serve
with flour tortillas and accompany with sliced green onion, shredded lettuce, and salsa, if desired. Serves 4.

Heavenly Recipes (North Dakota)

Chicken Enchiladas

6 boneless, skinless chicken
  breast halves (1½ pounds)
1 tablespoon butter
1 cup chopped onion
1 green bell pepper, cored,
  seeded, and chopped
1 red bell pepper, cored,
  seeded, and chopped
8 ounces grated Cheddar
  cheese
1 (4-ounce) can diced green
  chiles
1 cup purchased green chile
  salsa

½ cup chopped fresh cilantro
4 teaspoons ground cumin
Salt and freshly ground black
  pepper
12–15 (7-inch) flour tortillas
10 ounces Monterey Jack
  cheese, grated
1 cup whipping cream
½ cup chicken broth
Chopped avocado for garnish
Chopped tomatoes for garnish

Place chicken in pan of rapidly boiling water to cover, and simmer for 15–20 minutes till tender. Remove from heat; drain, cool and shred chicken. Preheat oven to 350°.

In medium skillet, melt butter over medium heat. Cook onion and bell peppers until just soft, 5–8 minutes. Transfer to large bowl. Add chicken, Cheddar cheese, green chiles, salsa, cilantro, and cumin. Season with salt and pepper to taste and mix well.

Grease a 10x15x2-inch baking pan or 2 smaller pans. In each flour tortilla, place ⅓ cup chicken mixture along an edge. Roll up from filling side and place seam-side-down in the pan. Sprinkle Monterey Jack cheese over enchiladas. Combine cream and chicken broth and pour over enchiladas. Cover pan with foil and bake for 30 minutes. Remove foil and continue baking for 10 minutes or until thoroughly heated. Garnish with avocado and tomatoes, if desired. Can serve tortilla soup with this dish.

From the High Country of Wyoming (Wyoming)

The Statehouse in Boise, Idaho, and dozens of other buildings in the city are geothermally heated from underground hot springs. In fact, Idaho is well sprinkled with public and private hot springs.

The World's Easiest Chicken

1 jar Russian dressing
1 small jar apricot jam

½ envelope onion soup mix
4 chicken breasts

In a large baking dish, combine Russian dressing, apricot jam, and onion soup mix. Place chicken breasts in dish; cover with the mixture. Bake at 350° for one hour. For best flavor, keep basting chicken with the mixture throughout the hour.

Favorite Recipes of Rainbow Valley Lutheran Church
(North Dakota)

Dutch Oven Chicken Dinner

This recipe was a favorite of the crew and wranglers at Teton Trail Rides when the Rudds operated the concession in Grand Teton National Park from 1950 to 1993. It makes a hearty outdoor meal.

4 large boneless chicken
  breasts
1–1½ cups cubed potatoes
1–1½ cups cubed zucchini
1–1½ cups cubed carrots
1–1½ cups chopped cabbage
1 (16-ounce) can garbanzo
  beans

1 medium onion, chopped
¼ cup chopped green pepper
2–3 garlic cloves, chopped
1 (16-ounce) can chicken broth
1 (10½-ounce) can cream of
  chicken soup
Salt and pepper

On outdoor barbecue, grill chicken breasts until brown on both sides. Place cut-up potatoes, zucchini, carrots, and cabbage in bottom of a 12-inch Dutch oven. Mix in garbanzo beans (with juice), onion, green pepper, and garlic cloves. Place chicken breasts over top of vegetables. Pour chicken broth over meat and vegetables. Spoon out and spread cream of chicken soup over top of chicken. Season with salt and pepper as desired. Cover and cook on low to medium heat on outdoor grill for 1–1½ hours, until vegetables are tender.

The Pure Food Club of Jackson Hole (Wyoming)

Sweet and Sour Chicken

½ cup vinegar
¾ cup sugar
¼ cup water
½ teaspoon salt
3 tablespoons ketchup

2 tablespoons soy sauce
2 pounds drummettes
½ cup cornstarch
Crisco

Combine vinegar, sugar, water, salt, ketchup, and soy sauce and set aside. This makes enough sweet and sour sauce for 2 pounds of chicken drummettes.

Roll chicken drummettes in cornstarch. Brown in Crisco. Place in baking dish. Pour mixture over chicken. Bake at 350° for 20 minutes. Turn chicken and bake 15 minutes.

Horse Prairie Favorites (Montana)

Oven Barbecued Chicken

Everyone wants this recipe.

5–6 pounds chicken thighs
Garlic powder
3 eggs, beaten
2 cups granulated sugar

1 cup pineapple juice
1½ cups ketchup
1 cup white vinegar
2 teaspoons soy sauce

Wash chicken thighs and pat dry. Sprinkle with garlic powder and let set for about 5 minutes. Dip chicken in beaten eggs. Fry until nearly done. Spray large oven pan with non-stick spray. Mix together the granulated sugar, juice, ketchup, vinegar, and soy sauce. Put chicken in pan and pour the sauce over chicken. Cover pan with aluminum foil and bake 30–45 minutes in 300° oven, or until sauce is thick. Put chicken on platter and spoon remaining sauce over top.

In the Kitchen with Kate (Kansas)

Juicy Baked Chicken and Mushrooms

A delicious low-calorie way to make chicken. The unflavored gelatin gives the chicken a saucy texture.

2 tablespoons dried parsley	½ teaspoon onion powder
2 tablespoons dried chives	½ teaspoon salt (optional)
8 ounces fresh mushrooms, sliced	½ teaspoon poultry seasoning
2 (5- to 6-ounce) chicken breasts, skinned	1½ teaspoons unflavored gelatin granules (½ package)
⅓ cup lemon juice	1 teaspoon paprika

Mix parsley, chives, and mushrooms in a 1-quart casserole. Place chicken on mushrooms. Pour lemon juice over chicken. Sprinkle remaining ingredients over chicken in order given. Cover. Microwave at MEDIUM-HIGH (70%) for 11–14 minutes or until tender. Let stand 3 minutes before serving. Yields 2 servings.

Easy Livin' Microwave Cooking (Nebraska)

Chicken Squares with Mushroom Sauce

3 cups diced, cooked chicken	4 beaten eggs
1 cup cooked rice	2 teaspoons salt
2 cups soft bread crumbs	¼ teaspoon poultry seasoning
⅓ cup diced celery	2 cups chicken broth
¼ cup pimiento, chopped	

Combine chicken, rice, bread crumbs, celery, and pimiento. To the beaten eggs, add salt, poultry seasoning, and broth (or use 2 chicken bouillon cubes dissolved in 2 cups hot water, then cooled); mix thoroughly. Stir into chicken mixture. Bake in greased 9x9x2-inch baking dish at 350° for 55 minutes. Cut into squares and serve with Mushroom Sauce.

MUSHROOM SAUCE:

⅔ cup milk	1 can cream of mushroom soup

Add milk to soup. Heat thoroughly. Serves 9.

Sharing God's Bounty (Kansas)

Chicken and Stuffing Casserole

4 cups stuffing mix
1 cup melted butter
4 cups chopped cooked
  chicken
2 cans cream of chicken
  soup
1 (13-ounce) can evaporated
  milk

1 (10-ounce) package frozen
  peas, thawed
1/4 cup minced onion
1 (2-ounce) jar chopped
  pimento, drained

Combine stuffing mix with melted butter in bowl; mix well. Press half the mixture into 9x13-inch baking dish. Combine chicken, soup, evaporated milk, peas, onion, and pimento in bowl; mix well. Spread in prepared dish; top with remaining stuffing mix. Bake at 350° for one hour. Yields 8 servings.

Y Cook? (North Dakota)

Hot Chicken Sandwich

1 loaf Pepperidge Farm
  Bread
3 cups chopped, cooked
  chicken
3 hard-boiled eggs, chopped
2 tablespoons chopped
  onions

1 cup sliced ripe olives
1 small can mushrooms
2/3 cup mayonnaise
1 can mushroom soup
1 cup sour cream
Slivered almonds
Paprika

Remove crust from bread and butter on both sides. Put 8 slices of bread in 9x13-inch pan. Mix together chicken, eggs, onions, olives, mushrooms, and mayonnaise. Put on bread. Put 8 slices of bread on top. Mix soup and sour cream together. Put on top of bread. Sprinkle with slivered almonds and paprika. Bake at 325° for 30 minutes.

St. Joseph's Table (South Dakota)

Chicken Pie

1 (4-pound) stewing or
   roasting fowl
Water, to barely cover
½ teaspoon salt
Shake of pepper
3 tablespoons butter
3 tablespoons flour

3 cups warm chicken broth
   (from stewing fowl)
1 cup cream
2 tablespoons chopped pimento
1 (4-ounce) jar button
   mushrooms, drained
Biscuits

Put fowl in large saucepan. Add water, salt, and pepper, and bring to a boil. Simmer until the meat falls from the bones (1½–2 hours). Cool. Discard skin. Remove meat from bones in large pieces. Place chicken pieces evenly in bottom of a 12-inch baking dish. In saucepan, melt butter; blend in flour; add broth gradually. Add cream. Beat all the while with a whisk. Add pimentos and mushrooms. Taste and adjust seasoning. Bring to boil before you pour over chicken. Top with uncooked biscuits (homemade, if possible). Preheat oven to 425°. Bake for 20–25 minutes.

Columbus Community Cookbook (Montana)

Guilt-Free Gourmet Turkey Burgers

1 pound lean ground turkey
1 small shredded zucchini
½ cup dry bread crumbs or
   crushed cornflakes
1 onion, chopped
2 tablespoons Worcestershire
1 egg white

1 tablespoon parsley
½ teaspoon salt
½ teaspoon pepper
½ green or red bell pepper,
   shredded
1 carrot, peeled and shredded

Combine all ingredients in large bowl; mix well. Form into patties (will be soft). Use spatula to transfer to broiler pan or fine wire vegetable rack for grilling. Cook well. Excellent with BBQ sauce, lettuce and tomato garnish.

The Kearney 125th Anniversary Community Cookbook (Nebraska)

Turkey Rolls

1¼ pounds diced cooked
chicken or turkey
1 (8-ounce) package cream
cheese, softened
Lemon pepper to taste

1 (8-ounce) can refrigerated
crescent rolls
1 (10¾-ounce) can cream of
mushroom soup
½ soup can of milk

Mix together well the meat, cream cheese, and lemon pepper. Set aside. Spread out crescent rolls, and separate into triangles. To make larger rolls, dough can be rolled thinner with a floured rolling pin. Place a large spoonful of meat mixture in center of each roll. Wrap dough around meat mixture, sealing edges. Bake as directed on crescent roll package until rolls are lightly browned. Mix and heat mushroom soup with milk to make a gravy. Spoon over warm rolls. Baked rolls can be frozen and reheated later.

The Pure Food Club of Jackson Hole (Wyoming)

Crock-Pot Dressing

1 cup butter
2 cups chopped onion
1 cup chopped celery
13 cups dried bread cubes
1 teaspoon poultry seasoning

1½ teaspoons salt
1½ teaspoons sage
½ teaspoon pepper
4 cups chicken broth
2 well-beaten eggs

Melt butter; add onion and celery; simmer. Mix all and cook in crockpot on LOW for 6–8 hours.

Years and Years of Goodwill Cooking (North Dakota)

Cornbread Dressing, Country Style

Here's the dressing to try out posthaste. My family enjoys it as a side dish rather than "stuffed into a bird." It is especially yummy served with chicken gravy, country style.

1 cup chopped white onion
1 cup chopped celery with
   some of the leaves
¼ cup water
6 cups crumbled cornbread
6 slices toasted regular bread,
   torn into small pieces

5 eggs, beaten slightly
1 tablespoon ground sage
¼ teaspoon seasoned salt
1 cup cubed cooked turkey or
   chicken
2–2½ cups chicken broth,
   purchased or homemade

Cook the onion and celery in water for about 5 minutes; drain. Combine the cornbread, regular bread, cooked onion and celery, eggs, sage, salt, and cooked chicken or turkey. Stir in enough of the chicken broth to make the stuffing extra moist. Turn into a greased 8x8x2-inch baking dish.

Bake, covered, at 400° for 30 minutes. Uncover and bake another 5–10 minutes more, until dressing is heated through and the top is a little crusty. This dressing can be made early in the day. Cover and refrigerate until ready to bake.

Note: If you don't have any leftover chicken or turkey in your refrigerator, stop by the local deli and pick up just enough to add to this extra-special cornbread delight.

Best-of-Friends, Festive Occasions Cookbook (Montana)

GAME

PHOTO ©2004 HANS ANDERSEN

A 12-foot-high bronze statue of Sakakawea (a.k.a. Sacagawea) and her baby son, Baptiste, stands at the entrance to the North Dakota Heritage Center on the state capitol grounds in Bismarck. The statue commemorates Sakakawea for her role in helping the Lewis and Clark Expedition establish friendly relations with the Shoshones.

Burger Pot Pie

When I think of old-fashioned meat pies like Grandma used to make, the first thing that comes to mind is her renowned potato pie crust. The following is a close rendition of her best.

2 pounds hash browns
1 egg, beaten
1 tablespoon granulated
  onion
½ teaspoon salt
1 tablespoon olive oil
1 pound lean ground venison
1 (16-ounce) can whole-kernel
  corn, undrained
1 (16-ounce) can green beans,
  undrained

1 (10-ounce) can tomato soup,
  undiluted
⅓ teaspoon oregano
⅓ teaspoon freshly ground
  black pepper
1 tablespoon sugar
1 cup grated Monterey Jack
  cheese

Combine hash browns, egg, granulated onion, and salt in mixing bowl; toss lightly. Press hash brown mixture into greased 9-inch-deep pie plate to form crust; bake crust in preheated 400° oven for 15–20 minutes; remove and set aside.

Heat olive oil in skillet; add lean ground venison. Cook over medium-high heat until venison is browned, stirring frequently to crumble; drain and set aside.

Combine corn, green beans, tomato soup, oregano, pepper, and sugar in mixing bowl; stir well; add browned venison. Pour filling mixture into hash brown pastry; bake in preheated 400° oven for 20 minutes. Remove, top with sprinkling of Monterey Jack cheese, and bake an additional 5 minutes or until cheese is melted and light golden brown. Cool slightly and cut into 6 pieces. Makes 6 servings.

98 Ways to Cook Venison (Idaho)

Country Hash

2 tablespoons olive oil
1 medium onion, diced
3 cups leftover venison roast,
  chopped
4–5 medium potatoes, diced
½ teaspoon salt

¼ teaspoon freshly ground
  black pepper
1½ cups milk
¾ cup Italian bread crumbs
6 large eggs

Heat olive oil in large skillet; add onion, venison roast, potatoes, salt and pepper. Cook, uncovered, over medium heat 20 minutes, turning frequently, until potatoes are cooked through. Drain. Reduce heat, then break eggs over hash mixture; cover. Cook additional 2–3 minutes, or until eggs reach desired degree of doneness. Makes 6 servings.

98 Ways to Cook Venison (Idaho)

Chicken Fried Venison Steak

1 elk or moose round steak,
  or 2 deer round steaks
1 cup flour
1 teaspoon dried thyme
1 teaspoon dried oregano
1 teaspoon salt

½ teaspoon pepper
1 or 2 cloves garlic, crushed
¼ cup olive oil
1 large onion, sliced or diced
Water to cover

Cut all fat and sinew from the steak. Cut steak into serving sizes. Mix flour, thyme, oregano, salt and pepper together. Coat both sides of steak pieces with the flour mixture.

In a large skillet, sauté the garlic in oil over medium heat. Turn the heat up to medium high, and brown the flour-covered steak. When browned, add leftover flour to oil. Mix together. Add onion. Cover meat and onion with water. Cover skillet. Turn heat on low and cook for 45 minutes or until tender. You may need to thin gravy a little before you serve it. It is good served over potatoes, noodles, or rice. Serves 4–6.

Cookin' in Paradise (Idaho)

Prime Rib of Venison

When you're having friends over for dinner, nothing is more impressive than a properly prepared prime rib of venison.

2 beef bouillon cubes
2 tablespoons beef soup mix
3 cups hot water
1 large onion, chopped
1 (6- to 7-pound) venison
   standing-rib roast

Salt
Garlic pepper
Spiced crab apples
Fresh parsley sprigs

Dissolve bouillon cubes and beef soup mix in 3 cups hot water; add chopped onion and stir well. Pour into baking dish. Sprinkle sides and back of venison prime rib with salt and garlic pepper, to taste.

Insert meat thermometer into thickest portion of roast. Place roast in preheated 400° oven; cook, uncovered, 30 minutes or until well browned. Baste with onion/soup stock; reduce heat to 325°. Bake, uncovered, for 1½ hours or until meat thermometer reaches 155°–160°, basting often with onion/soup stock. Slice between each rib. Serve with small bowl of stock; garnish with spiced crab apples and parsley twigs.

98 Ways to Cook Venison (Idaho)

Venison North Idaho

2 venison steaks, thick loin
½ clove garlic
1 tablespoon olive oil
2 tablespoons butter
Salt and pepper to taste
½ cup chopped mushrooms

½ bay leaf
1 teaspoon Worcestershire
2 tablespoons currant or apple
  jelly
¼ cup dry sherry
½ cup thick cream

Rub the surface of steak gently with the garlic. Heat olive oil and butter until sizzling in frying pan, and sauté steaks quickly in this until both sides are brown. Season with salt and pepper to taste. Combine rest of ingredients and pour over steaks. Bake in 350° oven for 70 minutes.

Recipes Logged from the Woods of North Idaho (Idaho)

Smoked Deer Ham

1 (5- to 8-pound) deer ham,
  trimmed neatly
½ cup Worcestershire
1 cup Italian dressing
1 tablespoon cayenne red
  pepper

1 tablespoon salt
1 tablespoon pepper
1 cup chopped onions
½ cup soft butter

Put ham in large container; cover with mixture of all remaining ingredients. Can slice holes in meat so it can soak inside better. Cover good; soak overnight or about 10 hours. Can turn over about 2 or 3 hours to marinate. Put on smoker and let smoke for 6 hours; turn and smoke 4 more hours or until tender.

The Oregon Trail Cookbook (Nebraska)

Teriyaki Elk Kabob

TERIYAKI MARINADE:

½ cup soy sauce
2 tablespoons molasses
¼ cup oil

2 teaspoons ground ginger
2 teaspoons dry mustard
6 garlic cloves, minced

Combine ingredients. Set aside.

1½ pounds elk steak, cubed
2 green peppers, cubed
15 cherry tomatoes
½ pound fresh mushrooms
1 medium onion, cubed

Zucchini, cubed
Cucumbers, cubed
Pitted olives (whole)
Red peppers, cubed

Marinate meat for 15 minutes. Drain. Place ingredients on skewers, alternating meat and vegetables. Grill 5–10 minutes, turning frequently and basting with Teriyaki Marinade.

Cookin' at Its Best (Idaho)

Wyoming is home to the world's largest single elk herd. The National Elk Refuge, located just outside the town of Jackson, is the largest established elk preserve in North America. Up to 9,000 elk winter on the refuge, and visitors can enjoy close-up views on daily sleigh rides from December through April.

Bou Bobs

Use caribou, mule deer, or whitetail, but use an adult animal—two years old or more. Mature animals have a more complex flavor and firmer texture to the meat, which the red wine vinegar and soy sauce complement. Make sure, however, that the meat you use is tender. Kabobs cook very fast, and there's no time for tenderizing.

1 pound tender caribou
¼ cup red wine vinegar
¼ cup soy sauce

¼ cup vegetable oil
1 teaspoon ground lemon peel
½ teaspoon pepper

Dry the caribou meat off with a paper towel, and cube it into 2-inch chunks. In a large bowl or resealable plastic bag, combine the red wine vinegar, soy sauce, oil, lemon peel, and pepper. Add the meat cubes, cover or seal, and marinate 24 hours in the refrigerator.

Start 40 briquettes, or preheat a propane barbecue and turn down to medium-high heat. Meanwhile, drain off and save the marinade. Pat the caribou chunks dry with paper towels, then place on skewers.

When the charcoals are white hot, and you can only hold your hand at cooking level for 4–5 seconds, lightly brush the meat chunks with the marinade and place on the grill. Cook about 5 minutes per side, then serve hot with risotto. Yields 4 servings.

Game on the Grill (Montana)

Wild Game Dip

This is an excellent accompaniment to all wild game dishes.

2 cups apricot preserves
¼ cup fresh lemon juice
½ cup white wine

2 tablespoons teriyaki sauce
¼ teaspoon cayenne pepper
Salt and pepper to taste

In saucepan, combine apricot preserves, lemon juice, wine, teriyaki sauce, cayenne pepper, salt and pepper. Stir until well blended. Cook and reduce to thicken. Yields 1½–2 cups.

Wonderful Wyoming Facts and Foods (Wyoming)

Basic Jerky

½ cup salt
½ tablespoon garlic salt
½ tablespoon pepper

5 pounds lean meat (elk, caribou, deer, beef, etc.)
Garlic powder (optional)

Make a mixture of salt, garlic salt, and pepper. Cut meat into 2-inch-wide strips, 1 inch thick. Roll strips in seasoning, or "dredge," as the television cooks say. Place meat in a crock and weight down with a plate. Brine this way in refrigerator for 5 days, then remove and rinse. Dry and place in smoker. Smoke about 18 hours or until the meat is a purple color when you cut into it. At this point you can rub garlic powder into it, if you like. Five pounds raw meat makes 1 pound jerky.

Variation: Mix brine ingredients with 1 quart of water, bring to a boil, and place the meat in the boiling mixture for 10 minutes. Remove and place immediately in the smoker.

Don Holm's Book of Food Drying, Pickling and Smoke Curing (Idaho)

Quail Cook-In-A-Bag

1 tablespoon flour
1 large oven cooking bag
6 quail
Salt and pepper to taste
1 cup chopped onion
½ cup chopped green pepper

1 pound fresh mushrooms, sliced
1 bay leaf
1 cup dry sherry
Juice of ½ lemon
1 cup water

Grease a large roasting pan. Put flour in oven cooking bag and shake, making sure that the inside of bag is evenly coated. Split birds lengthwise in half and sprinkle flesh with salt and pepper. Place birds in the bag and add the onion, green pepper, mushrooms, bay leaf, sherry, lemon juice, and water. Tie the bag, lay in pan, and punch 12 holes in the top of the bag. Roast at 350° for 45 minutes. This method of roasting creates its own gravy and bastes the birds at the same time.

The Oregon Trail Cookbook (Nebraska)

River Roast Wild Goose

1 young wild goose (about 10
  pounds) with giblets
Salt and pepper
8 medium onions, peeled
2–3 branches fresh sage or
  1 tablespoon dried sage,
  crushed

8 thick slices fatty bacon
2 tablespoons flour
1 cup strong stock made from
  giblets

Preheat oven to 325°. Rinse goose, drain and pat dry with paper towels, inside and out. Sprinkle cavity and all surfaces with salt and pepper. With a sharp knife, cut a quarter inch deep X in the root end of each onion. Fill goose body with onions and the fresh or dried sage. Close the cavity and tie legs together with butchers cord. Place in roasting pan on rack, breast-side-up. Cover with bacon slices and roast for about 2 hours. Remove bacon strips and dust goose with half of the flour. Continue roasting until crisp and done, about 30 minutes more. Transfer to heated platter and keep warm.

Skim fat from pan juices and add remaining flour to juices, stirring over medium heat until smooth and thickened. Add stock slowly, stirring. Bring to boil and adjust seasoning with salt and pepper to taste. Serve on side as sauce. Serves 6. Serve with hot applesauce and baby Brussels sprouts.

The Oregon Trail Cookbook (Nebraska)

In 1861, George Armstrong Custer graduated from West Point at the bottom of his class. However, during the Civil War (1861–1865), his skills at war propelled him to the temporary rank of brigadier general. After the war, Custer was required to revert to his previous rank of captain in the small regular army, but was always respectfully referred to as "General Custer." In 1866 he was appointed lieutenant colonel of the newly authorized 7th Cavalry. Sioux and Cheyenne warriors defeated Custer on June 25, 1876, at the Battle of Little Big Horn in Montana, which resulted in his death and a total loss of his troops. Little Bighorn Battlefield National Monument, near Hardin, Montana, is the site of the battle, commonly referred to as Custer's Last Stand. He remains the youngest general in U.S. history.

Creamed Pheasant
with Caramelized Onions

No matter what else I cook, this is what people remember. It harkens back to the classic pheasant fried in butter, then baked in cream sauce, but this is a lot easier. With the caramelized onions, I think it tastes a lot better, too.

2 tablespoons butter	**2 tablespoons Dijon mustard**
½ onion, thinly sliced	**¼ teaspoon white pepper**
¼ cup extra dry sherry	**1 pheasant, cleaned**
½ cup heavy cream	**1 tablespoon flour**

In a large skillet, melt the butter over medium heat, then add the onion slices and sauté until the onions are golden brown—caramelized. Turn the heat off and let onions sit.

Preheat a propane barbecue for 10 minutes, then turn down to medium-low heat. Or start 3 dozen charcoal briquettes on one side of the barbecue and wait 25 minutes. Optimum cooking temperature is 350° for both units.

While the barbecue heats up, combine the sherry, cream, mustard, and pepper in a small bowl. Mix thoroughly. Pat the pheasant down inside and out with paper towels and set it in a plastic oven bag that has been shaken with 1 tablespoon of flour. Pour the cream sauce and caramelized onions over the pheasant and close the bag. Make 6 small slits in the top of the bag, per package directions. Now place it on a clean drip pan for easy handling.

Place the pheasant in the barbecue, on the top shelf or over the unlit burner, and cook 60 minutes. Remove the pheasant from the bag, and serve with the cream sauce and mashed potatoes. Serves 4.

Game on the Grill (Montana)

Flint Ridge Pheasant

Those of us who cook for hunters always welcome a new recipe for fish or fowl. Here's one that we cheered for! This casserole is also wonderful for chicken; use 3 skinless, boneless chicken breast halves.

2 cups cooked wild rice
  (⅔ cups dry)
1 cup julienned (matchstick)
  1-inch carrot strips, cooked
5 slices bacon
1–2 tablespoons oil, butter or
  margarine
2 skinless, boneless pheasant
  breast halves, cut in
  2x2-inch pieces
Salt and pepper to taste
5 medium mushrooms, sliced

5 green onions, sliced
1 can cream of chicken soup
¼ cup cream or milk
¼ cup sherry or dry, white
  wine
1 cup (4 ounces) shredded
  mozzarella cheese
1 (14-ounce) can artichoke
  hearts, drained, quartered
¼ cup grated Parmesan
  cheese

Put the wild rice in 9x9x2-inch baking dish that has been sprayed with nonstick vegetable spray. Layer the carrots over the wild rice.

In large skillet, cook bacon until crisp; drain and crumble over the carrots. Pour off grease from skillet and add a tablespoon or two of oil. Sauté the pheasant until well browned on both sides (about 10 minutes). Transfer to baking dish.

In same skillet, sauté the mushrooms and green onions until tender, adding additional oil if needed. Add soup, cream and sherry, and mix well. Add mozzarella and gently stir in artichokes. Spread over the pheasant layer. Sprinkle with Parmesan. Cover dish with foil sprayed with nonstick vegetable spray. Bake at 350° for 30 minutes; remove foil and bake 15 more minutes until bubbly throughout. Serves 4–5.

Presentations (North Dakota)

Sautéed Duck Breasts with Roasted Apples on Pasta

4 boneless, skinless duck
  breasts
Salt and pepper to taste
2 tablespoons clarified butter
2 tablespoons butter
1 pound Granny Smith apples,
  skinned, thickly sliced
¼ cup chopped shallots

2 teaspoons chopped garlic
¼ cup apple jack brandy
2 cups heavy cream
Additional salt and pepper,
  if desired
Cooked pasta of your choice
½ cup Parmesan cheese

Place duck breasts between plastic wrap and pound out to even thickness. Salt and pepper breasts. In saucepan, sauté breasts in 2 tablespoons clarified butter for 2–3 minutes on each side, or to desired doneness; remove from pan and hold in a warm oven. In same saucepan, add 2 tablespoons butter, apples, shallots, and garlic, and sauté for 2 minutes. Deglaze the pan with apple jack; add cream, bring to a simmer, then adjust flavor with salt and pepper. Toss with pasta. Slice duck breasts and place on pasta; garnish with Parmesan cheese. Yields 4 portions.

Cooking on the Wild Side (Idaho)

Duck and Wild Rice Trail Casserole

2 pounds wild ducks
4 stalks celery
1 large onion, halved
Salt and pepper
1 (6-ounce) package long
  grain and wild rice
1 (4-ounce) can sliced
  mushrooms
½ cup chopped onion
½ cup margarine, melted
¼ cup all-purpose flour
¾ cup half-and-half
¾ cup white wine
2 tablespoons chopped fresh
  parsley
½ cup slivered almonds

Cook ducks with seasonings (celery, onion, salt and pepper), covered with water in Dutch oven for one hour or until tender. Remove ducks from stock. Let cool; strain stock and reserve. Cut meat into bite-sized pieces and set aside.

Cook rice according to directions on package. Drain mushrooms, reserving liquid. Add enough duck broth (stock) to make 1½ cups. Sauté chopped onion in margarine until tender; add flour, stirring until thick and smooth. Gradually stir in mushroom broth liquid. Cook over medium heat, stirring constantly, until thick and bubbly. Stir in duck, rice, half-and-half, wine and parsley. Spoon into a greased 2-quart shallow casserole. Sprinkle almonds on top. Cover and bake at 350° for 15–20 minutes until liquid is absorbed. Let rest 5 minutes before serving. Serves 6–8.

Note: You may substitute 3 cups cooked chicken for duck.

The Oregon Trail Cookbook (Nebraska)

SEAFOOD

White water plunges over 212 feet at the spectacular horseshoe rim of Shoshone Falls on the Snake River—52 feet further than Niagara Falls. October through April are the best times to view the falls, located near Twin Falls, Idaho.

Trout in Foil

6 whole trout, cleaned
Lemon pepper seasoning
1 lemon, thinly sliced
3 slices bacon, halved
1 onion, thinly sliced

3 medium potatoes, scrubbed
and thinly sliced
3 carrots, pared and thinly
sliced

Preheat oven to 350°. You will need 6 sheets of heavy-duty foil (each 4 inches longer than the trout). Lay trout on sheet of foil. Sprinkle lemon pepper the length of the cavity and line with lemon slices. Close cavity and top trout with a half slice of bacon. Top with onion, potato, and carrot slices; seal foil securely. Put foil-wrapped trout on a baking sheet. Bake 15 minutes; turn and bake 10 minutes longer (small trout less time, large trout more time). Makes 6 servings.

Yaak Cookbook (Montana)

Blodgett Lake Stuffed Trout

4 trout, cleaned (leave heads
and tails on)
1 tablespoon butter
4 slices bacon, cooked and
cut into 1-inch pieces
2 mushrooms, sliced
4 green scallion onions,
sliced thin

1 tablespoon lemon butter
(½ lemon juice and ½
melted butter)
1 teaspoon cumin
1 teaspoon ground red pepper
2 tablespoons white wine
1 lemon, sliced thin

Preheat oven to 375°. Put trout in greased 9x13-inch baking dish; set aside. Melt butter in skillet and sauté bacon pieces, green onions, and mushrooms. Drain off fat. Stuff the trout with bacon mixture. Brush top of trout with lemon butter. Sprinkle cumin and red pepper on top of trout. Place lemon slices on top of trout and bake for 30 minutes. Serve hot with steamed rice. Makes 4 servings.

Bitterroot Favorites & Montana Memories (Montana)

Papa's Favorite Trout

Jack Hemingway says, "This was Papa's favorite trout recipe. Mmmmm!"

1 dozen (6- to 8-inch) little
   brookies, filleted, but
   leave the blood line along
   backbone

Salt and pepper
1 stick butter
Juice of 2 lemons

Salt and pepper trout inside and out. Melt butter in a large skillet until it froths. Add trout and brown on both sides. Add lemon juice prior to turning trout over with spatula. Baste continuously until butter and trout are browned. Eat right away! Serves 6–8.

Ketchum Cooks (Idaho)

Sugar-Cured Rainbows

Rainbow trout are delicious when sugar-cured.

Split and open fish. Rub each with a handful of salt, then a handful of brown sugar. Place in layers in wooden barrel or crock, skin-side-down. Sprinkle each layer with black peppercorns. The top layer should be skin-side-up. Place in a cool spot overnight. Then wash in cool, fresh water for 20 minutes. Stack and press out moisture. Blot dry with towels.

   Smoke for 2–3 hours at about 85° until a nice pellicle (thin skin or film) is formed. Smoke another hour at 110°, then an hour at 120°, and longer, if necessary.

Don Holm's Book of Food Drying, Pickling and Smoke Curing
(Idaho)

 Nearly 85% of all the commercial trout sold in the United States is produced in the Hagerman Valley near Twin Falls, Idaho.

Platte River Catfish Fillets

2 tablespoons lemon juice
2 tablespoons white wine
½ cup dry bread crumbs
¼ teaspoon salt
⅛ teaspoon garlic powder
⅛ teaspoon pepper
1 pound catfish fillets
2 teaspoons oil

Heat oven to 450°. Spray 15x10x1-inch baking pan with non-stick cooking spray. In shallow dish, combine lemon juice and wine. In another shallow dish, combine bread crumbs, salt, garlic powder, and pepper. Dip fillets in liquid, then dip in crumbs to coat. Arrange coated fillets on sprayed pan; drizzle with oil. Bake at 450° for 8–10 minutes or until fish flakes easily with fork. Makes 4 servings.

The Oregon Trail Cookbook (Nebraska)

Dutch Oven Halibut

3 tablespoons olive oil
6–8 cloves garlic, minced
4 tablespoons chopped fresh
 tarragon
¼ cup lemon juice
2 cups white wine or cooking
 liquid
4–5 pounds halibut, cut into
 chunks, or fillets

Heat olive oil in 12-inch Dutch oven. Add garlic, and sauté for a few minutes, stirring constantly. Add fresh tarragon, lemon juice, and white wine or cooking liquid. Stir to blend all ingredients. Add halibut chunks or fillets; mix to coat the halibut with all the flavors. Cover and put Dutch oven into firepan. Put 6–8 briquets under the Dutch oven and 15 briquets on the lid. Cook 20–30 minutes depending upon the size of the chunks or fillets. When done, take off fire and remove halibut. Serve the juice as a sauce to be poured over halibut, or as an excellent dip for bread.

More Cee Dub's Dutch Oven and Other Camp Cookin' (Idaho)

Walleye Whopper

BATTER:

1 cup cold water
¼ cup dry white wine
1 cup all-purpose flour

1½ teaspoons baking
  powder
¼ teaspoon salt

Combine water and wine. Whisk in flour, baking powder, and salt until smooth.

4 (4- to 6-ounce) skinless
  boneless walleye fillets
¼ cup all-purpose flour
Cooking oil for deep-fat
  frying

4 warm buns
4 lettuce leaves
Tartar sauce

Rinse fillets and pat dry with paper towels. Halve crosswise. Coat fillets with flour, dip in batter. Fry fillets in large skillet of hot oil for 3–5 minutes. Remove; drain on paper towels. Keep warm. Serve on buns with lettuce and tartar sauce. Makes 4 sandwiches.

The Kearney 125th Anniversary Community Cookbook (Nebraska)

 The South Fork of the Snake River in Idaho is considered one of the best fly fishing rivers in North America with its large population of trout. One-fourth of Idaho residents own a fishing license. Another 200,000 non-residents also buy licenses.

Fillet of Salmon with Tomato Beurre Blanc

Beurre Blanc is French for white wine butter sauce. Many chefs today are adding additional ingredients to give the old classic a new twist. This Tomato Beurre Blanc is light and tangy and is a perfect accompaniment to the broiled salmon. You can grill the salmon, if you prefer.

⅔ cup sour cream, divided
2 tablespoons Dijon-style
  mustard
2 (8-ounce) salmon fillets
2 teaspoons olive oil
1 pound (4 large) tomatoes,
  peeled, seeded and chopped
Salt and pepper to taste

⅛ teaspoon fresh thyme leaves
  (or ½ teaspoon dried)
1 tablespoon minced shallot
2 tablespoons white wine
2 tablespoons white wine
  vinegar
½ cup butter (1 stick), cut into
8 pieces and very cold

Mix only ½ cup sour cream and mustard together, and coat salmon on both sides. Set aside.

Preheat broiler. Heat oil in a skillet over medium heat and add tomatoes, cooking for about 10–15 minutes, until juices are thick and somewhat reduced. Season with salt and pepper and stir in thyme. In a separate skillet over medium heat, combine shallot, white wine, and vinegar. Cook until the mixture is almost evaporated, with only about 1 tablespoon left. Whisk in remaining sour cream and heat through, about 2 minutes. Turn heat to the lowest setting.

While swirling pan, add butter, 1 piece at a time. When the piece is almost completely melted, add the next piece of butter and continue to swirl the pan. After 3 or 4 pieces have been added, remove pan from heat and continue to swirl and add butter. After the last piece has been added and melted, pour butter mixture into the warm tomato mixture. Season with more salt and pepper, if necessary. Keep warm while broiling the salmon, but watch the heat. Too much heat will "break" the sauce, and it will separate. Broil the salmon until opaque, about 3–5 minutes per side. Spoon 2–3 tablespoons sauce on a plate and top with salmon. Garnish with fresh thyme sprig and/or lemon wedge. Makes 2 servings.

Recipe from B Bar Guest Ranch, Emigrant, Montana
The Great Ranch Cookbook (Montana)

Orange and Herb Salmon

Halibut steaks, sea bass or snapper may be substituted for salmon.

½ tablespoon olive oil
Zest of 1 orange, finely
  grated
¼ cup orange juice, freshly
  squeezed
2 teaspoons garlic, minced
2 teaspoons dried tarragon

Salt to taste
Coarsely ground black pepper
  to taste
4 salmon steaks
2 teaspoons freshly snipped
  chives

Combine olive oil, orange zest, orange juice, garlic, tarragon, salt and pepper in medium mixing bowl to make marinade. Place salmon steaks in oven-proof dish. Pour marinade over steaks. Marinate for at least one hour at room temperature (or let marinate in refrigerator overnight). Preheat grill or oven to 450°.

Place steaks directly on the grill; spoon some of the marinade over steaks. If preparing in the oven, fish may be baked in marinade. Bake for 7–8 minutes, turning after 4 minutes or until salmon is just cooked through. Fish should flake easily when tested with a fork. Place on serving platter and sprinkle with chives. Serves 4.

Treasures of the Great Midwest (Kansas)

Seafood Giovanni

2 large onions, chopped
2 bell peppers, chopped
3 cups fresh mushrooms,
  sliced
Butter
3 cups canned tomatoes,
  drained and chopped

1 (8-ounce) package vermicelli
  pasta, cooked
3 cups flaked crabmeat,
  shrimp, or prawns (small)
2 cups sour cream
1 cup grated sharp cheese

Sauté onions, bell peppers, and mushrooms in butter. Add tomatoes, cooked vermicelli pasta, and crabmeat. Mix well. Add sour cream. Mix well again. Turn into greased 9x13-inch casserole. Sprinkle with grated cheese. Bake in moderate oven, 300°–350° for 30 minutes. Makes 12 servings.

Recipe from Time After Time B&B, Victor, Montana
Recipes from Big Sky Country (Montana)

Feta Shrimp Bake

This is always a favorite dish on Rocky Mountain River Tours' Middle Fork float trips.

1¼ cups chopped onion
4 garlic cloves, minced
⅛ cup olive oil
6 fresh tomatoes, chopped
½ cup chopped fresh parsley
1 tablespoon chopped fresh
  basil
2 teaspoons fresh marjoram
2 teaspoons grated lemon peel

Salt and freshly ground pepper
  to taste
1 teaspoon allspice
3 pounds shrimp, peeled and
  cleaned
1½ pounds feta cheese,
  crumbled
1 pound linguini pasta, cooked

In a Dutch oven or skillet, sauté onion and garlic in oil. Add tomatoes, parsley, basil, marjoram, and lemon peel. Simmer about 10 minutes. Season with salt, pepper, and allspice. If preparing conventionally, pour mixture into 2-quart casserole dish.

Put the shrimp on top of mixture. Sprinkle with feta cheese. Bake in Dutch oven for about 20 minutes, or in 350° conventional oven for 30–40 minutes, until the shrimp is done. Serve on top of linguini. Yields 8 servings.

The Outdoor Dutch Oven Cookbook (Idaho)

CAKES

PHOTO © GILLETTE CONVENTION & VISITORS BUREAU

Theodore Roosevelt named Devils Tower near Gillette, Wyoming, as the nation's first National Monument in 1906. This 1,267-foot-tall rock formation is a sacred site of worship for many American Indians. It was featured in the movie Close Encounters of the Third Kind.

Punch Bowl Cake

1 chocolate cake, baked and cut into small pieces
1 large package chocolate pudding, prepared
1 jar caramel sauce
1 (12-ounce) container Cool Whip
3 Skor or Heath bars, broken into pieces

Put cake pieces in bowl (glass looks best). Mix in chocolate pudding, then caramel sauce. Spread Cool Whip on top. Sprinkle candy on top. Refrigerate. Dip out with ice cream scoop. Rich and very yummy!

Rainbow's Roundup of Recipes (South Dakota)

Almost Better Than Harrison Ford Cake

1 package German chocolate cake mix
1 can sweetened condensed milk
1 jar caramel topping
1 (8-ounce) carton Cool Whip
Heath bar crumbles

Make and bake cake according to package directions and pour into a greased and floured 9x13-inch pan. Remove from oven and poke holes in cake with the handle of a wooden spoon. Pour condensed milk over all the holes. Pour caramel topping over all. Frost with Cool Whip and sprinkle with crumbles. Refrigerate.

Recipes from the Heart / Epsilon Omega Sorority (Nebraska)

"I Like Ike" was the presidential campaign slogan for Dwight D. Eisenhower, and an awful lot of people surely liked him. Eisenhower served as president from 1953 to 1961. Eisenhower was the only general to serve as president in the 20th century, and he never held an elected office prior to his presidency. The home, library, and final resting place of the former president and five-star general can be seen at the Eisenhower Center in Abilene, Kansas.

Twice the Guilt Cake

CAKE:

1 cup sugar
1 teaspoon vanilla
2 eggs
2 cups flour
1 teaspoon salt
1 teaspoon baking soda

1 (15-ounce) can crushed
   pineapple, undrained
½ cup brown sugar
½ cup coconut
½ cup chopped pecans
Whipped cream topping

Combine sugar, vanilla, and eggs. Beat 2 minutes at medium speed. At LOW speed add flour, salt, soda, and pineapple. Mix 1 minute. Pour into greased 9x13-inch pan. Sprinkle mixture of brown sugar, coconut, and pecans on top. Bake at 350° for 30–35 minutes. Just before Cake is done, prepare Sauce.

SAUCE:

½ cup butter
½ cup light cream

½ cup sugar
½ teaspoon vanilla

Heat ingredients together and pour mixture over warm cake. Cool and serve with whipped cream topping.

Recipe from Stoneheart Inn, St. Ignatius, Montana
Montana Bed & Breakfast Guide & Cookbook, 2nd Edition
(Montana)

Rave Reviews Coconut Cake

"Rave Reviews" says it all.

1 package Duncan Hines
   Yellow Cake Mix
1 (3-ounce) package instant
   vanilla pudding
1⅓ cups water
4 eggs
¼ cup oil

2 cups flaked coconut
1 cup pecans, finely chopped
1 (15-ounce) can cream cheese
   frosting
Extra coconut (¾ cup)
Margarine (2 teaspoons)

With an electric mixer, blend 2 minutes the cake mix, pudding, water, eggs, oil, coconut, and pecans. Pour into a greased and floured 9x13-inch pan. Bake about 45 minutes at 325°. Top with frosting. Sprinkle with extra coconut that has been sautéed in a little melted margarine until golden.

If It Tastes Good, Who Cares? II (North Dakota)

Poppy Seed Cake

¾ cup whole poppy seed
¾ cup cold water
2¼ cups cake flour
1⅓ cups sugar
2½ teaspoons baking powder
½ teaspoon salt

½ cup soft shortening
1½ teaspoons vanilla
¼ cup milk
3 egg whites, stiffly beaten
 (save yolks)

Soak poppy seed in cold water for 30 minutes. Heat oven to 350°. Grease well and flour 2 round layer cake pans. Sift dry ingredients into a mixing bowl. Add shortening, vanilla, and poppy seed-water combination, and beat 2 minutes at medium speed. Scrape sides and bottom often. Add milk, then fold in egg whites. Pour into prepared pans. Bake 30–35 minutes. Cool.

NUT FILLING:
1 cup sweet cream
1¼ cups sugar
4 egg yolks

1 cup ground nuts
½ cup coconut
1 teaspoon vanilla

Stir together the cream and sugar in saucepan till sugar is dissolved. Beat egg yolks slightly and add to cream mixture. Cook till thickened, about 7 minutes. Stir constantly. Cool, then add nuts and coconut, then vanilla. Cool and spread between layers and on top of the last layer. Let filling flow onto the sides.

Homemade Memories (Kansas)

Rhubarb Cake Quicky

1 box yellow or vanilla
 cake mix
3 cups rhubarb, thinly sliced
½ cup nuts, chopped

1 cup sugar
1 pint whipping cream, NOT
 whipped

Mix cake as directed and pour into greased and floured 13x9-inch pan. Sprinkle rhubarb and nuts over cake batter. Sprinkle sugar over rhubarb and nuts. Pour unwhipped cream over top. Bake in 350° oven for 40 minutes.

Ritzy Rhubarb Secrets Cookbook (North Dakota)

Simply Great Pineapple Cake

1 (18¼-ounce)box yellow or
   lemon cake mix with
   pudding in the mix
¾ cup vegetable oil

4 eggs, unbeaten
1 (11-ounce) can Mandarin
   oranges with juice

Mix ingredients in order given. Blend; beat with electric mixer, medium speed, for 2 minutes. Bake at 325° in 3 (8-inch) greased and floured pans for 20–24 minutes, or at 350° in 9x13-inch pan for 28–34 minutes. When cool, spread with the following icing.

ICING:

1 (15-ounce) can crushed
   pineapple
1 (3½-ounce) package dry
   instant vanilla pudding
   mix

1 (12-ounce) container whipped
   topping
Dash of salt

Mix crushed pineapple and instant pudding. Fold in the topping; spread on cake. Serves 15. Store cake in refrigerator.

REC Family Cookbook (North Dakota)

Victorian Applesauce Cake

1½ cups sugar
2 cups flour
1½ teaspoons baking soda
1½ teaspoons salt
2 tablespoons cocoa
½ teaspoon ground cloves
½ teaspoon nutmeg
½ teaspoon cinnamon

½ teaspoon allspice
½ cup shortening
1½ cups applesauce, divided
2 eggs
¾ cup chopped dates
¾ cup raisins
¾ cup chopped nuts
¾ cup chopped cherries

Sift together all dry ingredients into mixing bowl. Cut in shortening. Add 1 cup applesauce and eggs; beat 2 minutes. Add remaining ½ cup applesauce. Beat 1 minute. Mix in dates, raisins, nuts, and cherries. Pour into greased 9x9-inch cake pan, sprinkle with topping, and bake in 350° oven for 50–55 minutes.

TOPPING:

¼ cup finely chopped nuts

2 tablespoons sugar

Sprinkle over top of cake before baking.

Lewis and Clark Fare (Montana)

Stack Cake

Stack Cake was a traditional pioneer wedding cake put together at the wedding celebration. Each guest brought a layer of cake. The layers were put together with homemade applesauce, then stacked. The bride's popularity was measured by the number of stacks she had and by the number of layers in each stack.

The cakes were usually quite colorful and flavorful, as the guests proudly showed off their baking skills with many different types of cakes being brought to the bride.

Following is a typical 6-layer molasses cake, although you may choose to vary your layers.

1 cup butter	**Salt to taste**
1 cup sugar	**1 cup milk**
1 cup molasses	**1 quart applesauce**
3 eggs	**Whipped cream**
4 cups flour	**Pecans or walnuts, chopped**
1 teaspoon baking soda	

Cream together butter and sugar. Fold in molasses. Add eggs, one at a time, beating to incorporate. Mix together flour, baking soda, and salt. Add to creamed mixture alternately with milk, beating after each addition.

Grease and flour 3 (8-inch) round cake pans. Fill each with 1⅓ cups batter and refrigerate remainder for 3 more cakes. Bake at 375° for 15 minutes, or until done. Cool 5 minutes; remove from pans and cool on wire rack. Bake next 3 cakes.

When cool, spread applesauce between layers. Spread top with whipped cream and nuts. Serves 24.

Wonderful Wyoming Facts and Foods (Wyoming)

Apple Crisp Cake

⅓ cup milk
¼ cup sugar
½ teaspoon salt
2 tablespoons butter
¼ cup very warm water

1 package dry yeast
1 egg, beaten
1½ cups sifted flour
3 apples, pared and thinly
   sliced

Scald milk; stir in sugar, salt, and butter; cool to luke warm. Measure very warm water into large mixing bowl. Sprinkle in yeast, stirring until dissolved. Add lukewarm milk mixture. Add beaten egg and flour. Stir until blended; spread batter in well-greased 9x13x2-inch baking pan. Arrange apple slices on top.

TOPPING:
¼ cup soft butter
½ cup brown sugar
½ cup sifted flour

1 teaspoon cinnamon
½ teaspoon nutmeg

Cut butter into mixture of brown sugar, flour, and spices. Sprinkle over apples; cover. Let rise in warm place until double in bulk, about 1 hour. Bake at 400° for 30 minutes.

Recipes Logged from the Woods of North Idaho (Idaho)

Easy Strawberry Cake

1 white cake mix
4 cups sliced fresh
   strawberries

1 cup granulated sugar
1 pint whipping cream

Prepare batter for 2-layer size cake; mix according to package directions; turn into greased and floured 9x13-inch pan. Cover batter with strawberries; sprinkle strawberries with sugar. Pour whipping cream over ingredients in pan. Bake at 350° for 50–60 minutes or until cake springs back when touched lightly. Cream and strawberries sink to bottom, forming a lush custard layer.

Sharing Our Best (Wyoming)

Cranberry Cake with Cream Sauce

3 tablespoons butter, softened
1 cup sugar
1 egg
2 cups all-purpose flour*
2 teaspoons baking powder
1 teaspoon nutmeg
1 cup milk
2 cups cranberries
2 tablespoons grated orange or lemon peel

In a mixing bowl, cream the butter and sugar. Beat in egg. In a separate bowl, combine flour (*for persons living in high altitude areas, ⅓ cup of additional flour should be added), baking powder, and nutmeg. Add dry mixture to the butter/sugar/egg mixture alternately with milk, starting with and ending with milk. Stir in cranberries and peel of your choice. Grease a 7x11-inch baking dish. Bake at 350° for 35–40 minutes, or until a toothpick inserted near the center comes out clean. Top with Cream Sauce.

CREAM SAUCE:
1⅓ cups sugar
1 cup heavy cream
   (unwhipped)
⅔ cup butter

While cake is baking, combine the sauce ingredients in a saucepan. Cook and stir over medium heat until heated through. Cut warm cake into squares; serve with the warm Cream Sauce.

Recipes to Make You Purr (Wyoming)

Hootenholler Whiskey Cake

½ cup butter, softened
1 cup sugar
3 eggs, beaten
1 cup flour
½ teaspoon baking powder
¼ teaspoon salt
½ teaspoon nutmeg

¼ cup milk
¼ teaspoon baking soda
¼ cup molasses
1 pound raisins
2 cups chopped pecans
¼ cup bourbon

In a large bowl, cream butter with sugar and add eggs. Combine flour, baking powder, salt, and nutmeg. Add butter mixture and mix well. Add milk.

Combine baking soda and molasses. Mix well and add to batter. Stir in raisins, nuts, and bourbon. Pour batter into a greased and floured 9x5x3-inch loaf pan. Bake at 300° for 2 hours. Makes 1 loaf cake.

Note: This cake, wrapped in foil, keeps for weeks.

Bound to Please (Idaho)

Peanut Crunch Cake

1 package yellow cake mix
1 cup peanut butter
½ cup brown sugar
1 cup water
3 eggs

¼ cup vegetable oil
¾ cup chocolate chips, divided
¾ cup peanut butter chips,
  divided
½ cup chopped peanuts

Beat cake mix, peanut butter, and brown sugar on LOW speed until crumbly. Set aside ½ cup for topping. Add water, eggs, and oil to the remaining crumb mixture. Blend on LOW until moistened. Beat on HIGH 2 minutes. Stir in ¼ cup chocolate chips and ¼ cup peanut butter chips. Pour into greased 9x13-inch pan. Combine peanuts, remaining chips and reserved crumb mixture. Sprinkle over batter. Bake in 350° oven for 40–45 minutes or until toothpick inserted in the center comes out clean.

Ranch Recipe Roundup IV (Wyoming)

Burnt Sugar Candy Bar Cake

2¼ cups granulated sugar,
  divided
¾ cup hot water
3 cups all-purpose flour
½ teaspoon baking powder
¼ teaspoon baking soda
⅔ cup butter, softened

2 eggs, separated
2 teaspoons vanilla
1 recipe Brown Butter Frosting
1½ cups coarsely chopped
  candy bars (Hershey's, Mars,
  Nestle's Crunch, etc.)

Grease and flour 2 round baking pans. In a large skillet, cook ¾ cup sugar over medium-high heat until sugar just begins to melt. Reduce heat; cook until sugar is golden brown, about 1–3 minutes more, stirring mixture constantly. Carefully stir in hot water (syrup will form lumps). Bring to a boil; reduce heat. Continue stirring until mixture is free of lumps. Remove from heat. Pour syrup into a large measuring cup. Add additional water to equal 1¾ cups liquid. Set aside to cool.

Preheat oven to 350°. In a large mixing bowl, stir together flour, baking powder, and baking soda. In a separate bowl, beat together the 1½ cups sugar, butter, egg yolks, and vanilla with an electric mixer on medium speed for 1 minute, until smooth. Alternately add flour mixture and sugar syrup to egg mixture, beating on LOW speed after each addition just until combined. Clean beaters thoroughly.

In a medium mixing bowl, beat egg whites until stiff peaks form. Fold into batter; divide batter into baking pans; spread evenly. Bake for 25 minutes or until toothpick inserted in center comes out clean. Cool in pan; transfer to wire racks; cool completely. Prepare Brown Butter Icing.

BROWN BUTTER ICING:

½ cup plus 3 tablespoons
  butter (no substitute),
  divided
2 (3-ounce) packages cream
  cheese, softened

6½ cups sifted powdered
  sugar, divided
1 teaspoon vanilla
2–3 teaspoons milk

In a small saucepan, heat and stir ½ cup butter over low heat until melted. Continue heating until butter turns a nut-brown color. Remove from heat; cool for 5 minutes.

(continued)

(Burnt Sugar Candy Bar Cake continued)

In a large mixing bowl, beat together cream cheese with 3 table-spoons butter until combined. Beat in about 2 cups sifted powdered sugar. Beat in the browned butter and vanilla. Gradually beat in remaining powdered sugar and milk until frosting is of spreading consistency.

Spread ½ cup frosting over bottom cake layer. Sprinkle layer with ½ the chopped candy. Put on top layer, rounded side up, and frost sides and then top. Garnish with the rest of the coarsely chopped candy bar pieces, if desired.

Be Our Guest (Idaho)

Potato Cake

This recipe is about 140 years old. It's so moist, you don't need to frost it.

⅔ cup butter or shortening
2 cups flour
½ cup milk
2 teaspoons baking powder
¼–1 teaspoon ground cloves
½–1 teaspoon cinnamon
½ teaspoon salt
½ cup cocoa (or 2 squares chocolate, melted)

2 cups sugar
1 cup hot mashed potatoes
4 eggs (beat yolks and whites separately, add whites last)
¼–1 teaspoon nutmeg
1 teaspoon vanilla
1 cup chopped nuts

Combine all ingredients; mix well and bake in greased 9x13-inch cake pan at 375° for 40 minutes.

Idaho's Wild 100! (Idaho)

The Idaho potato, also called the Russet Burbank potato, was first developed in 1871 by Luther Burbank, an American botanist, horticulturist, and a pioneer in agricultural science. Over 30 varieties of potato are grown in the state of Idaho, but the Russet Burbank is by far the most produced potato crop in the state.

Filled Fudge Cake

If you like chocolate, you'll love this cake.

2 cups sugar
1 cup canola oil
1½ teaspoons salt
2 eggs
1 teaspoon vanilla
3 cups flour

2 teaspoons baking powder
2 teaspoons baking soda
¾ cup unsweetened cocoa
1 cup buttermilk
1 cup hot water
1 cup chopped nuts (optional)

Cream sugar, oil, and salt. Add eggs and vanilla. Mix together flour, baking powder, soda, and cocoa. Add to creamed mixture alternately with buttermilk and hot water. Mix well. Add nuts, if desired. Grease well a large Bundt or angel food cake pan. Pour ½ of batter into pan.

FILLING:

¼ cup sugar
1 teaspoon vanilla
1 (8-ounce) package cream
  cheese, softened

1 cup semisweet chocolate
  chips
½ cup coconut (optional)

Mix all Filling ingredients together well, and drop by spoonfuls on top of first layer of cake batter. Then cover with remaining batter. Bake at 350° for 1 hour. Do not turn out of pan until completely cool (3–4 hours). Turn out onto plate. Ice with thin chocolate glaze, if desired.

The Pure Food Club of Jackson Hole (Wyoming)

Four-Day Make-Ahead
Sour Cream Fudge Torte

FUDGE TORTE:

1 box devil's food cake mix   1 cup water
3 eggs   ½ cup oil

Heat oven to 350°. Grease and flour 2 (8-inch) cake pans. In large bowl, blend ingredients at LOW speed until moistened. Beat for 2 minutes at highest speed. Pour into pans. Bake for 30–40 minutes or until toothpick comes out clean. Cool cake in pans on cooling rack for 15 minutes. Remove from pans and cool completely. Split each layer in half, forming 4 layers. Fill and frost with Sour Cream Filling.

SOUR CREAM FILLING:

2 cups dairy sour cream   3 cups nondairy whipped
1 cup sugar   topping
3 cups flaked coconut

In large bowl, combine sour cream, sugar, and coconut. Gently fold in whipped topping. Use to fill between layers and to frost sides and top of Torte. Store covered in refrigerator.

Recipe from Big Horn B&B, Philipsburg, Montana
Recipes from Big Sky Country (Montana)

Black Joe Cake

2 cups sugar   1 teaspoon baking soda
2 cups flour   1 teaspoon vanilla
2 eggs   1 cup cold coffee
¾ cup cocoa   1 cup milk
½ cup oil   1 teaspoon salt
2 teaspoons baking powder

Put all ingredients in a mixing bowl. Stir together. Batter will be thin. Bake in a greased 9x9-inch cake pan at 350° for 35 minutes.

Recipe from Red Lodge Cafe, Red Lodge, Montana
Festival of Nations Cookbook (Montana)

Idaho Chocolate Cake

This cake is dark, dense and wonderfully fudgy.

1 (4-ounce) Idaho russet potato, peeled and grated	½ cup unsalted butter
2 cups sour cream	2 large eggs
1¾ cups cake flour	1½ teaspoons baking soda
1¾ cups sugar	1 teaspoon vanilla
¾ cup unsweetened cocoa	½ teaspoon salt

Position rack in center of oven and preheat to 350°. Butter a 9x13-inch baking pan and dust with flour. Place grated potato in work bowl. Combine all remaining ingredients and add half of the mixture to potato. Mix for 3 minutes, scraping bowl once. Transfer mixture to a larger bowl, add the balance of sour cream mixture, and beat an additional 3 minutes. Scrape sides of bowl once. Pour into prepared pan. Bake 35–40 minutes or until cake tester inserted in middle comes out clean. Cool completely in pan on rack. Invert onto cake dish and frost, if desired.

Idaho Cook Book (Idaho)

Cherry Chocolate Dump Cake

2 (21-ounce) cans cherry pie filling	1 (20-ounce) bottle cherry-flavored carbonated soda
1 chocolate cake mix, with pudding in the mix	

Place pie filling in the bottom of a greased 12-inch Dutch oven. Sprinkle dry cake mix over the fruit filling. Gently pour carbonated soda over the cake mix. Cover and bake, using 5 or 6 briquets under the Dutch oven, 20 on the outside rim of the lid, and 3 or 4 in the middle of the lid. Bake 35–45 minutes. Top with ice cream or whipped cream for an added treat.

Editor's Extra: Can bake in 375° oven for 35–45 minutes, uncovering for the last 10 minutes. Serve as you would cobbler.

More Cee Dub's Dutch Oven and Other Camp Cookin' (Idaho)

Black Forest Cake

Chocolate cake mix
1 large can cherry pie filling
3 cups whipping cream
¼ cup powdered sugar

1 tablespoon instant vanilla
  pudding
1 (4-ounce) chocolate bar (or
  chocolate chips)

Make cake according to package directions; bake in 3 (8-inch) round cake pans or in a spring form pan and cut into 3 layers.

Have cake layers ready and cooled. Transfer 1 layer to cake platter and spread with cherry pie filling. Beat whipping cream until thick; sift powdered sugar and instant pudding over cream and continue beating until cream makes stiff peaks. Put second layer of cake on top of cherries and spread with ⅓ of the whipped cream. Leave enough cream to frost remainder of cake. Top second layer with whipped cream, then add third layer and frost with remaining whipped cream. Use potato peeler to make curls on top of cake from chocolate bar. Or grate semisweet chocolate chips on top.

With Lots of Love (Wyoming)

Cheesecake Cups

Great for holiday entertaining—serve in red baking cups.

CUPS:
6 vanilla wafers
12 baking cups
1 (8-ounce) package cream
  cheese
⅓ cup brown sugar

1 egg
1 teaspoon vanilla
½ can cherry pie filling or ¼
  cup sour cream and 6 large
  strawberries

Place 2 medium-size paper baking cups in each cup of a microwave muffin pan or in 6 custard cups. Place a vanilla wafer in each cup. Set aside. Microwave cream cheese in a 2-quart microwave bowl for 1–2 minutes at defrost (30%) until soft. Stir in brown sugar, egg, and vanilla and beat until smooth. Pour into baking cups. Microwave 6 cups for 7–8 minutes at defrost (30%). Remove paper baking cups from dish(es). Cool at least one hour. Garnish with cherry pie filling and/or sour cream and sugar-sprinkled strawberries before serving. Keep refrigerated. Yields 6 servings.

Easy Livin' Microwave Cooking (Nebraska)

Lemon Cheesecake

Absolutely needs to be made the day before serving.

CRUST:

1½ cups graham crackers, processed very fine

1½ cups walnuts, processed very fine

9 tablespoons butter, melted

Combine, press into bottom and up sides of a springform pan, and bake 5 minutes at 350°.

FILLING:

3 (8-ounce) packages cream cheese, very soft

1⅓ cups sugar

3 eggs

¼ cup lemon juice

2 teaspoons vanilla extract

Beat together, fill partly baked Crust, and bake 40 minutes at 350°.

TOPPING:

2 cups sour cream

3 tablespoons sugar

1 teaspoon vanilla extract

Stir Topping ingredients together. Spread Topping on cheesecake after it has baked 40 minutes. Continue to bake 15 minutes longer (will not look set). Cool 30 minutes.

GLAZE:

¾ cup water

⅓ cup lemon juice

1 egg yolk

½ cup sugar

1½ tablespoons cornstarch

¼ teaspoon salt

1 tablespoon butter

Combine liquids of Glaze in saucepan. Stir in sugar, cornstarch, and salt. Boil over low heat and stir until thick. Remove from heat and add butter. Cool 20 minutes. Spread Glaze on the cheesecake, then cool and refrigerate until well chilled.

The Hearty Gourmet (Idaho)

Blender Red-Raspberry Cheesecake

RASPBERRY-CHEESE FILLING:

1 (8-ounce) package
  Neufchâtel cheese
2 cups (16 ounces) low-fat
  cottage cheese, drained
½ cup Egg Substitute or Egg
  Beaters or 2 large eggs
½ cup sugar or 12–14 packets
  sugar substitute

3 teaspoons cornstarch
  dissolved in 2 tablespoons
  skim milk
1 cup fresh or frozen red
  raspberries, cleaned and
  stems removed
2 drops red food coloring
  (optional)

Unwrap Neufchâtel cheese and place in a 2-quart microwave-safe bowl. Microwave for 40–60 seconds at MEDIUM-HIGH (70%), or until softened. Using a food processor, blender, or electric mixer and bowl, combine cheese and remaining filling ingredients until blended. Pour filling back into 2-quart bowl. Microwave for 7–8 minutes on HIGH (100%), or until very hot, stirring twice.

Microwave for 5–7 minutes at MEDIUM-HIGH (70%), or until almost set (center will jiggle slightly). Let cool. Refrigerate at least 4 hours. Yields 1 (9-inch) cheesecake.

Variation: Substitute one cup fresh or frozen blueberries or sliced strawberries for the raspberries.

Easy Livin' Low-Calorie Microwave Cooking (Nebraska)

"The great registry of the desert," Independence Rock, is located on the Sweetwater River 50 miles southwest of Casper, Wyoming. It proudly displays the hand-scratched names of more than 5,000 pioneers who passed by on their way westward on the Oregon Trail.

Snow White Cheesecake

BASE:

1 package graham crackers
  (⅓ of box)

1 teaspoon ground ginger

2 ounces butter (½ stick)

Crush crackers finely; add ginger and melted butter. Press evenly over base of a greased 8-inch spring form pan. Refrigerate while preparing Topping.

TOPPING:

1 (8-ounce) carton cottage
  cheese

1 (8-ounce) package cream
  cheese, softened

1 cup cream

½ cup superfine sugar

1 teaspoon vanilla

1 package unflavored gelatin

⅓ cup water

2 egg whites

Fresh fruit for garnish

In a blender or food processor, blend cottage cheese; add cream cheese and enough cream to process smoothly. Add sugar, vanilla, and remaining cream. Dissolve gelatin in water over a pan of hot water. Cool and add to cheese mixture, running machine constantly. Pour into a large bowl. Beat egg whites until soft peaks form; fold into cheese mixture. Spread evenly over Base and refrigerate until firm. Decorate top with any fresh fruit.

The Fine Art of Cooking (Montana)

 West Yellowstone in Montana claims to be the Snowmobile Capital of the World. On average, more than 150 inches of snow falls there each year, accumulating on the more than 400 miles of snowmobile trails found there.

God's Country White Chocolate Cheesecake

We endure plenty of ribbing when it comes to the prairie—people unfamiliar with its beauty think this must be "God's country, because no one else would want to live there." Maybe He knows something they don't and plans to visit when a sliver of this cake will be waiting at His place—it's truly a little slice of heaven.

1–3 tablespoons butter or margarine, softened
1 cup finely chopped, lightly toasted macadamia nuts
24 ounces white chocolate, chopped or broken
¾ cup heavy cream, scalded
3 (8-ounce) packages cream cheese, softened
1 cup sugar
¼ cup flour
4 eggs, room temperature (let sit out 30 minutes)
1 tablespoon vanilla or ¼ cup white crème de cacao
Sweetened whipped cream
12–14 macadamia nuts and/or 12–14 fresh raspberries dipped in 1 ounce melted white chocolate

Coat sides and bottom of 8- or 9-inch springform pan with butter. Sprinkle macadamia nuts over buttered surface, turning pan and shaking to distribute evenly. Chill in freezer 15 minutes.

Partially melt chocolate in double boiler or microwave. Add scalded cream, whisking until chocolate is melted and mixture is smooth. Set aside.

Beat the cream cheese, sugar, and flour. Add the chocolate mixture, then eggs, one at a time. Stir in vanilla and pour into prepared pan. Bake 20 minutes at 425°; reduce heat to 300° and bake 45–55 minutes more until cheesecake is nearly set. Turn off oven. Cool in oven 30 minutes. Cool one hour on rack, then refrigerate 6–24 hours.

At least 2 hours before serving, prepare raspberry sauce. Chill. Line baking sheet with waxed paper. Partially melt one ounce white chocolate, then stir until smooth. Dip macadamia nuts and raspberries halfway into melted chocolate. Invert onto waxed paper. Chill. Serve thin wedges of cheesecake with a small spoonful of Raspberry Sauce; garnish with whipped cream and top with a dipped macadamia nut and/or raspberry. Serves 12–14.

Presentations (North Dakota)

Chocolate Mousse Cheesecake

CRUST:

2½ cups crushed graham crackers

6 ounces butter or margarine, melted

Combine graham cracker crumbs and butter and press into a 9½x2½-inch spring form cake pan, lining sides and bottom. Place in refrigerator to chill and set.

FILLING:

2 large tablespoons cream cheese, softened
1 teaspoon vanilla extract
1 egg, lightly beaten
4 tablespoons powdered sugar

1½ cups chocolate syrup
1 pint whipping cream
1 ounce unflavored gelatin
½ cup hot water

In a bowl, beat cream cheese until smooth with electric mixer. Add vanilla, egg, and powdered sugar. Beat until smooth. Add chocolate syrup and mix thoroughly. Place whipping cream in a bowl and beat with electric mixer until soft peaks form. Fold into the cream cheese mixture. Heat the gelatin and ½ cup water in microwave for 30 seconds or until all of the gelatin granules have dissolved. While slowly stirring the cream cheese mixture, add the gelatin a little at a time. Pour all into graham cracker crust. Chill until set (about 2½ hours). Serves 10.

Wyoming Cook Book (Wyoming)

Established in 1910 as the country's 10th national park, Glacier National Park in Montana preserves over 1,000,000 acres of forests, alpine meadows, and lakes. The soul-stirring scenery of the park is so awesome that it's been referred to as "God's Backyard." The famous Going-to-the-Sun Road, a National Historic Civil Engineering Landmark, traverses through the heart of the park and crosses the Continental Divide, allowing visitors breathtaking views of the rugged Lewis and Livingston mountain ranges. Glacier Park's dramatic terrain was crafted by the movement of massive glaciers.

Amaretto Cheesecake

CRUST:

1½ cups chocolate wafer
   cookie crumbs
½ cup finely chopped
   toasted almonds

¼ cup butter, melted
2 tablespoons sugar
1 tablespoon amaretto

Place rack in middle of oven. Preheat oven to 375°. Grease a 9-inch spring form pan.

  Mix all ingredients together in large bowl till well blended. Press into bottom of spring form pan; bake till brown, about 7 minutes, but no longer than 9 minutes. Cool on a rack. Decrease oven temperature to 350°.

FILLING:

3 (8-ounce) packages cream
   cheese, at room temperature
1 cup sugar
4 eggs

⅓ cup whipping cream
⅓ cup finely chopped almonds
¼ cup Bailey's Irish Cream
¼ cup amaretto

Using an electric mixer, slowly beat cream cheese and sugar till light and fluffy. Add eggs, one at a time, beating well after each addition. Add the remaining ingredients for the Filling and beat till well blended. Pour Filling into Crust. Bake until just set, about 1 hour. Turn off oven and let the cheesecake cool inside oven with oven door open, approximately 30 minutes. Center of cheesecake should be completely set by this time. Remove cake from pan. Preheat oven again to 350°.

TOPPING:

1½ cups sour cream
1 tablespoon sugar

½ teaspoon vanilla

Blend ingredients in small bowl till smooth. Spread this mixture over cake. Bake 10 minutes. Cover with plastic wrap and refrigerate overnight.

Home at/on the Range with Wyoming BILS (Wyoming)

Pumpkin Walnut Cheesecake

CRUST:

⅛ cup sugar   Butter

1 cup graham cracker crumbs

Mix sugar and cracker crumbs together. Generously butter a 9x13-inch spring form pan and pat into bottom.

FILLING:

3 (8-ounce) packages cream   1 (16-ounce) can pumpkin
  cheese, softened   1 teaspoon cinnamon
¾ cup sugar   ½ teaspoon nutmeg
¾ cup brown sugar   ¼ teaspoon cloves
6 eggs (7 at high altitude)   ¼ cup heavy cream

Beat together cream cheese, sugars, eggs, pumpkin, spices, and cream. Pour into crust and bake at 325° for 1 hour and 35 minutes. Cheesecake is done when center is firm. Remove from oven, turn oven off, and close oven door.

TOPPING:

3 tablespoons butter,   ½ cup chopped walnuts
  softened   ½ cup brown sugar

Mix together butter, nuts, and sugar. Spread on hot cheesecake; return to oven until completely cool. Cheesecake may be frozen. Serves 12–14.

The Hole Thing Volume II (Wyoming)

COOKIES and CANDIES

PHOTO © WILLIAM H. MULLINS OUTDOOR PHOTOGRAPHY

The Appaloosa, with its unique spotted coat pattern, may be the oldest recognizable horse breed in the world. The Nez Perce Indians bred them for warhorses. The breed fell into decline at the end of the Nez Perce War in 1877. However, a few quality horses continued to be bred, mostly those captured or purchased by white settlers. Others were used in circuses and in Buffalo Bill Cody's Wild West Show. Today the Appaloosa is one of the most popular breeds in the United States, and it is the official state horse of Idaho.

Best in the West Sugar Cookies

These are the "melt-in-your-mouth" kind of cookies.

1 cup powdered sugar
1 cup white sugar
1 cup butter, softened
1 cup oil
2 eggs
1 teaspoon vanilla

4 cups plus 4 heaping
 tablespoons flour
1 teaspoon salt
2 teaspoons baking soda
1 teaspoon cream of tartar

Cream powdered sugar, white sugar, butter, and oil. Beat in eggs and vanilla. Sift and add remaining ingredients. Place walnut-size balls of dough on non-stick cookie sheet and flatten with fork. Bake 8–10 minutes at 375°.

The Best Little Cookbook in the West (South Dakota)

Basque Wedding Cookies

1 cup butter, softened
1 cup sifted confectioners'
 sugar, divided
1½ tablespoons grated
 lemon peel
1 tablespoon water

2½ cups sifted all-purpose
 flour
½ teaspoon salt
⅔ cup whole blanched
 almonds

Cream butter until light and fluffy. Stir in ¼ cup confectioners' sugar, peel, and water.

Mix flour with salt, and beat into butter mixture. Knead with hands until dough is light. Pinch off heaping teaspoonfuls of dough, press them flat, and wrap around a whole almond to cover completely. Shape like a tiny leaf and place 1 inch apart on greased baking sheet. Bake at 350° for 15 minutes. Take care not to overbake.

Remove from cookie sheet, cool 2 or 3 minutes, then roll in confectioners' sugar. Cool completely, then roll again. Makes 4 dozen.

Basque Cooking and Lore (Idaho)

Cornflake Macaroons

2 egg whites, beaten stiffly
1 cup granulated sugar
1 teaspoon vanilla
1 cup Angel Flake Coconut
1½ cups crushed cornflakes

Beat egg whites stiff. Gradually add sugar and vanilla. Fold in coconut and cornflakes. Drop by teaspoonfuls onto greased baking sheet. Bake 20 minutes in 325° oven.

Iola's Gourmet Recipes in Rhapsody (Nebraska)

Snow Flurries

These are my favorite holiday roll-out cookies. They're tasty and very tender.

1½ cups sugar
⅞ cup butter
⅔ cup shortening
1⅓ tablespoons lemon zest
3 eggs
1 teaspoon vanilla extract
½ teaspoon almond extract
½ teaspoon salt
½ teaspoon baking powder
4½ cups unbleached flour

Thoroughly cream sugar, butter, shortening, and lemon zest. Add eggs, 1 at a time, and stir. Beat batter until it becomes light. Add vanilla and almond extracts, and stir. Mix in salt and baking powder with the first cup of flour. Add the rest of flour 1 cup at a time, stirring after each addition.

Shape the dough into two rectangular shapes, and wrap in plastic wrap. Chill well before rolling.

Roll out on floured counter. Cut with floured cutters. Transfer to papered trays with metal spatula. Bake at 350° for about 10 minutes, until they barely start to brown. Makes 6–7 dozen.

Get Your Buns in Here (Wyoming)

Gingersnaps

¾ cup butter
1 egg
1 cup sugar
¼ cup molasses
2½ cups flour

2 teaspoons baking soda
1 teaspoon cinnamon
1 teaspoon cloves
1 teaspoon ginger

Preheat oven to 350° (and be sure the heating element is off when you begin baking the cookies, or they will burn before cooking). Cream together butter, egg, sugar, and molasses. Sift in flour, baking soda, and spices. Mix well and cover. Put in refrigerator for about an hour (the dough must be cold, or your cookies will not cook properly). Roll into walnut-size balls, roll in granulated sugar, and bake on ungreased cookie sheet 8–10 minutes.

Note: Want an easy way to measure molasses? Fill your ¼ cup measure with oil. Pour oil back into its original container; this coats the inside of the measuring cup with oil. Fill with molasses and add to other ingredients. All the molasses will slide right out—pretty slick!

With Lots of Love (Wyoming)

Old-Fashioned Sour Cream Cookies

½ cup soft butter
1½ cups sugar
2 eggs
1 cup sour cream (non dairy)
1 teaspoon vanilla

½ teaspoon baking powder
2¾ cups flour
½ teaspoon soda
⅛ teaspoon salt

Mix together butter, sugar, and eggs. Add sour cream and vanilla. Sift together dry ingredients and add to first mixture. Chill at least 1 hour. Drop onto greased cookie sheet and bake 8–10 minutes at 425°. Do not overbake.

Horse Prairie Favorites (Montana)

Chocolate Malt Ball Cookies

¾ cup brown sugar
1 teaspoon vanilla
1⅓ sticks margarine or
  vegetable shortening
1 egg
1¾ cups all-purpose flour
⅓ cup cocoa

½ teaspoon salt (if desired, or
  if shortening is used)
½ cup malted milk powder
  (not chocolate)
¾ teaspoon baking soda
2 cups malted milk balls,
  crushed

Beat together brown sugar, vanilla, and margarine in large bowl until mixed; beat in egg and mix well. Mix together flour, cocoa, salt, malted milk powder and baking soda. Add to creamed mixture and mix until blended. Stir in malted milk ball pieces. (To crush, put candy in sealable plastic bag and pound with rolling pin or a heavy spoon). Drop on ungreased cookie sheet by rounded tablespoonfuls 2 inches apart. Bake one sheet at a time at 375° for 7–9 minutes or until cookies are set. Do not overbake. Cool 2 minutes before removing to sheets of foil to cool completely. Makes about 3 dozen cookies.

In the Kitchen with Kate (Kansas)

Pineapple Drop Cookies

1 cup brown sugar
1 cup white sugar
1 cup shortening
2 eggs, well beaten
2 teaspoons vanilla
½ teaspoon salt

½ teaspoon baking soda
2 teaspoons baking powder
4 cups flour
1 cup crushed pineapple
1 cup finely chopped walnuts

Mix sugars, shortening, eggs, and vanilla together. Add dry ingredients alternately with pineapple. Add chopped nuts. Drop by teaspoon onto greased baking sheet. Bake at 375° for about 12 minutes.

Recipes from the Heart (Montana)

Lollipop Cookies

Will need wooden sticks and cookie decorations.

1 cup (2 sticks) butter,
  softened
1½ cups firmly packed
  brown sugar
2 eggs
2½ cups all-purpose flour
2 teaspoons baking powder

1 teaspoon each: cinnamon and
  nutmeg
½ teaspoon salt
¼ teaspoon baking soda
¼ cup milk
2½ cups quick cooking oats
  (not instant), uncooked

Cream butter and sugar in large mixing bowl until light and fluffy. Beat in eggs. Combine flour, baking powder, spices, salt, and baking soda. Add to butter mixture alternately with milk; mix well. Stir in oats. Cover and refrigerate 1 to 2 hours.

Preheat oven to 375°. Shape dough into 1½-inch balls. Place about 3 inches apart on unbuttered cookie sheets. Insert wooden stick (parallel with cookie sheet) halfway into each ball of dough. Flatten, using a flat bottom glass dipped in granulated sugar. Bake 13–15 minutes or until lightly browned. Cool on cookie sheet, 2–3 minutes. Transfer cookies to wire racks. Cool completely. Decorate as desired.

Sharing Our "Beary" Best II (South Dakota)

Perfect Raisin Cookies

2 cups raisins
1 cup water
1 cup chopped nuts
2 cups sugar
1 cup shortening
2 eggs

1 teaspoon vanilla
4 cups flour
1 teaspoon baking soda
1 teaspoon baking powder
½ teaspoon ground cloves
1 teaspoon cinnamon

Boil raisins and water for 5 minutes. Cool; add soda and nuts. Cream sugar, shortening, eggs, and vanilla. Combine flour, soda, baking powder, and spices. Add raisin mixture alternating with dry ingredients to creamed mixture. Drop by spoonful onto greased baking sheet and bake at 350° for 12–15 minutes. Cool and store with layers of waxed paper in covered buckets or crock.

Heavenly Recipes and Burnt Offerings (Montana)

One Cup Cookies

1 cup butter, softened
1 cup brown sugar
1 cup sugar
3 eggs
1 cup peanut butter
1 cup flour

1 teaspoon baking soda
1 cup oats
1 cup chopped walnuts
1 cup bran
1 cup shredded coconut
1 cup chocolate chips

Cream butter and sugars, then add eggs one at a time. Beat in peanut butter. Add flour and soda. Mix well; add remaining ingredients one at a time. Bake at 350° for 10 minutes.

Sharing Our Best (Idaho)

Chocolate-Peppermint Cream Cookies

1½ cups brown sugar
¾ cup butter
2 tablespoons water
2 cups chocolate chips

2 eggs
3 cups flour
1¼ teaspoons baking soda
1 teaspoon salt

In a saucepan, stir over low heat the brown sugar, butter, and water. Add chocolate chips; stir to melt chips. Beat in eggs and add flour, baking soda, and salt. Shape into balls and bake on cookie sheet at 350° for 8–10 minutes. Cool. Sandwich each pair together with 1 teaspoon Peppermint Cream.

PEPPERMINT CREAM:

3 cups powdered sugar,
  divided
⅓ cup soft butter
⅛ teaspoon peppermint
  extract

Dash of salt
¼ cup milk

Mix one cup powdered sugar, butter, extract, and salt. Beat in 2 cups powdered sugar alternately with milk.

Lakota Lutheran Church Centennial Cookbook (North Dakota)

Lemon Chocolate Chip Cookies

½ cup butter or margarine,
  softened
1 (18¼-ounce) box lemon
  cake mix

2 large eggs, slightly beaten
1 (12-ounce) package chocolate
  chips

Cut butter into cake mix until crumbly. Add eggs and chips, incorporating thoroughly. Chill in the refrigerator for 1 hour.

Preheat oven to 375°. Remove from fridge and roll into walnut-sized balls. Place balls on ungreased cookie sheets. Bake in preheated oven 10–12 minutes. Cool on baking rack. Store in airtight container.

This cookie dough can be rolled into a log, tightly wrapped and frozen, for use at a later date.

Elegant Cooking Made Simple (Idaho)

Macadamia Chip Cookies

I'm always looking for something new and different in the chocolate chip cookie world. This macadamia nut, chocolate chip combination is divinely decadent!

1 cup softened sweet butter
¾ cup granulated sugar
¾ cup firmly packed brown
  sugar
1 tablespoon vanilla extract
1 tablespoon Frangelico
  liqueur (optional)
1 tablespoon coffee liqueur
2 large eggs

2½ cups all-purpose flour
1 teaspoon baking soda
¼ teaspoon salt
2 (12-ounce) packages milk
  chocolate chips
1 cup chopped walnuts
½ cup chopped pecans
½ cup chopped macadamia
  nuts

Using large mixer bowl, cream first 6 ingredients until light and fluffy. Add eggs and beat well. Mix flour, baking soda, and salt in bowl. Stir into creamed mixture. Mix in chocolate chips and all chopped nuts by hand. Drop batter by ¼ cupfuls onto greased cookie sheets. Space cookies about 1 inch apart. Bake at 375° until cookies are light brown, about 15 minutes. Remove from oven, but be careful not to burn your mouth! Makes about 36 cookies.

Best-of-Friends, Festive Occasions Cookbook (Montana)

Wyoming Whopper Cookies

⅔ cup butter or margarine
1¼ cups packed brown
  sugar
¾ cup sugar
3 eggs, beaten
1½ cups chunky peanut
  butter

6 cups old-fashioned oats (not
  quick-cooking)
2 teaspoons baking soda
1½ cups raisins
2 cups semisweet chocolate
  chips

In large saucepan, melt butter over low heat. Blend in sugars, eggs, and peanut butter. Mix until smooth. Add oats, baking soda, raisins, and chocolate chips. Dough will be sticky. Drop onto greased baking sheet, 1 inch apart, with large ice cream scoop. Flatten slightly. Bake at 350° about 15 minutes. Remove cookies to a wire rack to cool. Yields 2 dozen.

Feeding the Herd (Wyoming)

Peanut Butter Middles

A grandchildren favorite.

1½ cups flour
½ cup cocoa
½ teaspoon baking soda
½ cup brown sugar
½ cup granulated sugar

½ cup margarine, softened
¼ cup peanut butter
1 egg
1 teaspoon vanilla

Combine flour, cocoa, and baking soda and set aside. Beat together brown and granulated sugars, margarine, peanut butter, egg, and vanilla. Add flour mixture. Form mixture into 40 balls.

FILLING:
1 cup peanut butter   1 cup powdered sugar

Blend peanut butter and powdered sugar and form into 40 balls. Wrap the chocolate mixture balls around the filling mixture balls and place on ungreased baking sheet. Flatten with a glass dipped in granulated sugar. Bake at 375° for 7–9 minutes or until slightly cracked.

In the Kitchen with Kate (Kansas)

Chrys' Devil Hermits

2 eggs
¼ cup milk
½ cup creamy peanut butter

1 family-size package fudge
   brownie mix
½ cup peanuts

Preheat oven to 350°. In mixing bowl, beat eggs until frothy. Add milk and peanut butter. Cream until smooth. Add brownie mix and peanuts. Drop by teaspoonfuls onto a greased baking sheet. Bake 8–10 minutes. Cool on a wire rack.

Recipes from the Heart (Montana)

Interstate Bar Cookies

½ cup margarine, softened
1 (2-layer) package cake mix
   (any flavor)
3 eggs
1 (8-ounce) package cream
   cheese, softened

1 cup brown sugar
1 cup powdered sugar
1 teaspoon vanilla

Combine margarine, cake mix, and one egg, beaten. Press into 9x13-inch pan. Beat together cream cheese, brown sugar, powdered sugar, 2 eggs, and vanilla. Pour over crust. Bake at 325° for 45 minutes. Cool. When cool, dust top of cookies with additional sifted powdered sugar.

125 Years of Cookin' with the Lord (Kansas)

Marshmallow Krispie Bars

1 (14-ounce) package
  caramels
¾ cup margarine, divided
1 (14-ounce) can sweetened
  condensed milk

2 (10-ounce) packages
  miniature marshmallows
8 cups crisp rice cereal

Melt caramels with ¼ cup margarine and condensed milk in saucepan over low heat, stirring to mix well; set aside. Melt ½ cup margarine and 1½ packages marshmallows in saucepan over low heat, stirring to mix well. Pour over cereal in large bowl; mix well. Press half the mixture in buttered 10x15-inch dish. Sprinkle with remaining ½ package marshmallows. Spread caramel mixture over marshmallows. Top with remaining cereal mixture. Let stand until firm. Cut into bars. Yields 70 servings.

Y Cook? (North Dakota)

Almond Bars

FIRST LAYER:
½ cup powdered sugar
1 cup margarine, softened

2 cups all-purpose flour

SECOND LAYER:
1 (8-ounce) package cream
  cheese, softened
2 eggs

½ cup white sugar
1 teaspoon almond flavoring

TOPPING:
¼ cup margarine, softened
1½ cups powdered sugar

1½ tablespoons milk
1 teaspoon almond flavoring

Combine ingredients in First Layer and press into 9x13-inch pan. Bake at 350° for 15 minutes. Beat Second Layer ingredients until creamy, and pour over First Layer immediately after removing from oven. Bake for 15 minutes. Let cool. Mix Topping ingredients and spread over bars. May put slivered almonds on top.

Heavenly Recipes (North Dakota)

Oatmeal-Cheesecake-Cranberry Bars

2 cups all-purpose flour
1¼ cups quick-cooking oatmeal
¾ cup packed brown sugar
1 cup butter, softened
12 ounces cream cheese, softened
½ cup sugar
2 eggs
2 teaspoons lemon juice
1 teaspoon vanilla
1 (16-ounce) can whole cranberry sauce
2 teaspoons cornstarch

In a large mixing bowl, stir together flour, oatmeal, and brown sugar. Add butter and use fingers to blend until mixture resembles coarse crumbs. Reserve 1½ cups of the crumbs. Press remaining crumbs into a greased 9x13-inch pan. Bake at 350° for 15 minutes.

In the same bowl, beat cream cheese and sugar with an electric mixer until light and fluffy. Beat in eggs, lemon juice, and vanilla. Spread over crust.

Stir together cranberry sauce and cornstarch; spoon carefully over cream cheese layer. Sprinkle with reserved crumbs. Bake 40 minutes more or until set. Cool and store in refrigerator. Bring to room temperature to serve. Makes 36 bars.

Another Cookbook (Idaho)

Date Bars

1 cup white sugar
4 level tablespoons butter
2 eggs, well beaten
1 pound dates, finely-chopped
4 tablespoons hot water
1 teaspoon baking powder
1½ cups flour (approximately)
Powdered sugar

Combine all ingredients together. Bake in 9x13-inch pan at 350° until golden brown; cool. Cut into squares and roll in powdered sugar.

Our Heritage (North Dakota)

Bing Bars

1 (12-ounce) package
  chocolate chips
¾ cup peanut butter
12 ounces Spanish peanuts,
  ground in blender
12 large marshmallows

1 (14-ounce) can sweetened
  condensed milk
½ cup butter
2 teaspoons cherry flavoring
1 (6-ounce) bag cherry chips

Melt chocolate chips and peanut butter together. Add ground peanuts. Put ½ of mixture in greased 9x13-inch pan. Set aside remainder.

Combine marshmallows, condensed milk, and butter in medium saucepan; bring to boil for 5 minutes. Add cherry flavoring and chips. Spread this mixture over first layer in pan, then spread remainder of chocolate mixture on top. Cut into bars when cool.

Spragg Family Cookbook (Idaho)

Rhubarb Dream Bars

CRUST:

2 cups flour
¾ cup powdered sugar

1 cup butter or margarine

Combine flour and sugar. Cut in butter until crumbs form. Press into 15x10-inch pan. Bake in 350° oven for 15 minutes (or a little less). While crust is baking, prepare filling.

FILLING:

4 eggs
2 cups sugar
½ cup flour

½ teaspoon salt
4 cups rhubarb, diced

Blend eggs, sugar, flour, and salt until smooth. Fold in rhubarb. Spread over hot crust and bake in 350° oven 35–40 minutes until filling is lightly browned. Cut bars when cool.

Ritzy Rhubarb Secrets Cookbook (North Dakota)

Apple Bars

2½ cups flour
1 teaspoon salt
1 cup shortening
2 egg yolks
Milk (about ½ cup)

1 cup cornflakes
12 apples, peeled and sliced
1–1½ cups sugar
1 teaspoon cinnamon
2 egg whites

Cut flour and salt into shortening. Beat egg yolks and add milk to make ⅔ cup. Mix well and add to flour mixture. Roll ½ of the dough between 2 sheets of waxed paper to fit a jellyroll pan. Crush cornflakes and spread on dough. Add apples, sugar, and cinnamon. Roll the rest of the dough for top. Beat egg whites and brush on top. Bake at 350° for 50–60 minutes. Frost with powdered sugar icing.

Incredible Edibles (North Dakota)

Sour Cream Raisin Bars

BAR:
1¾ cups oatmeal
1¾ cups flour
1 cup brown sugar

1 teaspoon baking soda
1 cup margarine, melted

Preheat oven to 350°. Combine oatmeal, flour, brown sugar, and baking soda. Add margarine and mix thoroughly. Pat ⅔ of mixture into bottom of a 9x13-inch pan. Bake for 15–20 minutes. Cool.

FILLING:
4 eggs yolks
1½ cups sugar
3 tablespoons cornstarch

2 cups sour cream
2 cups raisins

Mix and bring to a boil. Reduce heat. Boil 5–10 minutes, stirring constantly to avoid scorching. Pour over crumb layer and cover with remaining crumbs. Bake for 20 minutes. Cool and cut into bars.

Regent Alumni Association Cookbook (North Dakota)

Yaak Trail Bars

1 cup brown sugar
⅔ cup peanut butter
½ cup light corn syrup
½ cup butter, melted
2 teaspoons vanilla
1½ cups quick oats
1½ cups crisp rice cereal
1 cup semisweet chocolate
  pieces

1 cup raisins
½ cup coconut
½ cup raw, shelled sunflower
  seeds
⅓ cup wheat germ
2 tablespoons sesame seeds
Dash of cinnamon or more

Grease a 9x13x2-inch baking pan; set aside. Combine brown sugar, peanut butter, corn syrup, butter, and vanilla.

In another bowl, combine oats, cereal, chocolate pieces, raisins, coconut, sunflower seeds, wheat germ, sesame seeds, and cinnamon; stir in peanut butter mixture. Mix well. Press evenly into prepared pan. Bake in 350° oven for 25 minutes or until lightly browned. Cool. Cut into bars.

Yaak Cookbook (Montana)

Pecan Pie Bars

2 cups all-purpose flour
½ cup confectioners' sugar
1 cup butter or margarine,
  softened
1 (14-ounce) can sweetened
  condensed milk

1 egg
1 teaspoon vanilla extract
Pinch salt
1 (6-ounce) package toffee-
  flavored chips
1 cup chopped pecans

In mixing bowl, combine flour and sugar. Cut in butter until mixture resembles coarse meal. Press firmly into a greased 9x13-inch pan at least 2 inches deep. Bake at 350° for 15 minutes. Meanwhile, in another bowl, beat milk, egg, vanilla, and salt. Stir in toffee chips and pecans. Spread evenly over baked crust. Bake for another 20–25 minutes or until lightly browned. Cool, then refrigerate. When thoroughly chilled, cut into bars. Store in refrigerator. Makes 4 dozen.

The Pure Food Club of Jackson Hole (Wyoming)

Rocky Road Fudge Bars

BARS:

½ cup butter
1 (1-ounce) square
   unsweetened chocolate
1 cup sugar
1 cup flour
¾ cup nuts
1 teaspoon baking powder
1 teaspoon vanilla
2 eggs

Preheat oven to 350°. Grease and flour 9x13-inch pan. In large saucepan over low heat, melt butter and chocolate. Add remaining bar ingredients. Mix well and spread in prepared pan.

FILLING:

6 ounces cream cheese,
   softened
½ cup sugar
2 tablespoons flour
¼ cup butter
1 egg
½ teaspoon vanilla
¼ cup chopped nuts
1 (6-ounce) package chocolate
   chips
2 cups miniature
   marshmallows(or 2 cups
   regular size, cut-up)

In small bowl, combine cream cheese with next 5 ingredients. Blend until smooth and fluffy. Stir in nuts. Spread over chocolate mixture. Sprinkle with chocolate chips. Bake 25–30 minutes or until toothpick inserted in center comes out clean. Sprinkle with marshmallows and bake 2 minutes longer.

FROSTING:

¼ cup butter
1 (1-ounce) square
   unsweetened chocolate
2 ounces cream cheese
¼ cup milk
1 pound powdered sugar
   (about 3½ cups)
1 teaspoon vanilla

In large saucepan over low heat, melt butter, chocolate, cream cheese, and milk. Stir in powdered sugar and vanilla until smooth. Immediately pour over marshmallows.

Yesterday and Today Friendly Circle Cookbook (North Dakota)

Fudgy Chocolate Cookie Bars

1¾ cups flour
¾ cup powdered sugar
¼ cup Hershey's cocoa
1 cup cold butter
1 (12-ounce) package
  chocolate chips, divided

1 (14-ounce) can sweetened
  condensed milk
1 teaspoon vanilla
1 cup chopped walnuts

Combine flour, sugar, and cocoa; cut in butter until crumbly (can be done in food processor). Press firmly on bottom of a 9x13-inch baking dish. Bake 15 minutes at 350°.

Over medium heat, melt 1 cup chocolate chips in condensed milk and vanilla. Pour evenly over crust. Top with nuts and remaining 1 cup chips. Press down firmly. Bake 20 minutes or until set. Cool. Chill. Cut into bars. Store covered.

Wapiti Meadow Bakes (Idaho)

German Chocolate Caramel Brownies

1 (14-ounce) package
  caramels
1 (5-ounce) can evaporated
  milk, divided
1 package German chocolate
  cake mix

¾ cup margarine, melted
1 cup (6 ounces) chocolate
  chips

Melt caramels and ⅓ cup evaporated milk together. Mix together cake mix, margarine, ⅓ cup evaporated milk, and chocolate chips. Grease 9x13-inch pan. Press ½ dough in pan; spread with caramel mixture. Top loosely with rest of dough. Bake 30 minutes at 350°.

Home at the Range II (Kansas)

Triple Fudge Brownies

1 (3.9-ounce) package instant chocolate pudding mix
1 (18¼-ounce) package chocolate cake mix
2 cups (12 ounces) semisweet chocolate chips
Confectioners' sugar

Prepare pudding according to package directions. Whisk in cake mix. Stir in chocolate chips. Pour into greased 15x10x1-inch baking pan. Bake at 350° for 30–35 minutes or until the top springs back when lightly touched. Dust with confectioners' sugar. Yields 4 dozen.

Recipes from the Heart /Epsilon Omega Sorority (Nebraska)

Cinnamon Brownies

¾ cup baking cocoa
½ teaspoon baking soda
⅔ cup butter or margarine, melted, divided
½ cup boiling water
2 cups sugar
2 eggs, beaten
1 teaspoon vanilla extract
1⅓ cups all-purpose flour
1½–2 teaspoons cinnamon
¼ teaspoon salt
1 cup (6 ounces) semisweet chocolate chips

In a mixing bowl, combine cocoa and baking soda; blend in ⅓ cup melted butter. Add boiling water, stirring until thickened. Stir in sugar, eggs, vanilla, and remaining butter. Add flour, cinnamon, and salt. Fold in chocolate chips. Pour into a greased 9x13x2-inch baking pan. Bake at 350° for 30 minutes or until brownies test done. Cool.

FROSTING:
6 tablespoons butter, softened
½ cup baking cocoa
2⅔ cups powdered sugar
1–1½ teaspoons cinnamon
⅓ cup evaporated milk
1 teaspoon vanilla

Cream butter in a mixing bowl. Combine cocoa, sugar, and cinnamon; add alternately with milk to creamed butter. Beat to a spreading consistency; add vanilla. Add more milk, if necessary. Spread over the brownies. Yields 3 dozen.

Recipes Logged from the Woods of North Idaho (Idaho)

Orange Gumdrop Chews

1½ cups cut-up orange
  gumdrop slices
1⅓ cups flaked coconut
½ cup chopped pecans or
  walnuts

2 cups sifted all-purpose flour
3 eggs
1 tablespoon water
2 cups brown sugar
½ teaspoon salt

Mix cut-up orange slices, coconut, nuts, and flour. Beat eggs with water until foamy. Gradually add brown sugar and salt, beating till light and fluffy. Stir in gumdrop mixture. Spread evenly on greased 15x10½x1-inch pan. Bake in moderate 375° oven about 15 minutes or till done. Cool. Cut in bars. Makes 4 dozen.

Home at/on the Range with Wyoming BILS (Wyoming)

Moon Rocks

No bake!

2 cups sugar
3 tablespoons cocoa (optional)
½ teaspoon salt
½ cup butter or margarine
½ cup water

1 cup peanut butter
4 cups oatmeal
1 cup nonfat dry milk
1 cup raisins
1 teaspoon vanilla

Combine in large saucepan sugar, cocoa (if desired), salt, margarine, water, and peanut butter. Bring to rolling boil on medium heat; stir as needed to prevent sticking. Remove from burner and add oatmeal, powdered milk and raisins; mix well, then add vanilla. Drop by teaspoons onto wax paper or cookie sheet sprayed with nonstick spray. Let stand till cool.

Grandma Jane's Cookbook (Idaho)

WWW.WIKIPEDIA.ORG

Craters of the Moon National Monument and Preserve (Idaho), at 618 square miles, is the largest basaltic lava field in the lower 48 states. Sixty distinct lava flows form the Craters of the Moon lava field, each ranging in age from 15,000 to just 2,000 years old. Magma poured from fissures in the earth's crust to form cinder cones, craters, and fields of lava.

Vinegar Taffy

2 cups sugar
½ cup vinegar
⅛ teaspoon cream of tartar

⅛ teaspoon salt
2 tablespoons butter (no substitute)

Mix sugar, vinegar, cream of tartar, salt, and butter in saucepan. Cook to hard-ball stage. Pour onto a buttered plate. Let cool until you can handle it without burning yourself. Then butter hands and pull taffy until it becomes snowy white.

Sharing Our Best (Wyoming)

Popcorn Balls

⅔ cup corn syrup
2 cups sugar
⅔ cup boiling water
2 tablespoons vinegar
2 teaspoons cream of tartar

½ teaspoon baking soda
2 tablespoons butter
1 teaspoon food coloring
2 gallons of popped corn

Combine in large saucepan corn syrup, sugar, boiling water, and vinegar and bring to a boil. Add cream of tartar; stir until dissolved. Boil to soft-crack stage. Remove from heat and add soda, butter, and coloring. Mix well and pour over popped corn. Stir well. Dip hands in cold water and make balls.

Irma Flat Mothers' Club Cookbook (Wyoming)

Old-Fashioned Toffee

This is a delicious family favorite!

1½ cups (6 ounces) chopped
  walnuts or pecans
2 sticks (1 cup) butter
1½ cups brown sugar,
  packed

4 cubes (8 ounces) chocolate
  almond bark (or chocolate
  chips)

Spread nuts in a buttered 9x13-inch pan. Set aside. Combine butter and brown sugar in a 2-quart microwave-safe bowl. Microwave for 2 minutes at HIGH (100%). Stir until butter and brown sugar are completely dissolved. Microwave again for 7–9 minutes at MEDIUM-HIGH (70%), until mixture reaches 290° (soft crack stage), stirring two times (with a clean spoon each time). Pour syrup mixture over nuts. Microwave almond bark or chips in a 1-quart microwave-safe bowl for 2–3 minutes at MEDIUM-HIGH (70%). Stir. Spread over toffee. Cool and enjoy! Yields 2 pounds candy.

Easy Livin' Microwave Cooking for the Holidays (Nebraska)

Peanut Clusters

The chocolate bark/butterscotch chips combination is my family's favorite, but they are all delicious. This is a recipe that children can easily make on their own. It is foolproof. If the mixture is too thin to drop into nice mounds, let it cool a little to thicken.

1 (24-ounce) package almond
  bark, vanilla or chocolate
2 cups (12 ounces) baking
  chips (chocolate, vanilla,
  or butterscotch)

4⅔ cups (24 ounces) salted
  peanuts

Melt almond bark and chips together in the microwave or place in a low oven. Keep away from all water. Stir until smooth. Stir in peanuts. Drop teaspoonfuls onto waxed paper. Let cool to harden. Yields 5 dozen.

Mom's Camper Cooking (Kansas)

Holiday Chocolate Almond Wedges

(Candy Pizza)

2 cups (12 ounces) semisweet
  chocolate chips
8 cubes (16 ounces) white
  almond bark, divided
1 cup salted dry-roasted
  peanuts
1 cup miniature or 11 large
  marshmallows

1 cup crisp rice cereal
½ cup red candied cherries,
  chopped
½ cup green candied cherries,
  chopped
½ cup (2 ounces) slivered
  almonds or shredded coconut

Combine chocolate chips and 6 cubes (12 ounces) of the almond bark in a 2-quart microwave-safe bowl. Microwave for 3½–4½ minutes at MEDIUM-HIGH (70%), stirring twice. (Remember, the chips and bark will look soft and shiny but not melted; they will look melted only after stirring.) Stir until smooth.

Stir in peanuts, marshmallows, and cereal. Spread into a buttered 12-inch pizza pan. Sprinkle red and green cherries and almonds over the chocolate-cereal mixture. Microwave remaining 2 cubes (4 ounces) of white almond bark in a microwave-safe bowl for 1–1½ minutes at MEDIUM-HIGH (70%). Stir until smooth. Drizzle over the mixture in the pan. Chill slightly until firm. Cut into wedges. Enjoy! Yields 10–14 wedges.

Easy Livin' Microwave Cooking for the Holidays (Nebraska)

Fort Leavenworth, Kansas, is the oldest active U.S. Army post west of the Mississippi River, in operation for over 170 years. During the country's westward expansion, Fort Leavenworth was a stop for thousands of soldiers, surveyors, immigrants, American Indians, preachers, and settlers who passed through. The fort occupies 5,600 acres and supports 1,000 buildings and 1,500 quarters, including a 213-acre National Historic Landmark District, which was established in 1974. Fort Leavenworth also accommodates the Department of Defense's only maximum security prison, the United States Disciplinary Barracks. The nearby city of Leavenworth is the oldest city in Kansas, founded in 1854.

Beef Fudge

A must for every Montana cookbook!

1 cup ground cooked roast
  beef
½ pound butter or
  margarine
1 (14½-ounce) can
  evaporated milk

4 cups sugar
1 (12-ounce) bag chocolate
  chips
1 pint marshmallow crème
2 teaspoons vanilla
1 cup chopped nuts

Remove any hard crust from the beef before grinding. Cook butter, milk, and sugar to hard-ball stage. Stir often. Remove from heat. Stir in chips, marshmallow crème, vanilla, beef, and nuts. Beat all until firm. Pour into well-buttered 9x13-inch pan. Cut into squares. Refrigerate.

French Family Favorites (Montana)

Mashed Potato Fudge

¼ cup hot mashed potatoes
1 teaspoon butter
2¼ cups confectioners' sugar
½ teaspoon vanilla

Dash of salt
1⅓ cups flaked coconut
5–6 squares semisweet
  chocolate, melted, divided

Mix potatoes and butter; gradually add sugar. Beat until thoroughly blended. Stir in vanilla, salt, and coconut. Line an 8-inch-square pan with wax paper. Pour in ¼ of the melted chocolate, then the coconut mixture, and finally the remaining chocolate for top layer. Refrigerate. Cut into 1-inch squares. Yields 64 (1-inch) squares.

The Hole Thing Volume II (Wyoming)

See's Fudge

My grandmother told me this was the See's Candy original fudge recipe. It is yummy!!

1 cup chopped nuts
1 (6-ounce) package chocolate
  chips
1 stick butter, softened
1 teaspoon vanilla

2 cups sugar
1 (5-ounce) can (⅔ cup)
  evaporated milk
1¼ cups miniature
  marshmallows

Using a large bowl, add nuts, chocolate chips, butter, and vanilla. Set aside. Using a large heavy pot, add sugar, canned milk, and marshmallows. Boil 6 minutes, stirring constantly. Pour over chocolate chip mixture and stir until it gets creamy and chocolate chips melt. Pour into buttered flat casserole or platter. Cool, then cut.

Sharing Our Best (Idaho)

Spud Candy

Tastes like Mounds candy bars.

¾ cup instant potatoes,
  prepared per package
  directions
1 teaspoon vanilla
4 cups powdered sugar, sifted

4 cups flaked coconut
1 (12-ounce) package chocolate
  chips
⅓ bar paraffin

Combine potatoes, vanilla, sugar, and coconut. Mix well and chill overnight. Shape into balls and chill again. Melt chocolate and paraffin in double boiler. Dip candy in chocolate and place on waxed paper to set.

Tastes from the Country (Idaho)

PIES and OTHER DESSERTS

Castle Rock, a beautiful 70-foot-high chalk spire, is visible for miles. Several important fossil discoveries have been made at this 70-million-year-old natural landmark in northwest Kansas.

Montana Huckleberry Pie

Picking huckleberries in western Montana is like going to heaven. It's hard to explain, really, what the magic is. I think perhaps it's the place where huckleberries grow. Picture a steep mountainside, with conifer woods above, and a green valley below. There's a river meandering through the valley. You are sitting in the late afternoon sun on the edge of the deep green woods. Wind is soughing in the pine trees. Listen! It is the only sound you hear. Oh yes, there are some small birds calling and chirping, but they are musical notes that blend in with the soughing of the wind. The sun is hot but there's a breeze. I could sit on that mountainside in the berry patch forever. This is as close to paradise as I can imagine.

3 tablespoons flour	Pastry for double-crust 9-inch
¾ cup sugar (more if berries are very tart)	pie (do try whole-wheat pastry flour)
4 cups fresh or frozen huckleberries (blueberries)	

Mix flour and sugar with berries. Set aside. Roll out a little more than half the pastry dough to ⅛-inch thickness and fit into a 9-inch pie pan. Pour the berries into the pie shell. (If you use commercial blueberries, sprinkle 1 tablespoon lemon juice on top.) Roll remaining pastry a little thinner than for the bottom crust. Prick with your favorite design. Brush the edge of the bottom crust with cold water, and place the upper crust on pie. Press crusts together at the rim and trim off the excess dough. Flute the edge.

Bake in a preheated 450° oven for 10 minutes. Reduce the heat to 350° and bake about 40 minutes.

Note: Montana huckleberries are really blueberries. The scientific name of the genus is Vaccinium and that is the blueberry genus. But these wild berries are a world apart from the commercial blueberry, so they deserve a distinct title. We Montanans will fight for the name "huckleberry."

The Kim Williams Cookbook and Commentary (Montana)

Montana Huckleberry Chocolate Fleck Pie

What better way to combine two wonderful foods—chocolate and Montana huckleberries! This is a great dessert to make a few days before needed, and a favorite for Christmas dinner.

PIE CRUST:

½ cup butter
2 tablespoons sugar

1 cup flour

Combine butter and sugar. Do not cream. Add flour. Mix just until dough will form. Place ¼ cup of mixture crumbled in small pan. Press remaining mixture evenly over bottom and sides of 9-inch pie pan with well floured fingers. Bake at 375° until light golden brown. Bake crumbs 10–12 minutes, and crust 12–15 minutes.

PIE FILLING:

½ cup semisweet chocolate
  chips
⅔ cup sugar
¼ cup water
1 unbeaten egg white

1½ teaspoons vanilla
1 teaspoon lemon juice
1 cup whipping cream
½ cup huckleberries

Melt chocolate chips in double boiler. Cool to lukewarm. Combine in small bowl the sugar, water, egg white, vanilla, and lemon juice; beat with electric mixer at highest speed until soft peaks form when beaters are raised (3–5 minutes). Beat whipping cream until thick. Fold melted chocolate slowly into whipped cream mixture then fold into egg white mixture. Fold huckleberries into the mixture. Put into pie crust; sprinkle with baked crumbs and freeze.

Recipe by Vivian Schaap, Lone Mountain Ranch, Big Sky, Montana
Montana Celebrity Cookbook (Montana)

In land area, Montana can accommodate Virginia, Maryland, Delaware, Pennsylvania, and New York, and still have room for the District of Columbia. Montana covers more than 147,000 square miles, making it the fourth largest state in the nation after Alaska, Texas, and California. The name Montana comes from the Spanish word montaña, meaning "mountain," even though the eastern part of the state consists of gently rolling pastureland.

Bing Huckleberry Pie

¾ cup sugar
¼ cup flour
1 tablespoon cornstarch
2 cups ripe Bing cherries,
  halved and pitted

½ teaspoon almond extract
2 cups huckleberries
1 double pie crust
1 tablespoon butter or
  margarine

Mix dry ingredients. Wash, drain, and prepare Bing cherries. Sprinkle almond extract over. Gently combine with huckleberries and the dry mixture. Transfer into bottom crust. Dot with butter or margarine. Cover with top crust. Seal edges, and cut slits near the center. Cover with foil.

Bake at 375° about 20 minutes. Remove foil and bake 25 minutes longer. Cool and serve with whipped cream topping.

Huckleberry Haus Cookbook (Idaho)

Cherries in the Snow

This is our Christmas dessert.

1 (3-ounce) package cream
  cheese, softened
½ cup sugar
½ teaspoon vanilla

½ pint heavy cream
Graham cracker crust
1 can cherry pie filling

Blend cream, sugar, and vanilla. In separate bowl, whip the cream. Mix whipped cream into cream cheese mixture. Pour into graham cracker crust. Top with cherry pie filling and chill overnight.

Note: This doubles nicely using an 8-ounce package of cream cheese.

Mountain Brook's Wacky Wonders of the Woods (Montana)

Sour Cream Rhubarb Pie

FILLING:

3 tablespoons flour
½ teaspoon salt
1¼ cups sugar
1 egg
1 cup sour cream

1 teaspoon vanilla
½ teaspoon lemon extract
3 cups chopped rhubarb
1 (9-inch) unbaked pie crust

TOPPING:

⅓ cup sugar
⅓ cup flour
Pinch of salt

1 teaspoon cinnamon
¼ cup soft butter

Sift together flour, salt, and sugar. Add egg, sour cream, vanilla, and lemon extract. Add the rhubarb and pour into a 9-inch unbaked crust. Bake at 400° for 15 minutes. Reduce heat to 350° and bake for 25 minutes.

Mix all ingredients for Topping together with a fork. Sprinkle Topping over pie and return to oven for 15 minutes. Serves 6–8.

The Hole Thing Volume II (Wyoming)

Apple-Cranberry Streusel Custard Pie

1 (14-ounce) can sweetened
  condensed milk
1 teaspoon cinnamon
2 eggs, beaten
½ cup water
1½ cups fresh or frozen
  cranberries
2 medium apples, pared and
  sliced

1 (9-inch) unbaked pie shell
¼ cup firmly packed brown
  sugar
¼ cup sifted all-purpose flour
2 tablespoons cold butter or
  margarine
¼ cup chopped nuts

Place rack in lowest position of oven and preheat to 425°. In large mixing bowl, combine milk and cinnamon. Add eggs, water, and fruit. Mix well. Pour into pastry shell.

In medium mixing bowl, combine sugar and flour, and cut in margarine until crumbly. Stir in nuts and sprinkle mixture over top of pie. Bake 10 minutes, then reduce heat to 375° and bake 30–40 minutes, until golden.

Idaho Cook Book (Idaho)

Idaho Centennial Apple Pie

CHEESECAKE FILLING:

1 (8-ounce) package cream cheese, softened	1 egg
⅓ cup sugar	½ teaspoon vanilla
	Pastry for 2 (9- or 10-inch) pies

Combine cream cheese, sugar, egg, and vanilla in a small bowl with an electric mixer until light. Pour into one unbaked pie crust. (At this point, you can put it in a gallon freezer bag and freeze to make later.)

APPLE FILLING:

1 cup sugar	6 cups peeled and sliced apples (Jonathan when in season)
3 tablespoons cornstarch	
½ teaspoon cinnamon	¼ cup apple juice
¼ teaspoon salt	2 tablespoons butter

Combine sugar, cornstarch, cinnamon, and salt in a large saucepan. Add apples, apple juice, and butter. Place on medium heat. Bring to a boil. Reduce heat. Cover and simmer for 2 minutes. Spoon over Cheesecake Filling.

Roll dough for top crust. Lift onto filled pie. Trim ½ inch beyond edge of pie plate. Fold under the bottom crust and flute. Decorate with pastry scraps and cut vents in crust. Bake at 400° for 40 minutes or until nicely browned.

Another Cookbook (Idaho)

Crazy Horse Memorial scale model compared with mountain carving in its current shape in the distance.

Old-Fashioned Lemon Meringue Pie

1½ cups sugar
½ teaspoon salt
1½ cups water, divided
4 tablespoons butter
⅓ cup cornstarch

4 eggs, separated
¼ cup lemon juice
2 tablespoons lemon rind
1 (9-inch) baked pie shell

Combine sugar, salt, one cup of water and butter. Heat until sugar is dissolved. Blend cornstarch with ½ cup of cold water and add slowly to the hot mixture. Cook on low heat until clear, about 8 minutes. Beat egg yolks and add slowly; cook 3 minutes, stirring continually. Remove from heat and add lemon juice and rind. Cool. Pour in a baked pie shell. Set aside.

MERINGUE:

⅔ cup egg whites
¼ teaspoon salt

¼ teaspoon cream of tartar
⅔ cup sugar

Beat egg whites until foamy; add salt and cream of tartar. Continue beating and add sugar gradually until stiff peaks form. Pile on the lemon filling, sealing edges. Brown in a 375° oven for 10–15 minutes.

Taste the Good Life! Nebraska Cookbook (Nebraska)

The Crazy Horse Memorial is a mountain monument in the Black Hills of South Dakota in the form of Crazy Horse, an Oglala Lakota warrior, riding a horse and pointing into the distance. The mountain carving was begun in 1948 by sculptor Korczak Ziolkowski, who had worked on Mt. Rushmore under Gutzon Borglum. Ziolkowski was invited to the Black Hills by Lakota Chief Henry Standing Bear, whose invitation read: "My fellow chiefs and I would like the white man to know the red man has great heroes, too." It is not a federal or state project, but a nonprofit educational and cultural undertaking now carried on by Ziolkowski's family and financed primarily from admission fees. Ziolkowski was offered $10 million from the federal government on two occasions, but he turned the offers down, fearing that his plans for the memorial would be left behind. The monument is being carved out of Thunderhead Mountain on land considered sacred by some Native Americans, between Custer and Hill City, roughly 8 miles away from Mount Rushmore.

Peaches and Cream Streusel Pie

STREUSEL:

⅓ cup firmly packed dark
  brown sugar
⅓ cup all-purpose flour
⅓ cup old-fashioned
  rolled oats
½ teaspoon ground cinnamon

¼ teaspoon ground nutmeg
¼ cup chilled butter, cut into
  small pieces
¼ cup sliced almonds (about 1
  ounce)

Preheat oven to 350°. In a medium bowl, mix together brown sugar, flour, oats, cinnamon, and nutmeg. Using a pastry blender or 2 butter knives, cut the butter into the flour mixture until coarse crumbs form. Stir in nuts.

FILLING:

1 large egg
⅓ cup heavy cream
¼ cup sugar
1 teaspoon vanilla

1 teaspoon almond extract
½ teaspoon ground nutmeg
Pinch of salt

Mix egg, cream, sugar, vanilla, almond extract, nutmeg, and salt.

5 cups ripe, peeled, pitted,
  and sliced peaches
  (about 1½ pounds)

1 (8-inch) pie shell, baked

Arrange the sliced peaches in the bottom of baked pie shell; pour Filling over peaches. Sprinkle Streusel evenly over the cream mixture to edges of pie crust. Press Streusel down slightly. Bake pie until the Streusel is lightly browned, 30–35 minutes. Transfer pan to a wire rack to cool completely. Garnish with peach slices.

Note: If using frozen peaches, you will need 1 pound of unsweetened frozen, thawed, drained peaches.

Recipes to Make You Purr (Wyoming)

Sweet Potato Pie

Pastry for single-crust pie
1½ cups mashed sweet
 potatoes
⅔ cup brown sugar
1 tablespoon butter or
 margarine, melted

1 egg, slightly beaten
1 cup milk
1 teaspoon ground cinnamon
½ teaspoon ground ginger
⅓ teaspoon allspice
⅛ teaspoon salt

Line a pie plate with pastry, forming a high collar. Combine sweet potatoes, brown sugar, melted butter or margarine, egg, milk, spices and salt. Ladle into pie shell, and bake at 450° for 15 minutes; reduce heat and continue baking at 350° for 30 minutes or until a knife inserted in the center comes out clean. Makes 6 servings.

Reader's Favorite Recipes (Kansas)

Walnut Rum Pie

¾ cup sugar
½ cup butter, softened
½ cup flour
2 eggs, beaten
2 tablespoons dark rum

1 cup chocolate chips
1 cup coarsely chopped
 walnuts
1 (8-inch) pie shell, lightly
 baked

Combine sugar, butter, flour, and eggs, and beat until smooth. Add rum and beat until blended. Stir in chocolate chips and walnuts. Spoon into pie shell. Bake at 350° for 30–35 minutes, or until set and just golden brown.

Note: This is just enough for a smaller, 8-inch pie. Make 1½ recipes for 9-inch pan and double for 10-inch pan.

Wapiti Meadow Bakes (Idaho)

Edith's Buttermilk Raisin Pie

One of my favorite pies.

1½ cups raisins	1 teaspoon vinegar
1 cup water	1 tablespoon cornstarch
2 eggs	1 cup buttermilk
⅔ cup sugar	1 baked pie crust shell

Boil raisins in water until tender. Combine all other filling ingredients. Add this to the raisins and cook, stirring constantly until thickened. Pour into the baked shell. Serve with whipped topping.

A Taste of Prairie Life (South Dakota)

Wildcat Pie
(Vinegar Pie)

In the Old West, visitors at camps where Vinegar Pie was made asked for the recipe and refused to believe the cook when he told them there was nothing in the filling except suet, sugar, water, and vinegar. They thought there was a secret ingredient. Not so. The flavor came from sugar, bubbling and caramelizing through holes in the crust, and from the vinegar which substituted for fruit acid. If the cook had a few leftover dried peaches, he might cut them small and mix them in to heighten the illusion of fruit in his Vinegar Pie.

½ pound suet	1 cup sugar
1 cup water	Dried peaches (optional)
½ cup vinegar	Pastry dough (your own
Flour as needed	recipe)

Chop the suet and fry out. Discard the crackling. Add water and bring to a boil. Add the vinegar. Stir in flour slowly, creaming to form a paste. Add sugar and peaches, if desired, and pour into a dough-lined pie tin. Cover with dough, cut numerous openings for escaping steam, sprinkle sugar over top, and bake in 350° oven until the crust is crisp and brown. The result is surprisingly like a fruit pie.

Cow Country Cookbook (Montana)

Chocolate-Covered Cherry Pie

1 (14-ounce) can sweetened
  condensed milk
⅔ cup semisweet chocolate
  pieces
½ teaspoon salt

½ teaspoon vanilla
1 can cherry pie filling
1 (9-inch) pie shell, baked
Whipped cream for garnish
Stemmed cherries (optional)

Cook sweetened condensed milk over low heat, stirring occasionally, until mixture begins to boil. Let boil, stirring constantly until it thickens, about 4 minutes. Remove from stove; add chocolate pieces and stir until melted and well blended. Add remaining ingredients; stir until blended. Pour into cooled, baked pie shell. Chill 2–3 hours. Garnish with whipped cream and stemmed cherries, if desired.

The Best of Rural Montana Cookbook (Montana)

Chocolate Cream Cheese Pie

1 (3-ounce) package cream
  cheese, softened
2 tablespoons sugar
1 tablespoon milk
1 (8-ounce) carton whipped
  topping, thawed, divided
1 (8- or 9-inch) graham
  cracker crust in pan

1 (3.9-ounce) package instant
  chocolate pudding
1¾ cups milk
Coconut or chopped nuts
  (optional)

In small bowl, beat cream cheese, sugar, and 1 tablespoon of milk until smooth. Fold in half of whipped topping. Spread over graham cracker crust. Chill.

In large bowl, beat pudding and milk with wire whisk or hand mixer on LOW speed for 2 minutes. Pour pudding over cream cheese mixture. Chill.

Before serving, spread remaining whipped topping over top. Sprinkle with coconut or nuts, if desired. Yields 6–8 servings.

Irene's Country Cooking (Wyoming)

Milk Chocolate Pie

1 cup milk chocolate chips
½ cup milk, divided
1 (8-ounce) package cream
cheese, softened

1 (8-ounce) carton Cool Whip,
thawed
1 chocolate crumb pie crust
Milk chocolate kisses (optional)

In a microwave dish or double boiler, combine chocolate chips and
¼ cup milk. Cook until chips are melted; stir until smooth. In a
mixing bowl, beat cream cheese and remaining milk until smooth.
Gradually beat in the chocolate mixture. Fold in the whipped topping. Pour into crust. Freeze for 4–6 hours or overnight. Garnish
with kisses and whipped topping, if desired.

Favorite Recipes (Wyoming)

Krunch Kone Koffee Pie

10 sugar ice cream cones,
ground fine
¼ cup margarine, melted
½ cup hot fudge sauce
1 quart vanilla ice cream

1½ tablespoons instant coffee
1 teaspoon hot water
1 (8-ounce) tub whipped
topping
½ chocolate bar, grated

Grind ice cream cones and combine with melted margarine. Press
into 9-inch pie plate to form crust. Place in freezer. Microwave
hot fudge sauce until pourable. Pour into prepared crust and
return to freezer. Put ice cream in a medium bowl. Add instant
coffee that has been stirred into hot water. Beat until blended and
pour on top of fudge sauce. Return to freezer until solid. Top with
whipped topping and grated chocolate bar. Freeze. Let set at
room temperature for 5 minutes before serving.

Cooking with Iola (Nebraska)

Butter Brickle Ice Cream Pie

The caramel sauce can be made up to three days in advance and refrigerated . . . if you trust yourself to have this sweet treat in your house that long!

1½ cups pecans, coarsely
   chopped (save 8 whole
   pecans for garnish)
2 egg whites
¼ cup sugar

¼ teaspoon salt
1 quart butter brickle ice
   cream (or butter pecan or
   butter crunch), softened

Lightly toast all the pecans in a 350° oven for 5–8 minutes. Cool on a paper towel before using. Beat egg whites until frothy. Gradually add sugar and salt and beat until stiff. Fold in cooled chopped nuts and spread meringue in bottom and up side of well-buttered 9-inch pie pan. Prick bottom and sides with fork to eliminate bubbles. Bake at 350° for 15–20 minutes. Watch closely. Cool completely. Spread ice cream over crust. Cover with foil and freeze. To serve, cut into wedges, top with sauce and one whole pecan. Serves 8.

CARAMEL SAUCE:

1 cup firmly packed brown
   sugar
½ cup half-and-half or
   evaporated milk

¼ cup light corn syrup
2 tablespoons butter or
   margarine
1 tablespoon vanilla

Combine all ingredients except vanilla. Bring to a boil over medium heat, stirring occasionally. Boil about 4 minutes, stirring occasionally. Remove from heat, stir in vanilla, and let cool 30 minutes. Store in refrigerator.

Presentations (North Dakota)

Magic Peach Cobbler

1 stick butter
1 cup flour
⅔ cup sugar
1½ teaspoons baking powder
¾ cup milk

4 cups sliced fresh peaches
¼ cup sugar
Cinnamon and nutmeg
 (optional)

Melt butter in 9x13-inch pan. Mix flour, ⅔ cup sugar, baking powder, and milk. Pour this over melted butter, DON'T STIR. Add peaches on top. Sprinkle ¼ cup sugar on top of peaches. Bake at 350°–375° for at least 45 minutes. Should be nice and brown.

Note: May sprinkle a little cinnamon and nutmeg along with the sugar on top.

Story, Wyoming's Centennial Community Cookbook (Wyoming)

Huckleberry-Apple Crisp

2 cups huckleberries
2 cups peeled and sliced tart
 apples
1 tablespoon lemon juice
½ cup packed brown sugar
1 cup all-purpose flour

¾ cup sugar
1 teaspoon baking powder
1 egg, slightly beaten
½ cup butter, melted
½ teaspoon cinnamon

Butter a ½-quart baking dish. Put in huckleberries and apples. Sprinkle with lemon juice and brown sugar. Mix next 3 ingredients; stir in egg and mix until crumbly. Sprinkle over fruit. Top with melted butter and cinnamon. Bake at 350° for 45 minutes. Serve warm or at room temperature.

The Rocky Mountain Wild Foods Cookbook (Idaho)

Apple Dumplings

4–6 tablespoons butter or
  solid shortening
1¾ cup all-purpose flour
3 tablespoons sugar
½ teaspoon salt

3 teaspoons baking powder
¾ cup milk
4 medium apples, peeled and
  sliced

Preheat oven to 375°. Cut shortening into dry ingredients with pastry blender or knives until mixture is consistency of coarse cornmeal. Make well in the center of these ingredients. Pour in milk. Stir lightly until all ingredients are moistened and dough cleans the sides of the bowl; not more than ½ minute. Turn dough onto lightly floured surface. Knead 10 times. With floured rolling pin, roll dough into 9x12-inch rectangle about ½-inch thick. Cover with apples. Starting on the long end, roll-up jellyroll-style. Pinch side edge together. Cut tube into 10–12 slices and place in greased 9x13-inch cake pan. Pour sauce over slices and bake for 45 minutes or until apples are tender.

SAUCE:

1 cup white sugar
1 cup brown sugar, packed
1 cup margarine

2 cups water
1 teaspoon cinnamon

Combine all ingredients in saucepan; bring to a full boil. Boil one minute. Pour over sliced apple roll.

St. Joseph's Table (South Dakota)

Blackberry Dumplings

2 (10-ounce) packages frozen   ¼ cup sugar
   blackberries

Pour berries into 2-quart saucepan; stir in sugar. Warm over lowest heat setting, stirring occasionally.

DUMPLINGS:

1 cup biscuit mix   1 small egg
⅓ cup milk   1 tablespoon sugar

Stir all ingredients together to form soft dough (do not overwork). Increase heat under berries to medium-high, stirring constantly to a full boil. Drop Dumplings in 1 tablespoon at a time; reduce heat, and cook 10 minutes uncovered; cover and cook 10 minutes.

Elegant Cooking Made Simple (Idaho)

Bondurant Bread Pudding

1 loaf French bread, sliced   2 tablespoons vanilla extract
2 quarts low-fat milk   1½ cups dark raisins
4 eggs   ¼ pound unsalted butter,
2 cups sugar   melted

Soak bread in milk; crush by hand until well mixed and crumbled. Beat eggs in a separate bowl; gradually add sugar, vanilla, and raisins. Mix well. Pour butter into bottom of a shallow 3-quart baking pan. Add egg mixture to bread/milk combination and blend together until fully soaked. Pour into pan, allowing butter to rise to the top. Bake at 325° for 1 hour or until firm and slightly golden. Allow to cool. Serve with Whiskey Sauce.

WHISKEY SAUCE:

¼ pound butter   1 egg
1 cup sugar   ¼ cup whiskey
¼ cup boiling water

In top of double boiler, cream together butter and sugar. Beat in boiling water. Stir constantly until sugar is dissolved. Beat egg separately and add slowly to mixture. Stir and cook 2–3 minutes. Allow mixture to cool before adding whiskey. Serves 8–10.

The Hole Thing Volume II (Wyoming)

Old-Fashioned Shortcake

2 cups all-purpose flour
1 tablespoon baking powder
1 teaspoon salt
1 tablespoon granulated
  sugar
6 tablespoons fat (butter,
  margarine or shortening)

¾ cup milk
1 beaten egg (optional)
Melted butter, margarine or
  shortening
1 quart fresh or cooked fruit or
  berries
Whipped cream, as desired

Sift dry ingredients together twice; cut in fat until mixture resembles coarse corn meal. Add milk all at once, mixing until the dough leaves the side or cleans the bowl. An egg also may be added (with the milk) for a richer dough, if desired. Dough should be soft.

Turn onto lightly floured board and knead about 20 times or until dough is just smooth. Divide dough into 2 equal parts. Pat and roll out one portion to fit a pie or cake pan, making a layer about ¼-inch thick. Brush top with melted butter, margarine or shortening. Shape second portion of dough the same way and lightly place over the dough already in the pan. Bake at 425° for 12–15 minutes or until light golden brown. Cool slightly. Gently separate layers. Add fruit as filling; top with whipped cream as desired. Makes 8 servings.

Reader's Favorite Recipes (Kansas)

Moon Cake

1 cup water
½ cup butter or margarine
1 cup flour
4 eggs
1 (8-ounce) package cream
  cheese, softened

2 small boxes vanilla instant
  pudding, prepared
Cool Whip
Chocolate fudge ice cream
  topping
Chopped nuts

Bring water and butter to boil. Add flour all at once and stir rapidly until mixture forms a ball. Remove from heat and cool a little. Add eggs, one at a time, until shiny. Spread into ungreased 11x15-inch jellyroll pan. Bake at 400° for 30 minutes (watch!) Cool—Do not prick surface! Beat cream cheese until creamy. Slowly blend pudding into beaten cream cheese. Spread on cooled crust and refrigerate for 20 minutes. Top with Cool Whip. Drizzle with chocolate fudge sauce (ice cream topping) and sprinkle with chopped nuts (slivered almonds are good).

Heavenly Delights (Nebraska)

The Snake River Birds of Prey Natural Conservation Area is home to the largest concentration of nesting raptors in North America. Twenty-four species of predatory birds can be found there such as hawks, eagles, falcons, and owls. The area is home to a significant portion of prairie falcons, North America's only indigenous falcon. The NCA covers 484,873 acres and is located 35 miles south of Boise, Idaho.

Tornadoes

In this whimsical dessert, funnel clouds of pecan meringue touch down on dots of whipped cream and pools of brilliantly colored fruit sauce. It's not Oz, but it's close.

¾ cup pecan pieces
5 large egg whites
¼ teaspoon cream of tartar
1 cup sugar
1 teaspoon vanilla extract

2 cups fresh or frozen
    raspberries, blackberries, or
    strawberries
Sugar to taste
1 cup heavy cream, whipped

Preheat the oven to 300°. Grind the pecans to a fine paste in the bowl of a food processor. In a separate bowl, beat the egg whites and cream of tartar until soft peaks form. Gradually beat in the sugar and vanilla extract until stiff peaks form. Fold in the pecans. Fit a pastry bag with a #4 star tip and spoon in the meringue batter. Line 2 baking sheets with parchment paper. Pipe 24 (2-inch) mounds of meringue onto the parchment to form inverted funnel shapes. Bake for about 10 minutes, then turn down the heat to 100° and leave the meringues to dry out for 1–2 hours, or until crisp. Store in airtight containers or serve immediately.

Purée the fruit in a food processor and add sugar to taste. Place 3 teaspoonfuls of whipped cream randomly on each dessert plate. Spoon about 3 tablespoons of the fruit sauce around the whipped cream. Place the pointed end of each meringue in a dot of whipped cream and serve. Makes 2 dozen (serves 6–8).

Pure Prairie (Kansas)

Shannon's Fruit Tart

CRUST:

¾ cup butter
1 cup flour (heaping)

⅓ cup powdered sugar
Dash of salt

Combine ingredients with a fork or hands and press out on either a pizza round or cookie sheet. Spread as thin as possible without tearing. Bake 20 minutes at 325°—careful not to burn.

SPREAD:

1 (8-ounce) package cream
  cheese, softened
⅓ cup powdered sugar
1 cup whipping cream,
  whipped

Fruit
Apricot preserves
Water

Combine cream cheese, powdered sugar, and whipped cream and spread over cooled Crust. Arrange your choices of sliced fruit in an interesting pattern on the freshly prepared Crust. Brush a glaze of apricot preserves and water mixed and warmed to a syrup-like texture over the fruit, and refrigerate until ready to serve.

Potluck (Montana)

The Bridger-Teton National Forest in Wyoming is the second largest national forest in the lower 48 states, encompassing 3.4 million acres. The forest includes Gannett Peak (shown above), the tallest mountain in Wyoming, and the Gros Ventre landslide, one of the largest readily visible landslides on earth. Seven of the largest glaciers outside of Alaska are located within the forest boundaries.

Festive Cranberry Torte

CRUST:

1½ cups graham cracker
  crumbs
½ cup chopped pecans

¼ cup sugar
6 tablespoons butter or
  margarine, melted

In mixing bowl combine graham cracker crumbs, pecans, sugar, and melted margarine. Press onto bottom and up sides of 8-inch spring form pan. Chill.

FILLING:

2 cups ground fresh
  cranberries
1 cup sugar
1 tablespoon frozen orange
  juice concentrate, thawed

2 egg whites
1 teaspoon vanilla
⅛ teaspoon salt
1 cup whipping cream
1 recipe Cranberry Glaze

In large mixing bowl combine cranberries and sugar; let stand 5 minutes. Add unbeaten orange juice concentrate, egg whites, vanilla, and salt. Beat on LOW speed of electric mixer till frothy. Then beat at HIGH speed 6–8 minutes or till stiff peaks form. Whip cream to soft peaks; fold into cranberry mixture. Turn into Crust; freeze. Serve with Cranberry Glaze.

CRANBERRY GLAZE:

½ cup sugar
1 tablespoon cornstarch

¾ cup fresh cranberries
⅔ cup water

In saucepan stir together sugar and cornstarch; stir in cranberries and water. Cook and stir till bubbly. Cook, stirring occasionally, just till cranberry skins pop. Cool to room temperature. (Do not chill.) Makes 1 cup.

To serve, remove torte from pan. Place on serving plate. Spoon Cranberry Glaze in center. Makes 10 servings.

Home at/on the Range with Wyoming BILS (Wyoming)

Huckleberry Crème Caramel

Be sure to have your custard ramekins ready for when your sugar has caramelized.

1 cup sugar
¼ cup water
2 cups milk
2 teaspoons vanilla

6 whole eggs
½ cup + 2 tablespoons white
   sugar
4 tablespoons huckleberries

In heavy skillet over medium-high heat, combine sugar and water; stir until like a wet sand. Cook, stirring occasionally until sugar mixture turns to caramel. Immediately pour equal portions of the caramel into 4 (6-ounce) oven-safe ramekins. Set aside.

In saucepan, combine milk and vanilla. Bring to a scald. In a mixer or bowl, beat eggs and sugar until fluffy, stirring rapidly; slowly add ¼ cup of the scalded milk. Still stirring, slowly add the rest of the milk to finish custard.

Pour custard over the caramel in the ramekins. Sprinkle 1 tablespoon of huckleberries into each custard. Bake custards in water bath in preheated 300° oven for 20–30 minutes, or until set. (To test, use a small paring knife stuck into middle of custard; it should come out clean.) Serves 4.

A Taste of Jackson Hole II (Wyoming)

Mile High Strawberry Dessert

1 cup flour
½ cup butter
¼ cup brown sugar
½ cup chopped walnuts
1 (10-ounce) package
   strawberries, halved

½ cup sugar
1½ teaspoons lemon juice
2 egg whites
1 (8-ounce) container Cool
   Whip

Combine the first 4 ingredients and pour into 9x13-inch baking pan. Bake at 350° for about 15–18 minutes or until lightly browned. Crumble with a fork. Blend together the sugar, strawberries, lemon juice, and egg whites in a large bowl. Beat with an electric mixer for 20 minutes. Fold in the Cool Whip. Sprinkle about ½ the crumb mixture in a 9x13-inch pan. Spread the strawberry mixture over the crumbs and top with remaining crumbs. Freeze. Do not thaw before serving.

Yesterday and Today Friendly Circle Cookbook (North Dakota)

Simple Raspberry Dessert

CRUST:

1½ cups graham cracker
   crumbs

⅓ cup margarine, softened
¼ cup sugar

Combine ingredients well; pat into 9x13-inch pan.

CENTER:

1 (8-ounce) package cream
   cheese, softened

1 cup powdered sugar
1 medium container Cool Whip

Combine cream cheese and powdered sugar; add Cool Whip. Beat well and spread on Crust.

TOPPING:

⅔ cup sugar
1½ cups water
2 tablespoons cornstarch
1 small package raspberry
   Jell-O

2 small packages frozen
   raspberries, thawed and
   drained

Bring sugar, water, cornstarch, and Jell-O to boil. Cool slightly; add raspberries, pour over Center layer.

Brisbin Community Cookbook (Montana)

Apricot Tortoni

½ cup chopped almonds
3–4 tablespoons melted
  butter
1⅓ cups vanilla wafer
  crumbs
1 teaspoon almond extract
1 (12-ounce) jar apricot
  preserves

2 tablespoons apricot brandy
3 pints vanilla ice cream,
  softened, divided
1 cup whipping cream
¼ cup sugar
½ teaspoon almond extract, or
  1 teaspoon vanilla extract

Cook almonds in butter in skillet until toasted. Combine with wafer crumbs and 1 teaspoon almond extract in bowl; mix well. Press ⅓ of the mixture evenly in bottom of 9x13-inch glass dish. Combine apricot preserves with apricot brandy in bowl; mix well. Spoon ½ the ice cream over crumb mixture. Spoon ½ the preserve mixture over ice cream. Layer ½ of remaining crumb mixture over ice cream. Repeat layers, ending with crumbs.

Freeze several days before serving. The day before serving, combine whipping cream, sugar, and ½ teaspoon almond extract in mixer bowl; beat until thickened. Spoon over frozen mixture. Cut into 2-inch squares. Serve in champagne glasses. Yields 15 servings.

Cheyenne Frontier Days "Daddy of 'em All" Cookbook (Wyoming)

PHOTO © WIND RIVER VISITORS COUNCIL.

Ancient Indian petroglyphs (carvings or line drawings on rock) are scattered throughout Wyoming and Montana. Castle Gardens is one of the largest petroglyph sites in Wyoming, and includes depictions of medicine men, warriors, and hunters.

Filthy Wilma

CRUST:

1¼ cups flour

1 stick butter, melted

1 cup chopped nuts

Combine ingredients and press in bottom of greased 9x13-inch pan. Bake at 375° for 15 minutes.

FIRST LAYER:

1 (8-ounce) package cream cheese, softened

1 cup powdered sugar

1 medium (12-ounce) carton Cool Whip

Combine ingredients, blend well and spread on cooled Crust.

SECOND LAYER:

1 (3-ounce) package vanilla instant pudding

1 (3-ounce) package instant chocolate pudding

3 cups milk (or half-and-half)

1 teaspoon vanilla

Mix all ingredients together and spread on top of First Layer.

TOP LAYER:

1 (12- to 16-ounce) carton Cool Whip

1 package slivered almonds

Combine Cool Whip and almonds and spread on top. Refrigerate.

Cooking with Cops, Too (Idaho)

Amaretto Huckleberry Dessert

2 cups frozen huckleberries
1 cup sugar
1 tablespoon cornstarch

2 tablespoons amaretto liqueur
Coffee-flavored ice cream
Whipped cream

Combine huckleberries, sugar, and cornstarch in a saucepan. Bring to boil over moderate heat, stirring. Boil 2–3 minutes. Remove from heat and cool to room temperature. Stir in amaretto.

Place 2 scoops coffee ice cream in serving bowls, pour huckleberry mixture over, and garnish with whipped cream. Makes 8 servings.

Huckleberry Haus Cookbook (Idaho)

Easy Huckleberry Ice Cream

1½ cups huckleberries
½ cup sugar
1 tablespoon plus 1 teaspoon
 Clear Jel (or cornstarch)

½ teaspoon almond extract
1 half-gallon vanilla ice cream

Place huckleberries in a blender and process at LOW speed, in short intervals, just enough to break the berries. In a saucepan, combine berries with sugar and Clear Jel. Cook, stirring constantly, over moderate heat until mixture thickens. Remove from heat and cool. Stir in almond extract.

Put vanilla ice cream in a mixing bowl and let soften just enough to mix. Pour huckleberry mixture over and mix well. Transfer into plastic ice cream pail and freeze overnight.

Huckleberry Haus Cookbook (Idaho)

PHOTO © CITY OF SHERIDAN, WYOMING CONVENTION & VISITORS BUREAU

Each July, for over 70 years, Sheridan, Wyoming, has hosted the largest single go-round PRCA (Professional Rodeo Cowboys Association) rodeo in the country. Rodeo is the official state sport of Wyoming.

Listed below are the cookbooks that have contributed recipes to this book, along with copyright, author, publisher, city, and state, when applicable.

All About Bar-B-Q Kansas City Style ©1997 Pig Out Publications, Rich Davis and Shifra Stein, Kansas City, MO

Amana Lutheran Church 125th Anniversary Cookbook, Amana Lutheran Church Women, Scandia, KS

Amish Country Cooking ©1988 Andy & Millie Yoder, Rexford, MT

Another Cookbook, Kay Rose, Idaho Falls, ID

Ashton Area Cookbook, Ashton Area Development Committee, Ashton, ID

Bacon is not a Vegetable, Idaho State University Outdoor Program, Pocatello, ID

Basque Cooking and Lore ©1991 Darcy Williamson, Caxton Press, Caldwell, ID

Be Our Guest, St. Mark's Episcopal Church, Moscow, ID

The Best Little Cookbook in the West ©1996 Loaun Werner Vaad, Chamberlain, SD

The Best of Rural Montana Cookbook ©2001 Montana Electric Cooperatives' Association, Rural Montana Magazine, Great Falls, MT

Best-of-Friends, Festive Occasions Cookbook ©1993 Darlene Glantz Skees, Farcountry Press, Helena, MT

Bitterroot Favorites & Montana Memories ©2002 Bitterroot Favorites & Montana Memories, Laura Green Blount, Hamilton, MT

Blew Centennial Bon-Appetit, Blew Family, Phillipsburg, KS

Bound to Please ©1983 The Junior League of Boise, ID

Breakfast and More ©1992 Porch Swing Publications, Carole Eppler, Cheyenne, WY

Brisbin Community Cookbook, Brisbin Women's Club, Livingston, MT

Cee Dub's Dutch Oven and Other Camp Cookin' ©1999 C.W. "Butch" Welch, Back Country Press, Grangeville, ID

Cee Dub's Ethnic & Regional Dutch Oven Cookin' ©2002 C.W. "Butch" Welch, Back Country Press, Grangeville, ID

Centerville Community Centennial Cookbook, Centerville Community Church, Centerville, KS

A Century of Recipes, Hospice Visions, Inc., Twin Falls, ID

Cheyenne Frontier Days "Daddy of 'em All" Cookbook, ©1995 Chuckwagon Gourmet, Cheyenne, WY

Columbus Community Cookbook, Brick-By-Brick, Columbus, MT

Cookin' at its Best, New Meadows Senior Citizens Center, New Meadows, ID

Cookin' in Paradise, Paradise Valley Volunteer Fire Department Auxiliary, Bonners Ferry, ID

Cookin' with Farmers Union Friends, North Dakota Farmers Union Youth Group, Center, ND

A Cooking Affaire II ©1991 Jan Bertoglio and JoLe Hudson, Medicine Lodge, KS

Cooking on the Wild Side ©1999 Cooking on the Wild Side, Kirt Martin, Snake River Grill, Hagerman, ID

Cooking with Cops, Too, Pocatello Police Department, Pocatello, ID

Cooking with Iola, Iola Eagle, McCook, NE

Cooking with the Ladies, Ladies of Redeemer Lutheran Church, Cheyenne, WY

The Cool Mountain Cookbook ©2001 Gwen Ashley Walters, Pen & Fork Communications, Carefree, AZ

Cow Country Cookbook ©1993 Clearlight Publishers, Dan Cushman, Sante Fe, NM

Don Holm's Book of Food Drying, Pickling and Smoke Curing ©1975 Donald R. Holm, Caxton Press, Caldwell, ID

Down Home Country Cookin', Center for Discovery, Cottonwood, ID

Eastman Family Cookbook, Thelma Eastman, Winfield, KS

Easy Livin' Low-Calorie Microwave Cooking ©1990 Karen Kangas Dwyer, Omaha, NE

Easy Livin' Microwave Cooking ©1989 Karen Kangas Dwyer, Omaha, NE

Easy Livin' Microwave Cooking for the Holidays ©1989 Karen Kangas Dwyer, Omaha, NE

Elegant Cooking Made Simple, Sandra S. Corety, Caldwell, ID

Favorite Recipes, Ladies of Grace Bible Baptist, Casper, WY

Favorite Recipes of Montana, Montana Farm Bureau Federation Women's Committee, Bozeman, MT

Favorite Recipes of Rainbow Valley Lutheran Church, Women of ELCA, Alamo, ND

Feeding the Herd, Jackson Hole CowBelles, Jackson, WY

Festival of Nations Cookbook, Festival of Nations, Red Lodge, MT

The Fine Art of Cooking, Art Associates of Missoula and Missoula Symphony Guild, Missoula, MT

Fire Hall Cookbook, Fisher River Volunteer Fire Company, Libby, MT

Fire Hall Cookbook #2, Fisher River Volunteer Fire Company, Libby, MT

First Ladies' Cookbook ©1996 Betty L. Babcock, Shodair Children's Hospital, Helena, MT

French Family Favorites, French Family, Lewistown, MT

From the High Country of Wyoming, Flying A Guest Ranch, Debbie Hanson, Pinedale, WY

Game on the Grill ©2001 Eileen Clarke, Voyager Press, Townsend, MT

Generations "Coming Home," Samaria Recreation District, Samaria, ID

Get Your Buns in Here ©1999 Laurel A. Wicks, Jackson, WY

Grandma Jane's Cookbook, Jane Ross, Eagle, ID

The Great Entertainer Cookbook ©1992, 2002 Buffalo Bill Historical Center, Cody, WY

The Great Ranch Cookbook ©1998 Gwen Ashley Walters, Pen & Fork Communications, Carefree, AZ

The Hagen Family Cookbook, Marilee Nelson, Noonan, ND

Hall's Potato Harvest Cookbook ©1993 The Hall Family, Mound, MN

The Hearty Gourmet, Diana Swift, Wapiti Meadow Ranch, Cascade, ID

Heavenly Delights, Sacred Heart Altar Society, Nelson, NE

Heavenly Recipes, Milnor Lutheran Church WELCA, Milnor, ND

Heavenly Recipes and Burnt Offerings, Women Missionary Ladies, New Life Assembly of God Church, Lewistown, MT

Hey Ma! Come Quick! The Hog's in the Garden Again!!, Idaho State University Outdoor Program, Pocatello, ID

The Hole Thing Volume II, St. John's Hospital Auxiliary, Jackson, WY

Home at/on the Range with Wyoming BILS, Wyoming/PEO Sisterhood, Chapter Y, Casper, WY

Home at the Range I, Chapter EX. P.E. O., Oakley, KS

Home at the Range II, Chapter EX. P.E. O., Oakley, KS

Home at the Range III, Chapter EX. P.E. O., Oakley, KS

Home at the Range IV, Chapter EX. P.E. O., Oakley, KS

Homemade Memories, Dorothy Schraedler, Timken, KS

Horse Prairie Favorites, Grant Volunteer Fire Department, Grant - Dillon, MT

Huckleberry Haus Cookbook ©1997 Reverend Stan Simonik, Kingman, AZ

Idaho Cook Book ©1998 Golden West Publishers, Janet Walker, Phoenix, AZ

Idaho's Favorite Bean Recipes, Idaho Bean Commission, Boise, ID

Idaho's Wild 100! ©1990 Idaho Department of Fish and Game, Boise, ID

If It Tastes Good, Who Cares? I ©1992 Spiritseekers Publishing, Pam Girard, Bismark, ND

If It Tastes Good, Who Cares? II ©1992 Spiritseekers Publishing, Pam Girard, Bismark, ND

In the Kitchen with Kate ©1995 Capper Press, Inc., Ogden Publications, Inc., Topeka, KS

Incredible Edibles, Lake Legion Heritage Corporations, Inc., Devils Lake, ND

Iola's Gourmet Recipes in Rhapsody, Iola Egle, McCook, NE

Irene's Country Cooking ©2002 Irene D. Wakefield, Cheyenne, WY

Irma Flat Mothers' Club Cookbook, Irma Flat Mothers' Club, Cody, WY

Jackson Hole à la Carte, Jackson Hole Conservation Alliance, Jackson, WY

The Joy of Sharing, Scottsbluff Cosmopolitans, Scottsbluff, NE

The Kansas City Barbeque Society Cookbook ©1998 Kansas City Barbeque Society, Kansas City, MO

The Kearney 125th Anniversary Community Cookbook ©1998 Cookbooks by Morris Press, Kearney, NE

Ketchum Cooks ©1995 Dee Dee McCuskey, Sun Valley, ID

The Kim Williams Cookbook and Commentary ©1983 Kim Williams, Bitterroot Educational Resources, Missoula, MT

Lakota Lutheran Church Centennial Cookbook, Lakota Lutheran Church , Lakota, ND

Lewis and Clark Fare, Whitehall Senior Citizens, Whitehall, MT

Mackay Heritage Cookbook, Charlotte McKelvey for South Custer Historical Society, Mackay, ID

Matt Braun's Western Cooking ©1996 The Caxton Printers, Ltd., Matt Braun, Caxton Press, Caldwell, ID

The Miracle Cookbook, The Boise Courtyard by Marriott, Boise, ID

Mom's Camper Cooking, Rita Hewson, Larned, KS

Montana Bed & Breakfast Guide & Cookbook, 2nd Edition ©2000 Janet & Steve Colberg, Summer Kitchen Press, Helena, MT

Montana Celebrity Cookbook, Susie Graetz, Intermountain Children's Home and Services, Helena, MT

More Cee Dub's Dutch Oven and Other Camp Cookin' ©2000 C.W. "Butch" Welch, Back Country Press, Grangeville, ID

Mountain Brook's Wacky Wonders of the Woods ©1995 Mountain Brook Ladies Club, Kalispell, MT

90th Anniversary Trinity Lutheran Church Cookbook, Trinity Ladies Fellowship, Great Bend, KS

98 Ways to Cook Venison ©1997 Ragged Mountain Press, Eldon R. Cutlip, Kooskia, ID

Norman Lutheran Church 125th Anniversary Cookbook, Norman Lutheran Church WELCA, Kindred, ND

North Dakota: Where Food is Love ©1994 Marcella Richman, Tower City, ND

Northern Lites: Contemporary Cooking with a Twist ©1997 Lites Ltd., Rose Chaney and Connie (Berghan) Church, Sandpoint, ID

Old-Fashioned Dutch Oven Cookbook ©1969 Donald R. Holm, Caxton Press, Caldwell, ID

125 Years of Cookin' with the Lord, Trinity Lutheran Church, Topeka, KS

Onions Make the Meal Cookbook, Idaho-Eastern Oregon Onion Committee, Parma, ID

The Oregon Trail Cookbook ©1993 Cookbooks by Morris Press, Kearney, NE

Our Daily Bread, Ashland United Methodist Church, Ashland, KS

Our Heritage, Rutland Community Club, Rutland, ND

The Outdoor Dutch Oven Cookbook ©1997 Ragged Mountain Press, Sheila Mills, Blacklick, OH

The Pea & Lentil Cookbook ©2000 USA Dry Pea and Lentil Council, Moscow, ID

Potatoes Are Not the Only Vegetable!, Idaho State University Outdoor Program, Pocatello, ID

Potluck ©1999 Archie Bray Foundation for the Ceramic Arts, Helena, MT

Presentations ©1993 Friends of Lied, Lied Center for Performing Arts, Towner, ND

Pumpkin, Winter Squash and Carrot Cookbook ©1994 Litchville Committee 2000, Jane Winge, Community Cookbooks, Litchville, ND

The Pure Food Club of Jackson Hole ©2001 Judy S. Clayton, Teton Views Publishing, Jackson Hole, WY

Pure Prairie ©1995 Pig Out Publications, Judith Fertig, Kansas City, MO

Quilter's Delight, Busy Day Recipes, Lemhi Piece Makers, Salmon, ID

Rainbow's Roundup of Recipes, Rainbow Bible Ranch, Sturgis, SD

Ranch Recipe Roundup IV ©2001 Maverick Press, Wyoming Livestock Roundup, Del Tinsley, Casper, WY

Rare Collection Recipes, Soroptimist International of Billings, MT

Reader's Favorite Recipes ©1995 Capper Press, Ogden Publications, Topeka, KS

REC Family Cookbook ©1987 North Dakota Association of Rural Electric Cooperatives, RTC Magazine, Mandan, ND

Recipes & Remembrances, Buffalo Lake Lutheran Church WMF, Eden, SD

Recipes & Remembrances, Covenant Women of Courtland, KS

Recipes from Big Sky Country ©2001 Tracy Winters, Montana Bed & Breakfast Association, Winters Publishing, Missoula, MT

Recipes form the Heart, Christ Lutheran Church Women, Libby, MT

Recipes from the Heart, Epsilon Omega Sorority, Dalton, NE

Recipes from the Heart: 100 Years of Recipes and Folklore, Pattie Sanders, Great Blend, KS

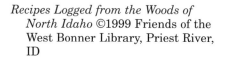

Recipes Logged from the Woods of North Idaho ©1999 Friends of the West Bonner Library, Priest River, ID

Recipes 1978–1998, Ellsworth County Hospital Auxiliary, Ellsworth, KS

Recipes Stolen from the River of No Return ©1999 Warren River Expeditions, Inc., Dave Warren, Salmon, ID

Recipes to Make You Purr, Humane Society of Park County, Cody, WY

Recipes Tried and True, Diana Swift, Wapiti Meadow Ranch, Cascade, ID

Recipes Worth Sharing ©1997 Janet Majure, Breadbasket Publishing, Lawrence, KS

Red River Valley Potato Growers Auxiliary Cookbook, R.R.V.P.G. Auxiliary, ND

Regent Alumni Association Cookbook, Regent Alumni Association, Regent, ND

Ritzy Rhubarb Secrets Cookbook, Community Cookbooks, ©1992 Litchville Committee 2000, Jane Winge, Litchville, ND

The Rocky Mountain Wild Foods Cookbook ©1995 Darcy Williamson, Caxton Press, Caldwell, ID

Salad Sampler from Quilting in the Country ©2000 Quilting in the Country, Jane Quinn, Bozeman, MT

Sausage & Jerky Handbook ©1994 Eldon R. Cutlip, Kooskia, ID

Savor the Inns of Kansas ©1994 Tracy M. Winters and Phyllis Y. Winters, Recipes from Kansas Bed & Breakfasts Cookbook and Directory, Winters Publishing, Greensburg, IN

Sharing God's Bounty, Recipes from the Tri-Parish, Clay Center, KS

Sharing Our "Beary" Best II, Teddy Bear Day Care, Groton, SD

Sharing Our Best, Kalif Shrine Buckskin Horse Patrol, Sheridan, WY

Sharing Our Best, Lalia Wilson, Pocatello, ID

Silver Celebration Cookbook, Peace Lutheran Church, Newton, KS

Simac Family Favorites, Jodi DeMars and Patsy Simac, Winifred, MT

Sisters Two II, Nancy Barth and Sue Hergert, Ashland, KS

Soup's On at Quilting in the Country ©1998 Quilting in the Country, Jane Quinn, Bozeman, MT

South Dakota Sunrise ©1997 Tracy Winters, Bed & Breakfast Innkeepers of South Dakota, Rapid City, SD

Sowbelly and Sourdough ©1995 Scott Gregory, Caldwell, ID

Spragg Family Cookbook, Karen Spragg, Aston, ID

St. Joseph's Table, St. Joseph's Catholic Church, Spearfish, SD

Story, Wyoming's Centennial Community Cookbook, Story Woman's Club, Story, WY

A Taste of Jackson Hole II ©2001 Christine Goodman, Jackson, WY

A Taste of Montana ©1999 Tracy Winters, Montana Bed & Breakfast Association, Winters Publishing, Missoula, MT

A Taste of Prairie Life ©1996 Loaun Werner Vaad, Chamberlain, SD

Taste the Good Life! Nebraska Cookbook, Morris Press, Kearney, NE

Tastes from the Country, Medicine Mt. Grange, Medimont, ID

Tastes & Tours of Wyoming ©1997 Wyoming Homestay and Outdoor Adventures

To Tayla with TLC, RCRH Medical Imaging Department, Rapid City, SD

Treasures of the Great Midwest ©1995 Junior League of Wyandotte & Johnson Counties, Kansas City, KS

Tried & True II, Spring Creek WELCA, Watford City, ND

Wapiti Meadow Bakes, Diana Swift, Wapiti Meadow Ranch, Cascade, ID

We Love Country Cookin', Marlene Grager and Donna Young, Sykeston, ND

Wheat Montana Cookbook ©1999 Wheat Montana, Wheat Montana Farms, Three Forks Books, Three Forks, MT

With Lots of Love ©2002 Taydie Drummond, A. Drummond Ranch B & B, Cheyenne, WY

Wolf Point, Montana 75th Jubilee Cookbook, Jubilee Cookbook Committee, Wolf Point, MT

Wonderful Wyoming Facts and Foods ©1989 Judy Barbour, Judy Barbour Books, Bandera, TX

Wyoming Cook Book ©1998 Golden West Publishers, Karin Wade, Phoenix, AZ

Y Cook? ©1994 The Fargo-Moorhead YWCA, Fargo, ND

Yaak Cookbook, The Yaak Women's Club, Troy, MT

Years and Years of Goodwill Cooking, Goodwill Circle of New Hope Lutheran Church, Upham, ND

Yesterday and Today Friendly Circle Cookbook, Beulah Congregation Church, Beulah, ND

You're Hot Stuff, Flo! ©1995 STAM-PEDE, Inc., Jerry Palen, The Saratoga Publishing Group, Inc., Saratoga, WY

PHOTO: WIKIMEDIA.ORG.

Opened in 1936, America's first ski resort, Sun Valley, is an affluent resort community in central Idaho. Sun Valley boasts 78 ski runs and world-renowned lodges. Among skiers, "Sun Valley" refers to the alpine ski area, which consists of Bald Mountain (shown here) and Dollar Mountain. Bald Mountain, or "Baldy," is often referred to as the best single ski mountain in the world.